SKINNY
SLOW COOKER

TASTE OF HOME BOOKS ● RDA ENTHUSIAST BRANDS, LLC ● MILWAUKEE, WI

Taste of Home

EDITORIAL

Editor-in-Chief: Catherine Cassidy

Vice President, Content Operations: Kerri Balliet
Creative Director: Howard Greenberg

Managing Editor, Print & Digital Books: Mark Hagen
Associate Creative Director: Edwin Robles Jr.

Editor: Christine Rukavena
Associate Editor: Molly Jasinski
Art Director: Raeann Sundholm
Layout Designers: Nancy Novak, Catherine Fletcher
Editorial Production Manager: Dena Ahlers
Editorial Production Coordinator: Jill Banks
Copy Chief: Deb Warlaumont Mulvey
Copy Editors: Chris McLaughlin, Ellie Piper, Dulcie Shoener
Contributing Copy Editors: Kristin Sutter, Michael Juley, Valerie Phillips
Editorial Intern: Maddie Rashid
Business Architect, Publishing Technologies: Amanda Harmatys
Solutions Architect, Publishing Technologies: John Mosey
Business Analyst, Publishing Technologies: Kate Unger
Junior Business Analyst, Publishing Technologies: Shannon Stroud
Editorial Services Administrator: Marie Brannon

Content Director: Julie Blume Benedict
Food Editors: Gina Nistico; James Schend; Peggy Woodward, RDN
Recipe Editors: Sue Ryon (lead), Irene Yeh

Test Kitchen & Food Styling Manager: Sarah Thompson
Test Cooks: Nicholas Iverson (lead), Matthew Hass, Lauren Knoelke
Food Stylists: Kathryn Conrad (lead), Shannon Roum
Prep Cooks: Bethany Van Jacobson (lead), Melissa Hansen, Aria C. Thornton
Culinary Team Assistant: Megan Behr

Photography Director: Stephanie Marchese
Photographers: Dan Roberts, Jim Wieland
Photographer/Set Stylist: Grace Natoli Sheldon
Set Stylists: Melissa Franco (lead), Stacey Genaw, Dee Dee Jacq
Set Stylist Assistant: Stephanie Chojnacki

Editorial Business Manager: Kristy Martin
Rights & Permissions Associate: Samantha Lea Stoeger
Editorial Business Associate: Andrea Heeg Polzin

BUSINESS

Vice President, Group Publisher: Kirsten Marchioli
Publisher: Donna Lindskog
Business Development Director, Taste of Home Live: Laurel Osman
Promotional Partnerships Manager, Taste of Home Live: Jamie Piette Andrzejewski

TRUSTED MEDIA BRANDS, INC.
President and Chief Executive Officer: Bonnie Kintzer

Chief Financial Officer: Dean Durbin
Chief Marketing Officer: C. Alec Casey
Chief Revenue Officer: Richard Sutton
Chief Digital Officer: Vince Errico
Senior Vice President, Global HR & Communications: Phyllis E. Gebhardt, SPHR; SHRM-SCP
General Counsel: Mark Sirota
Vice President, Magazine Marketing: Christopher Gaydos
Vice President, Operations: Michael Garzone
Vice President, Consumer Marketing Planning: Jim Woods
Vice President, Digital Product & Technology: Nick Contardo
Vice President, Digital Content & Audience Development: Diane Dragan
Vice President, Financial Planning & Analysis: William Houston
Publishing Director, Books: Debra Polansky

For other Taste of Home books and products, visit us at *tasteofhome.com*.

International Standard Book Number: 978-1-61765-580-7
Library of Congress Control Number: 2016940432

Cover Photographer: Grace Natoli Sheldon
Set Stylist: Melissa Franco
Food Stylist: Kathryn Conrad

Pictured on front cover: Slow-Cooked Lasagna Soup, page 16

Pictured on back cover (left to right): Slow Cooker BBQ Chicken, page 121; Strawberry Cream Cheese Pie, page 239; and Sesame Pulled Pork Sandwiches, page 145.

Printed in China
13579108642

GET SOCIAL WITH US

To find a recipe tasteofhome.com
To submit a recipe tasteofhome.com/submit
To find out about other *Taste of Home* products shoptasteofhome.com

 **LIKE US**
facebook.com/tasteofhome

 PIN US
pinterest.com/taste_of_home

 FOLLOW US
@tasteofhome

 TWEET US
twitter.com/tasteofhome

PUMPKIN SPICE
OVERNIGHT OATMEAL, 8

BLACK-EYED
PEAS & HAM, 44

ITALIAN TURKEY
SANDWICHES, 116

SLOW-COOKED
PEACH SALSA, 184

CONTENTS

Eat Right, *Save Time,* Feel Great!

With a hectic schedule, it's hard enough to sit the family down to a homemade meal, let alone one that cuts calories and satisfies everyone. The answer? Put your slow cooker to work with the healthy recipes in *Taste of Home Skinny Slow Cooker!*

Inside this handy cookbook, you'll discover 278 recipes to help you set your table with the comforting foods your family craves...all big on flavor and short on fat, calories or sodium. With dishes like *Gone-All-Day Stew* (*p. 83*) and *Slow-Cooked Pork Tacos* (*p. 172*), a hot, hearty and healthy entree is always at your fingertips. Losing weight has never tasted so good!

Every recipe features nutrition facts and most contain diabetic exchanges so you know that you're feeding your family right. You'll also find prep/cook guidelines with each dish to make meal planning a snap. Plus, two bonus chapters offer low-calorie sides, breads, desserts and more.

Watch for the At-a-Glance icons that are scattered throughout the book, too. Only have a few ingredients on hand? Check for the **(5) INGREDIENTS** icon, which spotlights recipes that call for five or fewer items—not including water, salt, pepper, oils and optional ingredients. Also, watch for the **FREEZE IT** icon when it comes to preplanning. These dishes go from the slow cooker to the freezer for nights when time is tight but a healthy meal is still your priority. Eating right has never been easier!

With these remarkable recipes at your fingertips, whipping up a family favorite is a snap—but so is cutting calories, losing weight and feeling great! Dig in to all the comfort, flavor and convenience your slow cooker offers, without an ounce of guilt. Let *Taste of Home Skinny Slow Cooker* show you how!

GARDEN CHICKEN
CACCIATORE, PAGE 125

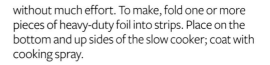

SLOW COOKER
BEEF TOSTADAS, PAGE 92

SLOW-COOK WITH CONFIDENCE
Follow these tips for slow-cooking success every time.

PREP NOW, COOK LATER
In most cases, you can prepare and load ingredients into the slow cooker insert beforehand and store it in the refrigerator overnight. But an insert can crack if exposed to rapid temperature changes. Let the insert sit out just long enough to reach room temperature before you place it in the slow cooker.

STICK WITH THAWED, NOT FROZEN
Although throwing frozen chicken breasts into the slow cooker may seem easy, it's not a smart shortcut. Foods thawing inside the slow cooker can create the ideal environment for bacteria to grow, so thaw frozen meat and veggies ahead of time. The exception is if you're using a prepackaged slow cooker meal kit and following the instructions as written.

LINE THE CROCK FOR EASE OF USE
Some recipes in this book call for a sling. Here's why:

▶ A sling helps you lift layered foods, such as *Mushroom Meat Loaf (p. 136)*, out of the crock

without much effort. To make, fold one or more pieces of heavy-duty foil into strips. Place on the bottom and up sides of the slow cooker; coat with cooking spray.

BROWN THE MEAT
Take a few extra minutes to brown your meat in a skillet before you place it in the slow cooker. Doing so will add rich color and more flavor to the finished dish.

NO PEEKING!
Don't lift that lid! It's tempting to check on your meal's progress, but resist the urge. Every time you open the lid, you'll have to add about 30 minutes to the total cooking time.

ADJUST COOK TIME AS NEEDED
Live at a high altitude? Slow cooking will take longer. Add about 30 minutes for each hour of cooking the recipe calls for; legumes will take roughly twice as long.

IN A RUSH?
Cooking one hour on high is roughly equal to two hours on low, so adjust the cooking time to suit your schedule.

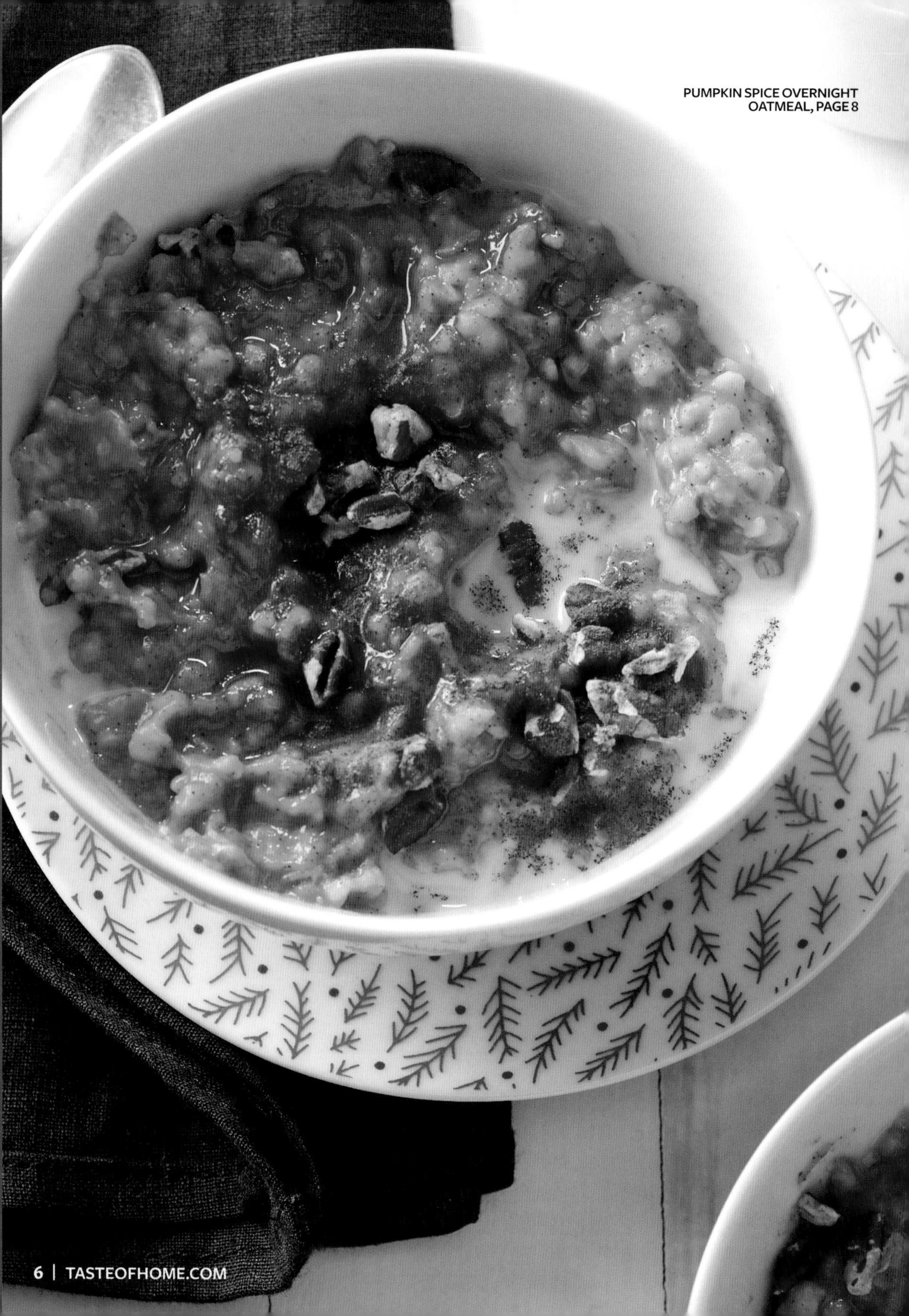

PUMPKIN SPICE OVERNIGHT OATMEAL, PAGE 8

BREAKFAST &
BRUNCH DISHES

8

10

12

CARROT CAKE OATMEAL

Set up this oatmeal in the slow cooker the night before so you can wake up to a healthy breakfast. For extra crunch, I garnish servings with ground nuts.

—DEBBIE KAIN
COLORADO SPRINGS, CO

PREP: 10 MIN. • **COOK:** 6 HOURS
MAKES: 8 SERVINGS

- 4½ **cups water**
- 1 **can (20 ounces) crushed pineapple, undrained**
- 2 **cups shredded carrots**
- 1 **cup steel-cut oats**
- 1 **cup raisins**
- 2 **teaspoons ground cinnamon**
- 1 **teaspoon pumpkin pie spice**
  Brown sugar, optional

In a 4-qt. slow cooker coated with cooking spray, combine the first seven ingredients. Cover and cook on low for 6-8 hours or until the oats are tender and the liquid is absorbed. Sprinkle with brown sugar if desired.
PER SERVING *1 cup (calculated without optional toppings) equals 197 cal., 2 g fat (trace sat. fat), 0 chol., 23 mg sodium, 46 g carb., 4 g fiber, 4 g pro.*

SLOW COOKER HAM & EGGS

This dish is great anytime, but I especially love to make it for Easter brunch. I like to serve the dish with hash browns or potato slices cooked up in the frying pan.

—ANDREA SCHAAK JORDAN, MN

PREP: 15 MIN. • **COOK:** 3 HOURS
MAKES: 6 SERVINGS

- 6 **large eggs**
- 1 **cup biscuit/baking mix**
- ⅔ **cup 2% milk**
- ⅓ **cup sour cream**
- 2 **tablespoons minced fresh parsley**
- 2 **garlic cloves, minced**
- ½ **teaspoon salt**
- ½ **teaspoon pepper**
- 1 **cup cubed fully cooked ham**
- 1 **cup (4 ounces) shredded Swiss cheese**
- 1 **small onion, finely chopped**
- ⅓ **cup shredded Parmesan cheese**

1. In a large bowl, whisk the first eight ingredients until blended; stir in remaining ingredients. Pour into a greased 3- or 4-qt. slow cooker.
2. Cook, covered, on low 3-4 hours or until the eggs are set. Cut into wedges.
PER SERVING *1 serving equals 315 cal., 18 g fat (9 g sat. fat), 256 mg chol., 942 mg sodium, 17 g carb., 1 g fiber, 21 g pro.*

PUMPKIN SPICE OVERNIGHT OATMEAL

There's nothing like a warm cup of oatmeal in the morning, and my spiced version comes from a slow cooker. Store leftovers in the fridge.

—JORDAN MASON BROOKVILLE, PA

PREP: 10 MIN. • **COOK:** 5 HOURS
MAKES: 6 SERVINGS

- 1 **can (15 ounces) solid-pack pumpkin**
- 1 **cup steel-cut oats**
- 3 **tablespoons brown sugar**
- 1½ **teaspoons pumpkin pie spice**
- 1 **teaspoon ground cinnamon**
- ¾ **teaspoon salt**
- 3 **cups water**
- 1½ **cups 2% milk**
  Optional toppings: toasted chopped pecans, ground cinnamon and additional brown sugar and milk

In a large bowl, combine the first six ingredients; stir in water and milk. Transfer to a greased 3-qt. slow cooker. Cook, covered, on low 5-6 hours or until oats are tender, stirring once. Serve with toppings as desired.
PER SERVING *1 cup (calculated without optional toppings) equals 183 cal., 3 g fat (1 g sat. fat), 5 mg chol., 329 mg sodium, 34 g carb., 5 g fiber, 6 g pro.* **Diabetic Exchanges:** *2 starch, ½ fat.*

HOW-TO

SERVE A STUNNING BRUNCH

- Measure, chop, cube or mix anything you can the night before to save time in the morning.
- Once you have your slow cooker going, move on to any last-minute details or recipes.
- Don't forget the coffee! Borrow a thermal carafe from a friend or local business, if you can, to keep it warm all morning long.

CARROT CAKE
OATMEAL

SLOW COOKER
HAM & EGGS

PUMPKIN SPICE
OVERNIGHT OATMEAL

OVERNIGHT VEGETABLE & EGG BREAKFAST

My eggs and veggies cook while you sleep and make a hearty breakfast for those who have to rush out the door. I use sliced potatoes, but frozen potatoes work, too.
—KIMBERLY CLARK-THIRY
ANCHOR POINT, AK

PREP: 15 MIN. • **COOK:** 7 HOURS
MAKES: 8 SERVINGS

- **4 pounds potatoes, peeled and thinly sliced (about 8 cups)**
- **1 medium green pepper, finely chopped**
- **1 package (10 ounces) frozen chopped spinach, thawed and squeezed dry**
- **1 cup sliced fresh mushrooms**
- **1 medium onion, finely chopped**
- **8 large eggs**
- **1 cup water**
- **1 cup 2% milk**
- **1¼ teaspoons salt**
- **¼ teaspoon pepper**
- **2 cups (8 ounces) shredded cheddar cheese**

1. In a greased 6-qt. slow cooker, layer first five ingredients. In a large bowl, whisk eggs, water, milk, salt and pepper; pour over top. Sprinkle with cheese.

2. Cook, covered, on low 7-9 hours or until potatoes are tender and eggs are set.

PER SERVING *1½ cups equals 354 cal., 15 g fat (7 g sat. fat), 217 mg chol., 668 mg sodium, 37 g carb., 4 g fiber, 19 g pro.*

OVERNIGHT VEGETABLE & EGG BREAKFAST

APPLE-CRANBERRY GRAINS

I made some changes to my diet in order to lose weight. My kids are skeptical when it comes to healthy food, but they certainly go for these wholesome grains.
—SHERISSE DAWE
BLACK DIAMOND, AB

PREP: 10 MIN. • **COOK:** 4 HOURS
MAKES: 10 SERVINGS

- **2 medium apples, peeled and chopped**
- **1 cup sugar**
- **1 cup fresh cranberries**
- **½ cup wheat berries**
- **½ cup quinoa, rinsed**
- **½ cup oat bran**
- **½ cup medium pearl barley**
- **½ cup chopped walnuts**
- **½ cup packed brown sugar**
- **1½ to 2 teaspoons ground cinnamon**
- **6 cups water**
  Milk
  Sliced apples, optional

In a 3-qt. slow cooker, combine the first 11 ingredients. Cook, covered, on low 4-5 hours or until grains are tender. Serve with milk. If desired, top with apple slices.

NOTE *Look for oat bran cereal near the hot cereals or in the natural foods section. Look for quinoa in the cereal, rice or organic food aisle.*

PER SERVING *¾ cup (calculated without milk) equals 286 cal., 5 g fat (1 g sat. fat), 0 chol., 8 mg sodium, 60 g carb., 5 g fiber, 5 g pro.*

THE SKINNY

GO FOR SKIM MILK

By serving Apple-Cranberry Grains with ½ cup skim milk instead of 2%, you'd save yourself about 20 calories and 2 grams of fat—and keep the protein!

APPLE-CRANBERRY
GRAINS

SLOW COOKER FRITTATA PROVENCAL

This meatless slow cooker meal makes an elegant brunch dish or a breakfast-for-supper option.

—CONNIE EATON PITTSBURGH, PA

PREP: 30 MIN. • **COOK:** 3 HOURS
MAKES: 6 SERVINGS

½ cup water
1 tablespoon olive oil
1 medium Yukon Gold potato, peeled and sliced
1 small onion, thinly sliced
½ teaspoon smoked paprika
12 large eggs
1 teaspoon minced fresh thyme or ¼ teaspoon dried thyme
1 teaspoon hot pepper sauce
½ teaspoon salt
¼ teaspoon pepper
1 log (4 ounces) fresh goat cheese, coarsely crumbled, divided
½ cup chopped soft sun-dried tomatoes (not packed in oil)

1. Layer two 24-in. pieces of aluminum foil; starting with a long side, fold up the foil to create a 1-in.-wide strip. Shape strip into a coil to make a rack for bottom of a 6-qt. oval slow cooker. Add water to slow cooker; set foil rack in water.

2. In a large skillet, heat oil over medium-high heat. Add potato and onion; cook and stir 5-7 minutes or until potato is lightly browned. Stir in the paprika. Transfer to a greased 1½-qt. baking dish (dish must fit in slow cooker).

3. In a large bowl, whisk the eggs, thyme, pepper sauce, salt and pepper; stir in 2 ounces cheese. Pour over the potato mixture. Top with remaining goat cheese. Place dish on foil rack.

4. Cook, covered, on low 3 hours or until eggs are set and a knife inserted near the center comes out clean.

NOTE *This recipe was tested with sun-dried tomatoes that are ready to use without soaking. When using other sun-dried tomatoes that are not oil-packed, cover with boiling water and let stand until soft. Drain before using.*

PER SERVING *1 wedge equals 245 calories, 14 g fat (5 g sat. fat), 385 mg chol., 338 mg sodium, 12 g carb., 2 g fiber, 15 g pro.* **Diabetic Exchanges:** *2 medium-fat meat, 1 starch, ½ fat.*

SLOW COOKER
FRITTATA PROVENCAL

PEAR-BLUEBERRY GRANOLA

Oatmeal fans will love this dish. Enjoy it as a delicious dessert when served with vanilla ice cream, but the pears, blueberries and granola also make a beautiful breakfast item.

—LISA WORKMAN BOONES MILL, VA

PREP: 15 MIN. • **COOK:** 3 HOURS
MAKES: 10 SERVINGS

- 5 medium pears, peeled and thinly sliced
- 2 cups fresh or frozen unsweetened blueberries
- ½ cup packed brown sugar
- ⅓ cup apple cider or unsweetened apple juice
- 1 tablespoon all-purpose flour
- 1 tablespoon lemon juice
- 2 teaspoons ground cinnamon
- 2 tablespoons butter
- 3 cups granola without raisins

In a 4-qt. slow cooker, combine the first seven ingredients. Dot with butter. Sprinkle granola over top. Cover and cook on low for 3-4 hours or until fruit is tender.
PER SERVING *¾ cup equals 267 cal., 7 g fat (1 g sat. fat), 6 mg chol., 35 mg sodium, 51 g carb., 10 g fiber, 7 g pro.*

HOT FRUIT SALAD

Round out a brunch easily with my spiced fruit compote. With its pretty color, this salad is nice around the holidays or for any special occasion.

—BARB VANDE VOORT
NEW SHARON, IA

PREP: 5 MIN. • **COOK:** 3 HOURS
MAKES: 16 SERVINGS

- 1 jar (25 ounces) unsweetened applesauce
- 1 can (21 ounces) cherry pie filling
- 1 can (20 ounces) unsweetened pineapple chunks, undrained
- 1 can (15 ounces) sliced peaches in juice, undrained
- 1 can (15 ounces) reduced-sugar apricot halves, undrained
- 1 can (15 ounces) mandarin oranges, undrained
- ¼ cup packed brown sugar
- 1 teaspoon ground cinnamon

Place the first six ingredients in a 5-qt. slow cooker; stir gently. Mix brown sugar and cinnamon; sprinkle over fruit mixture. Cook, covered, on low until heated through, 3-4 hours.
PER SERVING *¾ cup equals 141 cal., trace fat (trace sat. fat), 0 chol., 13 mg sodium, 35 g carb., 2 g fiber, 1 g pro.*

HOT FRUIT SALAD

RED BEAN VEGETABLE
SOUP, PAGE 31

SOUPS

32

16

29

HOME-STYLE
CHICKEN SOUP

HOME-STYLE CHICKEN SOUP

I've used this easy soup recipe on many occasions. Mom shared it with me, and we love it.
—**KATHY RAIRIGH** MILFORD, IN

PREP: 15 MIN. • **COOK:** 6¼ HOURS
MAKES: 4 SERVINGS

- 1 can (14½ ounces) reduced-sodium chicken broth
- 1 can (14½ ounces) diced tomatoes, undrained
- 1 cup cubed cooked chicken
- 1 can (8 ounces) mushroom stems and pieces, drained
- ¼ cup sliced fresh carrot
- ¼ cup sliced celery
- 1 bay leaf
- ⅛ teaspoon dried thyme
- ¾ cup uncooked egg noodles

In a 1½-qt. slow cooker, combine the first eight ingredients. Cover and cook on low for 6 hours. Stir in noodles; cover and cook on high for 15-20 minutes or until tender. Discard bay leaf.

PER SERVING *1 cup equals 137 cal., 3 g fat (1 g sat. fat), 37 mg chol., 671 mg sodium, 13 g carb., 3 g fiber, 14 g pro.* **Diabetic Exchanges:** *2 lean meat, 1 vegetable, ½ starch.*

SLOW-COOKED LASAGNA SOUP

Every fall and winter, our staff has a soup rotation, so this is my usual contribution. My co-workers love it.
—**SHARON GERST** NORTH LIBERTY, IA

PREP: 35 MIN.
COOK: 5 HOURS + STANDING
MAKES: 8 SERVINGS (2½ QUARTS)

- 1 package (19½ ounces) Italian turkey sausage links
- 1 large onion, chopped
- 2 medium carrots, chopped
- 2 cups sliced fresh mushrooms
- 3 garlic cloves, minced
- 1 carton (32 ounces) reduced-sodium chicken broth
- 2 cans (14½ ounces each) no-salt-added stewed tomatoes
- 2 cans (8 ounces each) no-salt-added tomato sauce
- 2 teaspoons Italian seasoning
- 6 lasagna noodles, broken into 1-inch pieces
- 2 cups coarsely chopped fresh spinach
- 1 cup cubed or shredded part-skim mozzarella cheese
  Shredded Parmesan cheese and minced fresh basil, optional

1. In a large skillet, cook the sausage over medium-high heat 8-10 minutes or until no longer pink, breaking into crumbles; drain. Transfer to a 5- or 6-qt. slow cooker.
2. Add the onion and carrots to the same skillet; cook and stir 2-4 minutes or until softened. Stir in the mushrooms and garlic; cook and stir 2-4 minutes or until the mushrooms are softened. Transfer to slow cooker. Stir in the broth, tomatoes, tomato sauce and Italian seasoning. Cook, covered, on low 4-6 hours or until the vegetables are tender.
3. Add the lasagna noodles; cook 1 hour longer or until tender. Stir in spinach. Remove insert; let stand 10 minutes. Divide mozzarella cheese among serving bowls; ladle soup over cheese. If desired, sprinkle with the Parmesan cheese and basil.

PER SERVING *1⅓ cups equals 266 cal., 8 g fat (3 g sat. fat), 36 mg chol., 725 mg sodium, 30 g carb., 5 g fiber, 18 g pro.* **Diabetic Exchanges:** *2 lean meat, 2 vegetable, 1½ starch.*

THE SKINNY

SCALE BACK SALT

Switching to no-salt-added ingredients can really make a big difference. By subbing no-salt-added stewed tomatoes and tomato sauce in this soup, we cut out more than 400 mg of sodium per serving.

SLOW-COOKED LASAGNA SOUP

SOUTHWESTERN CHICKEN SOUP

Here's the perfect recipe for a busy week, because the slow cooker does most of the work for you!

—**HAROLD TARTAR**
WEST PALM BEACH, FL

PREP: 10 MIN. • **COOK:** 7 HOURS
MAKES: 10 SERVINGS (2½ QUARTS)

- 1¼ pounds boneless skinless chicken breasts, cut into thin strips
- 1 tablespoon canola oil
- 2 cans (14½ ounces each) reduced-sodium chicken broth
- 1 package (16 ounces) frozen corn, thawed
- 1 can (14½ ounces) diced tomatoes, undrained
- 1 medium onion, chopped
- 1 medium green pepper, chopped
- 1 medium sweet red pepper, chopped
- 1 can (4 ounces) chopped green chilies
- 1½ teaspoons seasoned salt, optional
- 1 teaspoon ground cumin
- ½ teaspoon garlic powder

1. In a large skillet, saute the chicken in oil until lightly browned. Transfer to a 5-qt. slow cooker. Stir in the remaining ingredients.
2. Cover and cook on low for 7-8 hours or until the chicken and vegetables are tender. Stir before serving.
PER SERVING *1 cup equals 143 cal., 3 g fat (1 g sat. fat), 31 mg chol., 364 mg sodium, 15 g carb., 3 g fiber, 15 g pro. Diabetic Exchanges: 2 lean meat, 1 starch.*

FAMILY-PLEASING TURKEY CHILI

My children really love this chili. The leftovers are wonderful, too.

—**SHEILA CHRISTENSEN**
SAN MARCOS, CA

PREP: 25 MIN. • **COOK:** 4 HOURS
MAKES: 6 SERVINGS (2¼ QUARTS)

- 1 pound lean ground turkey
- 1 medium green pepper, finely chopped
- 1 small red onion, finely chopped
- 2 garlic cloves, minced
- 1 can (28 ounces) diced tomatoes, undrained
- 1 can (16 ounces) kidney beans, rinsed and drained
- 1 can (15 ounces) black beans, rinsed and drained
- 1 can (14½ ounces) reduced-sodium chicken broth
- 1¾ cups frozen corn, thawed
- 1 can (6 ounces) tomato paste
- 1 tablespoon chili powder
- ½ teaspoon pepper
- ¼ teaspoon ground cumin
- ¼ teaspoon garlic powder
- Optional toppings: reduced-fat sour cream and minced fresh cilantro

1. In a large nonstick skillet, cook the turkey, green pepper and onion over medium heat until meat is no longer pink. Add the garlic; cook 1 minute longer. Drain.
2. Transfer to a 4-qt. slow cooker. Stir in the tomatoes, kidney beans, black beans, broth, corn, tomato paste, chili powder, pepper, cumin and garlic powder.
3. Cover and cook on low for 4-5 hours or until heated through. Serve with optional toppings if desired.
PER SERVING *1½ cups (calculated without optional toppings) equals 349 cal., 7 g fat (2 g sat. fat), 60 mg chol., 725 mg sodium, 47 g carb., 12 g fiber, 27 g pro. Diabetic Exchanges: 3 lean meat, 2 starch, 2 vegetable.*

BUTTERNUT SQUASH SOUP

The golden color, smooth and creamy texture and comforting taste of this soup make it ideal for a chilly fall day. It has a slightly tangy taste from the cream cheese, and the cinnamon really comes through.

—**JACKIE CAMPBELL** STANHOPE, NJ

PREP: 30 MIN. • **COOK:** 6¼ HOURS
MAKES: 14 SERVINGS (2½ QUARTS)

- 1 medium onion, chopped
- 2 tablespoons butter
- 1 medium butternut squash (about 4 pounds), peeled and cubed
- 3 cans (14½ ounces each) vegetable broth
- 1 tablespoon brown sugar
- 1 tablespoon minced fresh gingerroot
- 1 garlic clove, minced
- 1 cinnamon stick (3 inches)
- 1 package (8 ounces) cream cheese, softened and cubed

1. In a small skillet, saute onion in butter until tender. Transfer to a 5- or 6-qt. slow cooker; add squash. Combine the broth, brown sugar, ginger, garlic and cinnamon; pour over squash. Cover and cook on low for 6-8 hours or until the squash is tender.
2. Cool slightly. Discard cinnamon stick. In a blender, process the soup in batches until smooth. Return all to slow cooker. Whisk in cream cheese; cover and cook 15 minutes longer or until cheese is melted.
PER SERVING *¾ cup equals 135 cal., 7 g fat (5 g sat. fat), 22 mg chol., 483 mg sodium, 17 g carb., 4 g fiber, 2 g pro. Diabetic Exchanges: 1½ fat, 1 starch.*

SOUTHWESTERN
CHICKEN SOUP

FAMILY-PLEASING
TURKEY CHILI

BUTTERNUT
SQUASH SOUP

**LOADED POTATO-
LEEK SOUP**

LOADED POTATO-LEEK SOUP

Growing up, my mother made potato and onion soup because it was affordable and fast. I've since trimmed the calories, and it's still a comforting family favorite.
—**COURTNEY STULTZ** WEIR, KS

PREP: 20 MIN. • **COOK:** 6 HOURS
MAKES: 6 SERVINGS (ABOUT 1½ QUARTS)

- 1 medium leek
- 1½ pounds potatoes (about 2 large), peeled and finely chopped
- 2 cups fresh cauliflowerets
- ¾ teaspoon rubbed sage
- ½ teaspoon salt
- ¼ teaspoon pepper
- 4 cups reduced-sodium chicken or vegetable broth
- 2 teaspoons olive oil
- 2 teaspoons lemon juice
  Sour cream, optional

1. Finely chop the white portion of leek. Cut leek greens into thin strips; reserve for the topping. In a 3- or 4-qt. slow cooker, combine the potatoes, cauliflower, seasonings, broth and chopped leek. Cook, covered, on low 6-8 hours or until vegetables are tender.
2. In a small skillet, heat oil over medium-high heat. Add reserved leek greens; cook 3-5 minutes or until light golden. Puree soup using an immersion blender. Or, cool soup slightly and puree in batches in a blender. Stir in lemon juice. Top with the leek greens and, if desired, sour cream.
PER SERVING *1 cup (calculated without sour cream) equals 108 cal., 2 g fat (trace sat. fat), 0 chol., 593 mg sodium, 20 g carb., 2 g fiber, 4 g pro.* **Diabetic Exchanges:** *1 starch, ½ fat.*

CHICKEN WILD RICE SOUP WITH SPINACH

I stir together this creamy chicken soup whenever we're craving something warm. Reduced-fat and reduced-sodium ingredients make it a healthier option.
—**DEBORAH WILLIAMS** PEORIA, AZ

PREP: 10 MIN. • **COOK:** 5¼ HOURS
MAKES: 6 SERVINGS (ABOUT 2 QUARTS)

- 3 cups water
- 1 can (14½ ounces) reduced-sodium chicken broth
- 1 can (10¾ ounces) reduced-fat reduced-sodium condensed cream of chicken soup, undiluted
- ⅔ cup uncooked wild rice
- 1 garlic clove, minced
- ½ teaspoon dried thyme
- ½ teaspoon pepper
- ¼ teaspoon salt
- 3 cups cubed cooked chicken breast
- 2 cups fresh baby spinach

1. In a 3-qt. slow cooker, mix the first eight ingredients until blended. Cook, covered, on low 5-7 hours or until rice is tender.
2. Stir in chicken and spinach. Cook, covered, on low 15 minutes longer or until heated through.
PER SERVING *1¼ cups equals 212 cal., 3 g fat (1 g sat. fat), 56 mg chol., 523 mg sodium, 19 g carb., 2 g fiber, 25 g pro.* **Diabetic Exchanges:** *3 lean meat, 1 starch.*

HEARTY BLACK BEAN SOUP

Cumin and chili powder give spark to this thick and hearty soup. If you have leftover meat—smoked sausage, browned ground beef or roast—toss it in during the last 30 minutes of cooking.
—**AMY CHOP** OAK GROVE, LA

PREP: 10 MIN. • **COOK:** 9 HOURS
MAKES: 8 SERVINGS

- 3 medium carrots, halved and thinly sliced
- 2 celery ribs, thinly sliced
- 1 medium onion, chopped
- 4 garlic cloves, minced
- 1 can (30 ounces) black beans, rinsed and drained
- 2 cans (14½ ounces each) reduced-sodium chicken broth or vegetable broth
- 1 can (15 ounces) crushed tomatoes
- 1½ teaspoons dried basil
- ½ teaspoon dried oregano
- ½ teaspoon ground cumin
- ½ teaspoon chili powder
- ½ teaspoon hot pepper sauce
  Hot cooked rice

In a 3-qt. slow cooker, combine the first 12 ingredients. Cover and cook on low for 9-11 hours or until the vegetables are tender. Serve with the rice.
PER SERVING *1 cup (calculated without rice) equals 129 cal., 0 fat (0 sat. fat), 0 chol., 627 mg sodium, 24 g carb., 6 g fiber, 8 g pro.* **Diabetic Exchanges:** *1½ starch, 1 lean meat.*

HOW-TO

PREPARING LEEKS

To prepare leeks, cut off the root end and tough green tops. Split the white portion in half and swish the pieces in a bowl of water to rinse away the sand between the layers. Then chop or slice. While leek tops aren't typically used in recipes, well-rinsed tops can be used to flavor homemade stock. Cut them into large pieces so they'll be easy to discard.

LEMON CHICKEN
& RICE SOUP

LEMON CHICKEN & RICE SOUP

When buying chicken for this soup, ask the butcher to cube it for you. It'll save you some prep time, and no mess!

—**KRISTIN CHERRY** BOTHELL, WA

PREP: 35 MIN. • **COOK:** 4¼ HOURS
MAKES: 12 SERVINGS (4 QUARTS)

- 2 tablespoons olive oil
- 2 pounds boneless skinless chicken breasts, cut into ½-inch pieces
- 5 cans (14½ ounces each) reduced-sodium chicken broth
- 8 cups coarsely chopped Swiss chard, kale or spinach
- 2 large carrots, finely chopped
- 1 small onion, chopped
- 1 medium lemon, halved and thinly sliced
- ¼ cup lemon juice
- 4 teaspoons grated lemon peel
- ½ teaspoon pepper
- 4 cups cooked brown rice

1. In a skillet, heat 1 tablespoon oil over medium-high heat. Add half of the chicken; cook and stir until browned. Transfer to a 6-qt. slow cooker. Repeat with remaining oil and chicken.
2. Stir broth, vegetables, lemon slices, lemon juice, peel and pepper into chicken. Cook, covered, on low 4-5 hours or until chicken is tender. Stir in rice; heat through.
PER SERVING *1⅓ cups equals 203 cal., 5 g fat (1 g sat. fat), 42 mg chol., 612 mg sodium, 20 g carb., 2 g fiber, 20 g pro. **Diabetic Exchanges:** 2 lean meat, 1 starch, 1 vegetable, ½ fat.*

COLORFUL MINESTRONE

What makes my minestrone different from others? Butternut squash, a leek and fresh kale!

—**TIFFANY ANDERSON-TAYLOR** GULFPORT, FL

PREP: 40 MIN. • **COOK:** 7½ HOURS
MAKES: 10 SERVINGS (3½ QUARTS)

- 1 medium leek (white portion only), thinly sliced
- 1 small onion, chopped
- 1 tablespoon olive oil
- 3 slices deli ham, chopped
- 2 garlic cloves, minced
- 2 quarts water
- 1 can (28 ounces) diced tomatoes, undrained
- 1 medium butternut squash, peeled, seeded and cubed
- 2 medium carrots, coarsely chopped
- 2 celery ribs, chopped
- 2 cups fresh baby spinach, cut into thin strips
- 1 cup thinly sliced fresh kale
- 1 medium potato, peeled and cubed
- 1 tablespoon minced fresh rosemary
- 1 teaspoon salt
  Pepper to taste
- 1 can (15 ounces) cannellini beans, rinsed and drained

1. In a small skillet, saute leek and onion in oil for 2 minutes or until vegetables are tender. Add ham and garlic; cook 1 minute longer.
2. Transfer ham mixture to a 5-qt. slow cooker. Stir in the water, vegetables, rosemary, salt and pepper. Cover and cook on low for 7-8 hours or until vegetables are tender.
3. Stir in beans; cover and cook 30 minutes longer.
PER SERVING *1½ cups equals 134 cal., 2 g fat (trace sat. fat), 3 mg chol., 477 mg sodium, 26 g carb., 7 g fiber, 5 g pro. **Diabetic Exchanges:** 2 vegetable, 1 starch.*

BEAN SOUP WITH CORNMEAL DUMPLINGS

This soup's great Southwestern flavor is a real winner with my family. I love it because I can have the soup already cooking when I get home from work. Then I simply make the dumplings and dinner is almost ready.

—JOAN HALLFORD
NORTH RICHLAND HILLS, TX

PREP: 15 MIN. • **COOK:** 6½ HOURS
MAKES: 6 SERVINGS

- 2 **cans (14½ ounces each) chicken broth**
- 1 **package (16 ounces) frozen mixed vegetables**
- 1 **can (15 ounces) black beans, rinsed and drained**
- 1 **can (15 ounces) pinto beans, rinsed and drained**
- 1 **can (14½ ounces) diced tomatoes, undrained**
- 1 **medium onion, chopped**
- 1 **tablespoon chili powder**
- 1 **tablespoon minced fresh cilantro**
- 4 **garlic cloves, minced**
- ¼ **teaspoon pepper**

CORNMEAL DUMPLINGS

- ½ **cup all-purpose flour**
- ½ **cup shredded cheddar cheese**
- ⅓ **cup cornmeal**
- 1 **tablespoon sugar**
- 1 **teaspoon baking powder**
- 1 **large egg**
- 2 **tablespoons milk**
- 2 **teaspoons canola oil**

1. In a 5-qt. slow cooker, combine the first 10 ingredients. Cover and cook on low for 6-8 hours or until vegetables are tender.
2. For dumplings, combine the flour, cheese, cornmeal, sugar and baking powder in a large bowl. In another bowl, combine the egg, milk and oil; add to dry ingredients just until moistened (batter will be stiff).
3. Drop by heaping tablespoons onto soup. Cover and cook on high for 30 minutes (without lifting cover) or until a toothpick inserted into a dumpling comes out clean.
PER SERVING *1 serving (1 cup) equals 334 cal., 6 g fat (3 g sat. fat), 46 mg chol., 774 mg sodium, 55 g carb., 12 g fiber, 16 g pro.*

VEGGIE MEATBALL SOUP FOR 3

It's a snap to put together this hearty soup before I leave for work. I just add uncooked pasta when I get home, and I have a few minutes to relax before supper is ready.

—CHARLA TINNEY TYRONE, OK

PREP: 10 MIN. • **COOK:** 4¼ HOURS
MAKES: 3 CUPS

- 1½ **cups reduced-sodium beef broth**
- 1 **cup frozen mixed vegetables, thawed**
- ¾ **cup canned stewed tomatoes**
- 9 **frozen fully cooked homestyle meatballs (½ ounce each), thawed**
- 2 **bay leaves**
- ⅛ **teaspoon pepper**
- ½ **cup uncooked spiral pasta**

In a 1½-qt. slow cooker, combine the first six ingredients. Cover and cook on low for 4-5 hours or until heated through. Stir in pasta; cover and cook 20-30 minutes longer or until tender. Discard bay leaves.
PER SERVING *1 cup equals 250 cal., 11 g fat (5 g sat. fat), 35 mg chol., 671 mg sodium, 26 g carb., 5 g fiber, 11 g pro.* **Diabetic Exchanges:** *1½ starch, 1½ fat, 1 lean meat, 1 vegetable.*

THE SKINNY

BRING ON THE BEANS

Beans are packed with protein and fiber, making recipes such as Bean Soup with Cornmeal Dumplings a smart choice. The nutritional one-two punch of fiber and protein means you'll stay fuller longer, which can save you from snacking between meals and adding more calories.

**VEGGIE MEATBALL
SOUP FOR 3**

FORGOTTEN
MINESTRONE

SLOW-COOKED
CHILI

VEGETABLE
PORK SOUP

FORGOTTEN MINESTRONE

This soup gets its name because the broth simmers for hours, allowing me to work on other things. But after one taste, you and your family will agree this full-flavored soup is truly unforgettable!

—MARSHA RANSOM
SOUTH HAVEN, MI

PREP: 15 MIN. • **COOK:** 8½ HOURS
MAKES: 8 SERVINGS (2 QUARTS)

- 1 **pound beef stew meat, cut into ½-inch cubes**
- 1 **can (28 ounces) diced tomatoes, undrained**
- 1 **medium onion, chopped**
- 2 **tablespoons minced dried parsley**
- 1 **teaspoon salt**
- 1½ **teaspoons ground thyme**
- 1 **beef bouillon cube**
- ½ **teaspoon pepper**
- 6 **cups water**
- 1 **medium zucchini, halved and thinly sliced**
- 2 **cups chopped cabbage**
- 1 **can (15 ounces) garbanzo beans or chickpeas, rinsed and drained**
- 1 **cup uncooked elbow macaroni Grated Parmesan cheese, optional**

1. In a 5-qt. slow cooker, combine the first nine ingredients. Cover and cook on low for 8-10 hours or until meat is tender.
2. Add the zucchini, cabbage, beans and macaroni; cover and cook on high for 30-45 minutes or until the macaroni and vegetables are tender. Sprinkle servings with cheese, if desired.
PER SERVING *1 cup (calculated without cheese) equals 202 cal., 5 g fat (2 g sat. fat), 35 mg chol., 661 mg sodium, 24 g carb., 5 g fiber, 16 g pro.* ***Diabetic Exchanges:*** *2 lean meat, 2 vegetable, 1 starch.*

SLOW-COOKED CHILI

This hearty chili can cook for up to 10 hours on low in the slow cooker. It's so good to come home to its wonderful aroma after a long day.

—SUE CALL BEECH GROVE, IN

PREP: 20 MIN. • **COOK:** 8 HOURS
MAKES: 10 SERVINGS (2½ QUARTS)

- 2 **pounds lean ground beef (90% lean)**
- 2 **cans (16 ounces each) kidney beans, rinsed and drained**
- 2 **cans (14½ ounces each) diced tomatoes, undrained**
- 1 **can (8 ounces) tomato sauce**
- 2 **medium onions, chopped**
- 1 **green pepper, chopped**
- 2 **garlic cloves, minced**
- 2 **tablespoons chili powder**
- 1 **teaspoon salt**
- 1 **teaspoon pepper**
  Shredded cheddar cheese, optional

1. In a large skillet, cook the beef over medium heat until no longer pink; drain.
2. Transfer to a 5-qt. slow cooker. Add next nine ingredients. Cover and cook on low for 8-10 hours. Garnish individual servings with cheese, if desired.
PER SERVING *1 cup (calculated without cheese) equals 260 cal., 8 g fat (3 g sat. fat), 57 mg chol., 476 mg sodium, 23 g carb., 7 g fiber, 25 g pro.* ***Diabetic Exchanges:*** *3 lean meat, 1½ starch, 1 vegetable.*

VEGETABLE PORK SOUP

Packed with nutritious veggies, tender pork and savory flavor, this healthy soup fills the house with a tantalizing aroma as it cooks.

—DEB HALL HUNTINGTON, IN

PREP: 20 MIN. • **COOK:** 7 HOURS
MAKES: 6 SERVINGS (2 QUARTS)

- 1 **pound pork tenderloin, cut into 1-inch pieces**
- 1 **teaspoon garlic powder**
- 2 **teaspoons canola oil**
- 1 **can (28 ounces) diced tomatoes**
- 4 **medium carrots, cut into ½-inch pieces**
- 2 **medium potatoes, cubed**
- 1 **can (12 ounces) light or nonalcoholic beer**
- ¼ **cup quick-cooking tapioca**
- 2 **bay leaves**
- 1 **tablespoon Worcestershire sauce**
- 1 **tablespoon honey**
- 1 **teaspoon dried thyme**
- ¼ **teaspoon salt**
- ¼ **teaspoon pepper**
- ⅛ **teaspoon ground nutmeg**

1. Sprinkle pork with garlic powder. In a large skillet, brown pork in oil; drain.
2. Transfer to a 4-qt. slow cooker. Add the remaining ingredients. Cover and cook on low for 7-8 hours or until the meat is tender. Discard bay leaves.
PER SERVING *1⅓ cups equals 258 cal., 4 g fat (1 g sat. fat), 42 mg chol., 357 mg sodium, 34 g carb., 5 g fiber, 18 g pro.* ***Diabetic Exchanges:*** *2 lean meat, 2 vegetable, 1½ starch.*

TOP TIP

FREEZE INDIVIDUAL SOUP PORTIONS

To freeze soup or chili in handy single-serving packets, line a measuring cup with a small freezer bag to hold the bag upright, then fill with soup. Freeze the bags flat, then stack them for efficient storage.

BROCCOLI
POTATO SOUP

BROCCOLI POTATO SOUP

For a soothing soup with nice texture, try this one with broccoli and chunks of potato. The red pepper flakes add a hint of spice, and the fresh herbs make it a truly delicious soup.

—CRYSTAL KELSO SANDY, OR

PREP: 25 MIN. • **COOK:** 4½ HOURS
MAKES: 8 CUPS (2 QUARTS)

- 1 **pound small red potatoes, cubed**
- 1 **large onion, chopped**
- 1 **large carrot, coarsely chopped**
- 7 **garlic cloves, minced**
- 3 **cups water**
- 1 **can (14½ ounces) condensed cream of broccoli soup, undiluted**
- 1 **teaspoon each minced fresh thyme, basil and parsley**
- 1 **teaspoon garlic powder**
- ½ **teaspoon salt**
- ½ **teaspoon crushed red pepper flakes**
- ¼ **teaspoon pepper**
- 2 **cups frozen chopped broccoli, thawed and drained**
- 1 **cup (4 ounces) shredded Havarti cheese**

1. Place potatoes, onion, carrot and garlic in a 4- or 5-qt. slow cooker. Add the water, soup and seasonings. Cover and cook on low for 4-5 hours or until heated through.

2. Stir in the broccoli and cheese. Cover and cook for 30 minutes or until broccoli is tender.

PER SERVING *1 cup equals 158 cal., 6 g fat (3 g sat. fat), 15 mg chol., 563 mg sodium, 20 g carb., 3 g fiber, 7 g pro.* **Diabetic Exchanges:** *1½ starch, 1 fat.*

BLACK BEAN 'N' PUMPKIN CHILI

My family is crazy about this slow cooker recipe because it uses ingredients you don't usually find in chili. Believe it or not, I discovered that pumpkin is what makes this dish so special. Cook up a big batch and freeze some for later; it tastes even better reheated.

—DEBORAH VLIET HOLLAND, MI

PREP: 20 MIN. • **COOK:** 4 HOURS
MAKES: 10 SERVINGS (2½ QUARTS)

- 2 tablespoons olive oil
- 1 medium onion, chopped
- 1 medium sweet yellow pepper, chopped
- 3 garlic cloves, minced
- 2 cans (15 ounces each) black beans, rinsed and drained
- 1 can (15 ounces) solid-pack pumpkin
- 1 can (14½ ounces) diced tomatoes, undrained
- 3 cups chicken broth
- 2½ cups cubed cooked turkey
- 2 teaspoons dried parsley flakes
- 2 teaspoons chili powder
- 1½ teaspoons ground cumin
- 1½ teaspoons dried oregano
- ½ teaspoon salt
  Cubed avocado and thinly sliced green onions, optional

1. In a large skillet, heat oil over medium-high heat. Add onion and pepper; cook and stir until tender. Add garlic; cook 1 minute longer.

2. Transfer to a 5-qt. slow cooker; stir in the next 10 ingredients. Cook, covered, on low 4-5 hours. If desired, top with avocado and green onions.

PER SERVING *1 cup equals 192 cal., 5 g fat (1 g sat. fat), 28 mg chol., 658 mg sodium, 21 g carb., 7 g fiber, 16 g pro.* **Diabetic Exchanges:** *2 lean meat, 1½ starch, ½ fat.*

BLACK BEAN 'N' PUMPKIN CHILI

RED BEAN
VEGETABLE SOUP

RED BEAN VEGETABLE SOUP

Cajun seasoning boosts my bean soup that's loaded with fresh vegetables. Yum!

—**RONNIE LAPPE** BROWNWOOD, TX

PREP: 15 MIN. • **COOK:** 6 HOURS
MAKES: 12 SERVINGS (3 QUARTS)

- 3 **large sweet red peppers, chopped**
- 3 **celery ribs, chopped**
- 2 **medium onions, chopped**
- 4 **cans (16 ounces each) kidney beans, rinsed and drained**
- 4 **cups chicken broth**
- 2 **bay leaves**
- ½ **to 1 teaspoon salt**
- ½ **to 1 teaspoon Cajun seasoning**
- ½ **teaspoon pepper**
- ¼ **to ½ teaspoon hot pepper sauce**

In a 5-qt. slow cooker, combine the peppers, celery, onions and beans. Stir in the remaining ingredients. Cover and cook on low for 6 hours or until the vegetables are tender. Discard bay leaves before serving.
PER SERVING *1 cup equals 158 cal., trace fat (trace sat. fat), 2 mg chol., 701 mg sodium, 29 g carb., 8 g fiber, 11 g pro.* **Diabetic Exchanges:** *2 starch, 1 lean meat.*

MANHATTAN CLAM CHOWDER

I came up with this simple, delicious soup years ago when my husband and I both worked. It's easy to dump all the ingredients into the slow cooker in the morning and come home to a prepared meal.

—**MARY DIXON** NORTHVILLE, MI

PREP: 10 MIN. • **COOK:** 8 HOURS
MAKES: 9 SERVINGS

- 3 **celery ribs, sliced**
- 1 **large onion, chopped**
- 1 **can (14½ ounces) sliced potatoes, drained**
- 1 **can (14½ ounces) sliced carrots, drained**
- 2 **cans (6½ ounces each) chopped clams**
- 2 **cups reduced-sodium tomato juice**
- 1½ **cups water**
- ½ **cup tomato puree**
- 1 **tablespoon dried parsley flakes**
- 1½ **teaspoons dried thyme**
- ½ **teaspoon salt**
- 1 **bay leaf**
- 2 **whole black peppercorns**

In a 3-qt. slow cooker, combine all ingredients. Cover and cook on low for 8-10 hours or until vegetables are tender. Discard bay leaf and peppercorns.
PER SERVING *1 cup equals 80 cal., trace fat (trace sat. fat), 14 mg chol., 612 mg sodium, 13 g carb., 3 g fiber, 4 g pro.* **Diabetic Exchanges:** *1 starch, 1 lean meat.*

SLOW-COOKED HAMBURGER SOUP

I work full time but my family sits down to a home-cooked meal just about every night, thanks in part to simple recipes like this. I love that I can make it in the slow cooker.

—**THERESA JACKSON** CICERO, NY

PREP: 15 MIN. • **COOK:** 8 HOURS
MAKES: 10 SERVINGS (2½ QUARTS)

- 1 **pound lean ground beef (90% lean)**
- 1 **medium onion, chopped**
- 2 **garlic cloves, minced**
- 4 **cups V8 juice**
- 1 **can (14½ ounces) stewed tomatoes**
- 2 **cups coleslaw mix**
- 2 **cups frozen green beans**
- 2 **cups frozen corn**
- 2 **tablespoons Worcestershire sauce**
- 1 **teaspoon dried basil**
- ½ **teaspoon salt**
- ¼ **teaspoon pepper**

In a large saucepan, cook the beef and onion over medium heat until meat is no longer pink. Add garlic; cook 1 minute longer. Drain. In a 5-qt. slow cooker, combine the remaining ingredients. Stir in beef mixture. Cover and cook on low for 8-10 hours or until the vegetables are tender.
PER SERVING *1 cup equals 145 cal., 4 g fat (2 g sat. fat), 28 mg chol., 507 mg sodium, 17 g carb., 3 g fiber, 11 g pro.* **Diabetic Exchanges:** *1 lean meat, 1 vegetable, ½ starch.*

HOW-TO

MAKE YOUR OWN CAJUN SEASONING

Can't find Cajun seasoning in the spice section of your grocery store? Go the DIY route! There are many different blends, but a typical mix includes salt, onion powder, garlic powder, cayenne pepper, ground mustard, celery seed and pepper.

SLOW COOKER
SPLIT PEA SOUP

SLOW COOKER SPLIT PEA SOUP

When I have leftover ham in the fridge, I always like to make this soup. Just throw the ingredients into the slow cooker, turn it on and dinner is set.

—PAMELA CHAMBERS
WEST COLUMBIA, SC

PREP: 15 MIN. • **COOK:** 8 HOURS
MAKES: 8 SERVINGS

- 1 **package (16 ounces) dried green split peas, rinsed**
- 2 **cups cubed fully cooked ham**
- 1 **large onion, chopped**
- 1 **cup julienned or chopped carrots**
- 3 **garlic cloves, minced**
- ½ **teaspoon dried rosemary, crushed**
- ½ **teaspoon dried thyme**
- 1 **carton (32 ounces) reduced-sodium chicken broth**
- 2 **cups water**

In a 4- or 5-qt. slow cooker, combine all ingredients. Cover and cook on low for 8-10 hours or until the peas are tender.

FREEZE OPTION *Freeze cooled soup in freezer containers. To use, thaw overnight in the refrigerator. Heat through in a saucepan over medium heat, stirring occasionally.*
PER SERVING *1 cup equals 260 cal., 2 g fat (1 g sat. fat), 21 mg chol., 728 mg sodium, 39 g carb., 15 g fiber, 23 g pro.* **Diabetic Exchanges:** *2½ starch, 2 lean meat.*

TOP TIP

SOUP-ER TOPPINGS
Make your split pea soup even more filling by topping the servings with diced vegetables of your choice. Be creative and discover a new combination you like!

FRESH PUMPKIN SOUP

LIME NAVY BEAN CHILI

I love using my slow cooker for tasty soups like this one. Just fill it in the morning and come home to a warm, wonderful meal—no matter how busy the day!

—**CONNIE THOMAS** JENSEN, UT

PREP: 15 MIN. + SOAKING
COOK: 5 HOURS • **MAKES:** 6 SERVINGS

- 1¼ **cups dried navy beans**
- 3 **cups water**
- 2 **bone-in chicken breast halves (7 ounces each), skin removed**
- 1 **cup frozen corn**
- 1 **medium onion, chopped**
- 1 **can (4 ounces) chopped green chilies**
- 4 **garlic cloves, minced**
- 1 **tablespoon chicken bouillon granules**
- 1 **teaspoon ground cumin**
- ½ **teaspoon chili powder**
- 2 **tablespoons lime juice**

FRESH PUMPKIN SOUP

This appealing soup harvests the fall flavors of just-picked pumpkins and tart apples, and is sure to warm you up on a crisp autumn day. I top the creamy puree with a sprinkling of toasted pumpkin seeds.

—**JANE SHAPTON** IRVINE, CA

PREP: 50 MIN. • **COOK:** 8 HOURS
MAKES: 9 SERVINGS (ABOUT 2 QUARTS)

- 8 **cups chopped fresh pumpkin (about 3 pounds)**
- 4 **cups chicken broth**
- 3 **small tart apples, peeled and chopped**
- 1 **medium onion, chopped**
- 2 **tablespoons lemon juice**
- 2 **teaspoons minced fresh gingerroot**
- 2 **garlic cloves, minced**
- ½ **teaspoon salt**

TOASTED PUMPKIN SEEDS
- ½ **cup fresh pumpkin seeds**
- 1 **teaspoon canola oil**
- ⅛ **teaspoon salt**

1. In a 5-qt. slow cooker, combine the first eight ingredients. Cover and cook on low for 8-10 hours or until the pumpkin and apples are tender.

2. Meanwhile, toss pumpkin seeds with oil and salt. Spread onto an ungreased 15x10x1-in. baking pan. Bake at 250° for 45-50 minutes or until golden brown. Set aside.

3. Cool soup slightly; process in batches in a blender. Transfer to a large saucepan; heat through. Garnish servings with toasted pumpkin seeds.

PER SERVING *1 cup soup with 1 tablespoon seeds equals 102 cal., 2 g fat (0.55 g sat. fat), 0 chol., 567 mg sodium, 22 g carb., 3 g fiber, 3 g pro.* **Diabetic Exchanges:** *1 starch, ½ fruit.*

1. Sort the beans and rinse with cold water. Place the beans in a large saucepan; add enough water to cover by 2 in. Bring to a boil; boil for 2 minutes. Remove from heat; cover and let soak for 1-4 hours or until beans are softened. Drain and rinse beans, discarding liquid.

2. In a 3-qt. slow cooker, combine the beans, 3 cups of water, chicken, corn, onion, chilies, garlic, bouillon, cumin and chili powder. Cover and cook on low for 5-6 hours or until a thermometer reads 170° and beans are tender.

3. Remove chicken breasts; set aside until cool enough to handle. Remove meat from bones; discard bones and cut meat into bite-size pieces. Return chicken to pot. Stir in lime juice just before serving.

PER SERVING *1 cup equals 250 cal., 2 g fat (1 g sat. fat), 30 mg chol., 532 mg sodium, 37 g carb., 12 g fiber, 22 g pro.* **Diabetic Exchanges:** *2 starch, 3 lean meat, 1 vegetable.*

SUMMER'S BOUNTY SOUP

This chunky soup, packed with garden-fresh veggies, is so versatile. You can add or omit just about any vegetable to make the most of what you have.

—VICTORIA HAHN
NORTHAMPTON, PA

PREP: 5 MIN. • **COOK:** 7 HOURS
MAKES: 14 SERVINGS
(ABOUT 3½ QUARTS)

- 4 medium tomatoes, chopped
- 2 medium potatoes, peeled and cubed
- 2 cups halved fresh green beans
- 2 small zucchini, cubed
- 1 medium yellow summer squash, cubed
- 4 small carrots, thinly sliced
- 2 celery ribs, thinly sliced
- 1 cup cubed peeled eggplant
- 1 cup sliced fresh mushrooms
- 1 small onion, chopped
- 1 tablespoon minced fresh parsley
- 1 tablespoon salt-free garlic and herb seasoning
- 4 cups reduced-sodium V8 juice

Combine all ingredients in a 5-qt. slow cooker. Cook, covered, on low 7-8 hours or until vegetables are tender.
PER SERVING *1 cup equals 67 cal., trace fat (trace sat. fat), 0 chol., 62 mg sodium, 15 g carb., 3 g fiber, 2 g pro. Diabetic Exchange: 2 vegetable.*

SPICY COWBOY CHILI

Toasting the peppers for this chili releases their earthy flavors, but wear gloves when handling dried peppers and seeds, as they can burn the skin.

—RACHEL SPRINKEL HILO, HI

PREP: 45 MIN. • **COOK:** 7 HOURS
MAKES: 14 SERVINGS (3½ QUARTS)

- 1 whole garlic bulb
- 2 to 3 tablespoons olive oil, divided
- 2 dried ancho chilies
- 2 dried chipotle chilies
- 1 bottle (12 ounces) dark beer
- 3 pounds beef stew meat, cut into ¾-inch pieces
- 2 large onions, chopped
- 3 cans (16 ounces each) kidney beans, rinsed and drained
- 3 cans (14½ ounces each) diced tomatoes, undrained
- 2 cans (8 ounces each) tomato sauce
- 2 tablespoons Worcestershire sauce
- 1 tablespoon chili powder
- 1 teaspoon pepper
- ½ teaspoon salt
  Shredded cheddar cheese, optional

1. Preheat oven to 425°. Remove papery outer skin from garlic bulb, but do not peel or separate the cloves. Cut off top of garlic bulb, exposing individual cloves. Brush cut cloves with 1 teaspoon oil. Wrap in foil. Bake 30-35 minutes or until cloves are soft. Unwrap and cool slightly. Squeeze garlic from skins; mash with a fork.
2. Meanwhile, in a large dry skillet over medium-high heat, toast chilies on both sides until puffy, about 3-6 minutes. (Do not blacken.) Cool. Remove stems and seeds; coarsely chop chilies. Place in a small bowl; cover with beer. Let stand to soften, about 30 minutes.
3. In the same skillet, heat 1 tablespoon oil over medium-high heat. Brown beef in batches, adding more oil if needed; transfer to a 6-qt. slow cooker. In the skillet, heat 2 teaspoons oil over medium heat. Add onions; cook and stir until tender. Add to beef.
4. Stir in the remaining ingredients, mashed garlic and beer-chilies mixture. Cover and cook on low 7-9 hours or until meat is tender. If desired, serve with cheese.
NOTE *You may substitute ½ teaspoon ground chipotle pepper for dried chipotle chilies; add ground chipotle to slow cooker along with mashed garlic and beer mixture.*
PER SERVING *1 cup equals 301 cal., 9 g fat (3 g sat. fat), 60 mg chol., 588 mg sodium, 27 g carb., 8 g fiber, 27 g pro. Diabetic Exchanges: 4 lean meat, 1½ starch, 1 vegetable.*

SUMMER'S BOUNTY SOUP

SPICY COWBOY
CHILI

CIOPPINO

CIOPPINO

If you're looking for a great seafood recipe to create in your slow cooker, this classic fish stew is just the ticket. It's full to the brim with clams, crab, fish and shrimp.

—LISA MORIARTY WILTON, NH

PREP: 20 MIN. • **COOK:** 4½ HOURS
MAKES: 8 SERVINGS (2½ QUARTS)

- 1 can (28 ounces) diced tomatoes, undrained
- 2 medium onions, chopped
- 3 celery ribs, chopped
- 1 bottle (8 ounces) clam juice
- 1 can (6 ounces) tomato paste
- ½ cup white wine or ½ cup vegetable broth
- 5 garlic cloves, minced
- 1 tablespoon red wine vinegar
- 1 tablespoon olive oil
- 1 to 2 teaspoons Italian seasoning
- 1 bay leaf
- ½ teaspoon sugar
- 1 pound haddock fillets, cut into 1-inch pieces
- 1 pound uncooked shrimp (41-50 per pound), peeled and deveined
- 1 can (6 ounces) chopped clams, undrained
- 1 can (6 ounces) lump crabmeat, drained
- 2 tablespoons minced fresh parsley

1. In a 4- or 5-qt. slow cooker, combine the first 12 ingredients. Cook, covered, on low 4-5 hours.
2. Stir in seafood. Cook, covered, 20-30 minutes longer or until fish just begins to flake easily with a fork and shrimp turn pink.
3. Remove bay leaf. Stir in parsley.
PER SERVING 1¼ cups equals 205 cal., 3 g fat (1 g sat. fat), 125 mg chol., 483 mg sodium, 15 g carb., 3 g fiber, 29 g pro. *Diabetic Exchanges: 3 lean meat, 2 vegetable.*

SLOW-COOKED HALIBUT CHOWDER

Mashed potato flakes are a great hands-free way to thicken the chowder as it simmers. When we lived in Alaska, we were spoiled with abundant fresh halibut, but feel free to substitute whatever fish you like.

—DONNA GOUTERMONT
SEQUIM, WA

PREP: 20 MIN. • **COOK:** 5½ HOURS
MAKES: 6 SERVINGS

- 2 cups water
- 2 cups 2% milk
- 2 medium potatoes, cubed
- 1 large onion, chopped
- 1 cup mashed potato flakes
- 1 can (8 ounces) tomato sauce
- 2 garlic cloves, minced
- 1 teaspoon celery salt
- 1 teaspoon dried parsley flakes
- ½ teaspoon ground mustard
- ¼ teaspoon chili powder
- ¼ teaspoon cayenne pepper
- 1 pound halibut fillets, cut into chunks
- 1 tablespoon butter

1. In a 3-qt. slow cooker, combine the first 12 ingredients. Cover and cook on low for 5 hours or until potatoes are tender.
2. Add halibut and butter. Cover and cook 30-45 minutes longer or until fish flakes easily with a fork.
PER SERVING 1¼ cups equals 254 cal., 6 g fat (3 g sat. fat), 37 mg chol., 534 mg sodium, 27 g carb., 2 g fiber, 21 g pro. *Diabetic Exchanges: 2 lean meat, 2 starch.*

VERMICELLI BEEF STEW

I love to try new recipes for my husband and myself, and also when we entertain friends and relatives. This stew is a little different from most because of the vermicelli.

—SHARON DELANEY-CHRONIS
SOUTH MILWAUKEE, WI

PREP: 20 MIN. • **COOK:** 8½ HOURS
MAKES: 8 SERVINGS (2 QUARTS)

- 1½ pounds beef stew meat, cut into 1-inch cubes
- 1 medium onion, chopped
- 2 tablespoons canola oil
- 3 cups water
- 1 can (14½ ounces) diced tomatoes
- 1 package (16 ounces) frozen mixed vegetables, thawed
- 1 tablespoon dried basil
- 1 teaspoon salt
- 1 teaspoon dried oregano
- 6 ounces uncooked vermicelli, broken into 2-inch pieces
- ¼ cup grated Parmesan cheese

1. In a large skillet, brown meat and onion in oil; drain. Transfer to a 5-qt. slow cooker. Stir in the water, tomatoes, vegetables, basil, salt and oregano. Cover and cook on low for 8-10 hours or until the meat and vegetables are tender.
2. Stir in vermicelli. Cover and cook for 30 minutes or until pasta is tender. Sprinkle with cheese.
PER SERVING 1 cup equals 294 cal., 10 g fat (3 g sat. fat), 55 mg chol., 455 mg sodium, 28 g carb., 5 g fiber, 22 g pro. *Diabetic Exchanges: 2 lean meat, 2 vegetable, 1 starch, 1 fat.*

TOP TIP

WHICH FISH?

If you'd like to swap out the halibut in Slow-Cooked Halibut Chowder, you can try one of these fish with similar textures: red snapper, catfish, sea bass, trout or salmon.

BROWN SUGAR-GLAZED
BABY CARROTS, PAGE 44

SLOW &
EASY SIDES

40

43

47

PARSLEY SMASHED POTATOES

I love potatoes but hate the work involved in making mashed potatoes from scratch. So I came up with a simple side dish made even easier thanks to my slow cooker. You can save the leftover broth to make soup the next day!

—**KATIE HAGY** BLACKSBURG, SC

PREP: 20 MIN. • **COOK:** 6 HOURS
MAKES: 8 SERVINGS

- 16 small red potatoes (about 2 pounds)
- 1 celery rib, sliced
- 1 medium carrot, sliced
- ¼ cup finely chopped onion
- 2 cups chicken broth
- 1 tablespoon minced fresh parsley
- 1½ teaspoons salt, divided
- 1 teaspoon pepper, divided
- 1 garlic clove, minced
- 2 tablespoons butter, melted
  Additional minced fresh parsley

1. Place potatoes, celery, carrot and onion in a 4-qt. slow cooker. In a small bowl, mix broth, parsley, 1 teaspoon salt, ½ teaspoon pepper and garlic; pour over vegetables. Cook, covered, on low 6-8 hours or until potatoes are tender.

2. Transfer potatoes from slow cooker to a 15x10x1-in. pan; discard cooking liquid and vegetables or save for other use. Using bottom of a measuring cup, flatten the potatoes slightly. Transfer to a large bowl; drizzle with butter. Sprinkle with the remaining salt and pepper; toss to coat. Sprinkle with additional parsley.

PER SERVING *2 smashed potatoes equals 114 cal., 3 g fat (2 g sat. fat), 8 mg chol., 190 mg sodium, 20 g carb., 2 g fiber, 2 g pro. **Diabetic Exchanges:** 1 starch, ½ fat.*

HONEY-BUTTER PEAS AND CARROTS

The classic combination of peas and carrots is made even better with a few flavor enhancers. Slow cooking allows the ingredients to meld for maximum richness.

—**THERESA KREYCHE** TUSTIN, CA

PREP: 15 MIN. • **COOK:** 5¼ HOURS
MAKES: 12 SERVINGS (½ CUP EACH)

- 1 pound carrots, sliced
- 1 large onion, chopped
- ¼ cup water
- ¼ cup butter, cubed
- ¼ cup honey
- 4 garlic cloves, minced
- 1 teaspoon salt
- 1 teaspoon dried marjoram
- ⅛ teaspoon white pepper
- 1 package (16 ounces) frozen peas

In a 3-qt. slow cooker, combine the first nine ingredients. Cook, covered, on low 5 hours. Stir in peas. Cook, covered, on high for 15-25 minutes longer or until vegetables are tender.

PER SERVING *½ cup equals 106 cal., 4 g fat (2 g sat. fat), 10 mg chol., 293 mg sodium, 16 g carb., 3 g fiber, 3 g pro. **Diabetic Exchanges:** 1 starch, 1 fat.*

TOP TIP

SERVE, THEN STORE
When food is finished cooking, remove it from the slow cooker within an hour. Promptly refrigerate any leftovers.

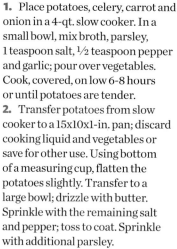

PARSLEY SMASHED POTATOES

HONEY-BUTTER
PEAS AND CARROTS

SIMPLE VEGETARIAN
SLOW-COOKED BEANS

SIMPLE VEGETARIAN SLOW-COOKED BEANS

When I have a hungry family to feed, I often go to these tasty beans with spinach, tomatoes and carrots. It's a veggie delight worth having on the menu frequently.

—JENNIFER REID FARMINGTON, ME

PREP: 15 MIN. • **COOK:** 4 HOURS
MAKES: 8 SERVINGS

- 4 cans (15½ ounces each) great northern beans, rinsed and drained
- 4 medium carrots, finely chopped (about 2 cups)
- 1 cup vegetable stock
- 6 garlic cloves, minced
- 2 teaspoons ground cumin
- ¾ teaspoon salt
- ⅛ teaspoon chili powder
- 4 cups fresh baby spinach, coarsely chopped
- 1 cup oil-packed sun-dried tomatoes, patted dry and chopped
- ⅓ cup minced fresh cilantro
- ⅓ cup minced fresh parsley

In a 3-qt. slow cooker, combine the first seven ingredients. Cook, covered, on low for 4-5 hours or until the carrots are tender, adding spinach and tomatoes during the last 10 minutes of cooking. Stir in cilantro and parsley.

PER SERVING *¾ cup equals 229 cal., 3 g fat (trace sat. fat), 0 chol., 672 mg sodium, 40 g carb., 13 g fiber, 12 g pro.*

(5) INGREDIENTS

EASY BEANS & POTATOES WITH BACON

Green beans and bacon are a combination I don't think you can beat, so I used them to crank up everyday potatoes .

—BARBARA BRITTAIN SANTEE, CA

PREP: 15 MIN. • **COOK:** 6 HOURS
MAKES: 10 SERVINGS

- 8 bacon strips, chopped
- 1½ pounds fresh green beans, trimmed and cut into 2-inch pieces (about 4 cups)
- 4 medium potatoes, peeled and cut into ½-inch cubes
- 1 small onion, halved and sliced
- ¼ cup reduced-sodium chicken broth
- ½ teaspoon salt
- ¼ teaspoon pepper

1. In a skillet, cook the bacon over medium heat until crisp, stirring occasionally. Remove to paper towels with a slotted spoon; drain, reserving 1 tablespoon drippings. Cover and refrigerate until serving.

2. In a 5-qt. slow cooker, combine the remaining ingredients; stir in reserved drippings. Cover and cook on low for 6-8 hours or until the potatoes are tender. Stir in bacon; heat through.

PER SERVING ¾ *cup equals 116 cal., 4 g fat (1 g sat. fat), 8 mg chol., 256 mg sodium, 17 g carb., 3 g fiber, 5 g pro.* **Diabetic Exchanges:** *1 starch, 1 fat.*

EASY BEANS & POTATOES WITH BACON

BLACK-EYED PEAS & HAM

We have slow-cooked black-eyed peas regularly at our house—they are just so good.

—DAWN FRIHAUF FORT MORGAN, CO

PREP: 20 MIN. + SOAKING
COOK: 5 HOURS
MAKES: 12 SERVINGS (¾ CUP EACH)

- 1 package (16 ounces) dried black-eyed peas, rinsed and sorted
- ½ pound fully cooked boneless ham, finely chopped
- 1 medium onion, finely chopped
- 1 medium sweet red pepper, finely chopped
- 5 bacon strips, cooked and crumbled
- 1 large jalapeno pepper, seeded and finely chopped
- 2 garlic cloves, minced
- 1½ teaspoons ground cumin
- 1 teaspoon reduced-sodium chicken bouillon granules
- ½ teaspoon salt
- ½ teaspoon cayenne pepper
- ¼ teaspoon pepper
- 6 cups water
  Minced fresh cilantro, optional
  Hot cooked rice

1. Rinse and sort the peas; soak according to package directions.
2. Transfer peas to a 6-qt. slow cooker; add the next 12 ingredients. Cover and cook on low for 5-7 hours or until peas are tender. Sprinkle with cilantro if desired. Serve with the rice.
NOTE *Wear disposable gloves when cutting hot peppers; the oils can burn skin. Avoid touching your face.*
PER SERVING *¾ cup (calculated without rice) equals 170 cal., 3 g fat (1 g sat. fat), 13 mg chol., 386 mg sodium, 24 g carb., 7 g fiber, 13 g pro.* **Diabetic Exchanges:** *1½ starch, 1 lean meat.*

FALL GARDEN MEDLEY

Here's a very colorful, tasty and healthy recipe to make for special occasions or anytime, especially in the fall and winter. It complements so many different meat dishes.

—KRYSTINE KERCHER LINCOLN, NE

PREP: 20 MIN. • **COOK:** 5 HOURS
MAKES: 8 SERVINGS

- 4 large carrots, cut into 1½-inch pieces
- 3 fresh beets, peeled and cut into 1½-inch pieces.
- 2 medium sweet potatoes, peeled and cut into 1½-inch pieces
- 2 medium onions, peeled and quartered
- ½ cup water
- 2 teaspoons salt
- ½ teaspoon pepper
- ¼ teaspoon dried thyme
- 1 tablespoon olive oil
  Fresh parsley or dried parsley flakes, optional

1. Place the carrots, beets, sweet potatoes, onions and water in a greased 3-qt. slow cooker. Sprinkle with salt, pepper and thyme. Drizzle with olive oil. Cover and cook on low for 5-6 hours or until tender.
2. Stir the vegetables and sprinkle with parsley if desired.
PER SERVING *¾ cup equals 83 cal., 2 g fat (trace sat. fat), 0 chol., 633 mg sodium, 16 g carb., 3 g fiber, 2 g pro.* **Diabetic Exchanges:** *1 vegetable, ½ starch.*

⑤ INGREDIENTS

BROWN SUGAR-GLAZED BABY CARROTS

When things get busy during the holidays, delicious glazed carrots come to the rescue. They cook while I'm preparing other parts of the meal, and I'm able to use my oven for other dishes, especially the turkey.

—ANNDREA BAILEY
HUNTINGTON BEACH, CA

PREP: 10 MIN. • **COOK:** 6 HOURS
MAKES: 6 SERVINGS

- 2 pounds fresh baby carrots
- 1 celery rib, finely chopped
- 1 small onion, finely chopped
- ¼ cup packed brown sugar
- 3 tablespoons butter, cubed
- ½ teaspoon salt
- ½ teaspoon pepper

In a 3-qt. slow cooker, combine all the ingredients. Cover and cook on low for 6-8 hours or until the carrots are tender.
PER SERVING *¾ cup equals 144 cal., 6 g fat (4 g sat. fat), 15 mg chol., 364 mg sodium, 23 g carb., 3 g fiber, 1 g pro.*

HOW-TO

CHOP AN ONION

1. To quickly chop an onion, peel and cut in half from the root to the top. Leaving the root attached, place flat side down on work surface.
2. Cut vertically through the onion, leaving the root end uncut.
3. Cut across the onion, discarding root end. The closer the cuts, the more finely the onion will be chopped.

BLACK-EYED
PEAS & HAM

FALL GARDEN
MEDLEY

BROWN SUGAR-
GLAZED BABY CARROTS

FIESTA CORN
AND BEANS

FIESTA CORN AND BEANS

Bursting with Southwestern flavors, this zesty veggie medley can serve as a side dish or a meatless meal. Add a dollop of yogurt for a cool, creamy finishing touch.

—**GERALD HETRICK** ERIE, PA

PREP: 25 MIN. • **COOK:** 3 HOURS
MAKES: 10 SERVINGS

- 1 **large onion, chopped**
- 1 **medium green pepper, cut into 1-inch pieces**
- 1 **to 2 jalapeno peppers, seeded and sliced**
- 1 **tablespoon olive oil**
- 1 **garlic clove, minced**
- 2 **cans (16 ounces each) kidney beans, rinsed and drained**
- 1 **package (16 ounces) frozen corn**
- 1 **can (14½ ounces) diced tomatoes, undrained**
- 1 **teaspoon chili powder**
- ¾ **teaspoon salt**
- ½ **teaspoon ground cumin**
- ½ **teaspoon pepper**
  Optional toppings: plain yogurt and sliced ripe olives

1. In a large skillet, saute the onion and peppers in oil until tender. Add the garlic; cook for 1 minute longer. Transfer to a 4-qt. slow cooker. Stir in the beans, corn, tomatoes and the seasonings.

2. Cover and cook on low for 3-4 hours or until heated through. Serve corn and beans with yogurt and olives if desired.

NOTE *Wear disposable gloves when cutting hot peppers; the oils can burn skin. Avoid touching your face.*

PER SERVING *¾ cup (calculated without optional toppings) equals 149 cal., 2 g fat (trace sat. fat), 0 chol., 380 mg sodium, 28 g carb., 7 g fiber, 8 g pro.* **Diabetic Exchanges:** *1 starch, 1 lean meat, 1 vegetable.*

SLOW-COOKED SAUSAGE DRESSING

Dressings are delicious but often are not the healthiest side. I've cut some of the fat but none of the good flavor. No one will mind.

—**RAQUEL HAGGARD** EDMOND, OK

PREP: 20 MIN. • **COOK:** 3 HOURS
MAKES: 12 SERVINGS (⅔ CUP EACH)

- ½ **pound reduced-fat bulk pork sausage**
- 2 **celery ribs, chopped**
- 1 **large onion, chopped**
- 7 **cups seasoned stuffing cubes**
- 1 **can (14½ ounces) reduced-sodium chicken broth**
- 1 **medium tart apple, chopped**
- ⅓ **cup chopped pecans**
- 2 **tablespoons reduced-fat butter, melted**
- 1½ **teaspoons rubbed sage**
- ½ **teaspoon pepper**

1. In a large nonstick skillet, cook the sausage, celery and onion over medium heat until the meat is no longer pink; drain. Transfer the mixture to a large bowl; stir in the remaining ingredients.

2. Place in a 5-qt. slow cooker coated with cooking spray. Cover and cook on low for 3-4 hours or until heated through and apple is tender, stirring once.

NOTE *This recipe was tested with Land O'Lakes light stick butter.*

PER SERVING *⅔ cup equals 201 cal., 8 g fat (2 g sat. fat), 17 mg chol., 640 mg sodium, 26 g carb., 3 g fiber, 7 g pro.*

COCONUT-PECAN SWEET POTATOES

Let sweet potatoes cook effortlessly while you tend to other things. A little coconut gives the classic dish a new twist.

—**RAQUEL HAGGARD** EDMOND, OK

PREP: 15 MIN. • **COOK:** 4 HOURS
MAKES: 12 SERVINGS (⅔ CUP EACH)

- ½ **cup chopped pecans**
- ½ **cup flaked coconut**
- ⅓ **cup sugar**
- ⅓ **cup packed brown sugar**
- ½ **teaspoon ground cinnamon**
- ¼ **teaspoon salt**
- ¼ **cup reduced-fat butter, melted**
- 4 **pounds sweet potatoes (about 6 medium), peeled and cut into 1-inch pieces**
- ½ **teaspoon coconut extract**
- ½ **teaspoon vanilla extract**

1. In a small bowl, combine the first six ingredients; stir in melted butter. Place the sweet potatoes in a 5-qt. slow cooker coated with cooking spray. Sprinkle with the pecan mixture.

2. Cook, covered, on low 4 to 4½ hours or until potatoes are tender. Stir in extracts.

NOTE *This recipe was tested with Land O'Lakes light stick butter.*

PER SERVING *⅔ cup equals 211 cal., 7 g fat (3 g sat. fat), 5 mg chol., 103 mg sodium, 37 g carb., 3 g fiber, 2 g pro.*

THE SKINNY

GREEK YOGURT IS THE PERFECT TOPPING

Add a tablespoon or two of low-fat plain Greek yogurt to Fiesta Corn and Beans servings—with no guilt attached! It's low in calories while providing calcium and other nutrients.

SPICED CARROTS & BUTTERNUT SQUASH

When I've got a lot going on, the slow cooker is my go-to tool for cooking veggies. Spicy seasonings complement the sweetness of squash and carrots beautifully.
—**COURTNEY STULTZ** WEIR, KS

PREP: 15 MIN. • **COOK:** 4 HOURS
MAKES: 6 SERVINGS

- **5** large carrots, cut into ½-inch pieces (about 3 cups)
- **2** cups cubed peeled butternut squash (1-inch pieces)
- **1** tablespoon balsamic vinegar
- **1** tablespoon olive oil
- **1** tablespoon honey
- **1** teaspoon ground cinnamon
- **½** teaspoon salt
- **½** teaspoon ground cumin
- **¼** teaspoon chili powder

Place carrots and squash in a 3-qt. slow cooker. In a small bowl, mix remaining ingredients; drizzle over vegetables and toss to coat. Cook, covered, on low 4-5 hours or until vegetables are tender. Gently stir before serving.

PER SERVING ⅔ cup equals 85 cal., 3 g fat (trace sat. fat), 0 chol., 245 mg sodium, 16 g carb., 3 g fiber, 1 g pro. **Diabetic Exchanges:** 1 vegetable, ½ starch, ½ fat.

TOP TIP

THE BEST SQUASH

Look for butternut squash with hard, deep-colored rinds and no blemishes. Store unwashed squash in a dry, cool place for up to 1 month.

SWEET POTATO STUFFING

Mom likes to make sure there will be enough stuffing to satisfy our large family. For holiday gatherings, she slow-cooks this tasty sweet potato dressing in addition to the traditional stuffing cooked inside the turkey.
—**KELLY POLLOCK** LONDON, ON

PREP: 15 MIN. • **COOK:** 4 HOURS
MAKES: 10 SERVINGS

- **¼** cup butter, cubed
- **½** cup chopped celery
- **½** cup chopped onion
- **½** cup chicken broth
- **½** teaspoon salt
- **½** teaspoon rubbed sage
- **½** teaspoon poultry seasoning
- **½** teaspoon pepper
- **6** cups dry bread cubes
- **1** large sweet potato, cooked, peeled and finely chopped
- **¼** cup chopped pecans

1. In a Dutch oven, heat the butter over medium-high heat. Add the celery and onion; cook and stir until tender. Stir in broth and seasonings. Add remaining ingredients; toss to combine.

2. Transfer to a greased 3-qt. slow cooker. Cook, covered, on low 4 hours or until heated through.

PER SERVING 1 cup equals 212 cal., 8 g fat (3 g sat. fat), 12 mg chol., 459 mg sodium, 33 g carb., 3 g fiber, 5 g pro. **Diabetic Exchanges:** 2 starch, 1½ fat.

SPICED CARROTS & BUTTERNUT SQUASH

SWEET POTATO
STUFFING

CHIPOTLE SHREDDED
BEEF, PAGE 91

BEEF

56

67

92

SPICY BEEF VEGETABLE STEW

This zesty beef stew is packed with richness and goes together quickly. Try pairing it with warm corn bread, sourdough or some French bread for a memorable meal.

—LYNNETTE DAVIS TULLAHOMA, TN

PREP: 10 MIN. • **COOK:** 8 HOURS
MAKES: 8 SERVINGS (3 QUARTS)

- 1   **pound lean ground beef (90% lean)**
- 1   **cup chopped onion**
- 1   **jar (24 ounces) meatless pasta sauce**
- 3½ **cups water**
- 1   **package (16 ounces) frozen mixed vegetables**
- 1   **can (10 ounces) diced tomatoes and green chilies**
- 1   **cup sliced celery**
- 1   **teaspoon beef bouillon granules**
- 1   **teaspoon pepper**

1. In a large skillet, cook beef and onion over medium heat until meat is no longer pink; drain.

2. Transfer to a 5-qt. slow cooker. Stir in the remaining ingredients. Cover and cook on low for 8 hours or until the vegetables are tender.

PER SERVING *1½ cup equals 177 cal., 5 g fat (2 g sat. fat), 35 mg chol., 675 mg sodium, 19 g carb., 5 g fiber, 15 g pro.* **Diabetic Exchanges:** *2 meat, 1 starch.*

SPICY BEEF VEGETABLE STEW

SHREDDED BEEF SANDWICHES

Coated with a tasty, cola-flavored sauce, the meat gets its zip from chili powder and cayenne pepper.

—MARIE ELAINE BASINGER CONNELLSVILLE, PA

PREP: 30 MIN. • **COOK:** 8¼ HOURS
MAKES: 8 SERVINGS

- ¾   **cup cola**
- ¼   **cup Worcestershire sauce**
- 2   **garlic cloves, minced**
- 1   **tablespoon white vinegar**
- 1   **teaspoon reduced-sodium beef bouillon granules**
- ½   **teaspoon chili powder**
- ½   **teaspoon ground mustard**
- ¼   **teaspoon cayenne pepper**
- 1   **beef rump roast or bottom round roast (2 pounds)**
- 2   **teaspoons canola oil**
- 2   **medium onions, chopped**
- ½   **cup ketchup**
- 8   **hoagie buns, split**

1. In a measuring cup, combine the cola, Worcestershire sauce, garlic, vinegar, bouillon and the seasonings; set aside. Cut roast in half. In a nonstick skillet, brown meat in oil on all sides.

2. Place onions in a 3-qt. slow cooker. Top with meat. Pour half the cola mixture over meat. Cover and cook on low for 8-10 hours or until meat is tender. Cover and refrigerate remaining cola mixture.

3. Remove meat from cooking liquid and cool. Strain cooking liquid, reserving the onions and discarding the liquid. When meat is cool enough to handle, shred with two forks. Return meat and onions to slow cooker.

4. Combine ketchup and reserved cola mixture; pour over meat and heat through. Serve on buns.

PER SERVING *1 sandwich equals 354 cal., 10 g fat (2 g sat. fat), 59 mg chol., 714 mg sodium, 40 g carb., 2 g fiber, 26 g pro.* **Diabetic Exchanges:** *3 lean meat, 2½ starch.*

SHREDDED
BEEF SANDWICHES

MUSHROOM POT ROAST

Between wholesome veggies and tender beef, this is one special entree that all ages will like. Serve mashed potatoes alongside to soak up every last drop of the beefy gravy.

—ANGIE STEWART TOPEKA, KS

PREP: 25 MIN. • **COOK:** 6 HOURS
MAKES: 10 SERVINGS

- 1 boneless beef chuck roast (3 to 4 pounds)
- ½ teaspoon salt
- ¼ teaspoon pepper
- 1 tablespoon canola oil
- 1½ pounds sliced fresh shiitake mushrooms
- 2½ cups thinly sliced onions
- 1½ cups reduced-sodium beef broth
- 1½ cups dry red wine or additional reduced-sodium beef broth
- 1 can (8 ounces) tomato sauce
- ¾ cup chopped peeled parsnips
- ¾ cup chopped celery
- ¾ cup chopped carrots
- 8 garlic cloves, minced
- 2 bay leaves
- 1½ teaspoons dried thyme
- 1 teaspoon chili powder
- ¼ cup cornstarch
- ¼ cup water
  Mashed potatoes

1. Sprinkle the roast with salt and pepper. In a Dutch oven, brown the roast in oil on all sides. Transfer to a 6-qt. slow cooker. Add mushrooms, onions, broth, wine, tomato sauce, parsnips, celery, carrots, garlic, bay leaves, thyme and chili powder. Cover and cook on low for 6-8 hours or until meat is tender.

2. Remove meat and vegetables to a serving platter; keep warm. Discard bay leaves. Skim fat from cooking juices; transfer to a small saucepan. Bring liquid to a boil. Combine cornstarch and water until smooth; gradually stir into the pan. Bring to a boil; cook, stir for 2 minutes or until thickened. Serve with mashed potatoes, meat and vegetables.

PER SERVING *4 ounces cooked beef with ⅔ cup vegetables and ½ cup gravy (calculated without the potatoes) equals 310 cal., 14 g fat (5 g sat. fat), 89 mg chol., 363 mg sodium, 14 g carb., 3 g fiber, 30 g pro.* **Diabetic Exchanges:** *4 lean meat, 2 vegetable, 1½ fat.*

MUSHROOM
POT ROAST

FLANK STEAK
FAJITAS

MUSHROOM-BEEF SPAGHETTI SAUCE

I got the recipe for this sauce in a recipe exchange and wish I could credit the person who gave it to me. My children love it! I added the mushrooms, but if you'd like it even chunkier, add some bell pepper and other veggies, too.

—MEG FISHER MARIETTA, GA

PREP: 20 MIN. • **COOK:** 6 HOURS
MAKES: 12 SERVINGS (1½ QUARTS)

- 1 **pound lean ground beef (90% lean)**
- ½ **pound sliced fresh mushrooms**
- 1 **small onion, chopped**
- 2 **cans (14½ ounces each) diced tomatoes, undrained**
- 1 **can (12 ounces) tomato paste**
- 1 **can (8 ounces) tomato sauce**
- 1 **cup reduced-sodium beef broth**
- 2 **tablespoons dried parsley flakes**
- 1 **tablespoon brown sugar**
- 1 **teaspoon dried basil**
- 1 **teaspoon dried oregano**
- 1 **teaspoon salt**
- ¼ **teaspoon pepper**
  Hot cooked spaghetti
  Shredded Parmesan cheese, optional

1. In a large nonstick skillet, cook the beef, mushrooms and onion over medium heat until meat is no longer pink; drain. Transfer to a 3-qt. slow cooker.
2. Stir in the tomatoes, tomato paste, tomato sauce, broth, parsley, brown sugar, basil, oregano, salt and pepper. Cover and cook on low for 6-8 hours. Serve with spaghetti. Sprinkle with cheese if desired.
PER SERVING *½ cup sauce (calculated without spaghetti) equals 115 cal., 3 g fat (1 g sat. fat), 19 mg chol., 493 mg sodium, 12 g carb., 3 g fiber, 10 g pro.* **Diabetic Exchanges:** *2 vegetable, 1 lean meat.*

FLANK STEAK FAJITAS

Flank steak turns out tender, juicy and delicious in the slow cooker to create these tempting fajitas. I like to serve them with a side of Spanish rice.

—TWILA BURKHOLDER
MIDDLEBURG, PA

PREP: 20 MIN. • **COOK:** 6 HOURS
MAKES: 6 SERVINGS

- 1 **beef flank steak (1½ pounds)**
- 1 **medium onion, sliced**
- 1 **cup tomato juice**
- 1 **jalapeno pepper, seeded and chopped**
- 2 **garlic cloves, minced**
- 1 **tablespoon minced fresh cilantro**
- 1 **teaspoon ground cumin**
- 1 **teaspoon chili powder**
- ¼ **teaspoon salt**
- 1 **medium green pepper, julienned**
- 1 **medium sweet red pepper, julienned**
- 6 **flour tortillas (8 inches), warmed**
  Shredded cheddar cheese, sour cream and guacamole, optional

1. Thinly slice steak across the grain into strips; place in a 5-qt. slow cooker. Add onion, tomato juice, jalapeno, garlic, cilantro, cumin, chili powder and salt. Cover, cook on low for 5 hours.
2. Add green and red peppers. Cover and cook 1 hour longer or until the meat and vegetables are tender.
3. Using a slotted spoon, spoon meat mixture down the center of each tortilla. Sprinkle with cheese if desired. Fold sides of tortilla over filling. Serve with cheese, sour cream and guacamole if desired.
NOTE *Wear disposable gloves when cutting hot peppers; the oils can burn skin. Avoid touching your face.*
PER SERVING *1 fajita (calculated without optional ingredients) equals 340 cal., 12 g fat (4 g sat. fat), 48 mg chol., 549 mg sodium, 33 g carb., 2 g fiber, 25 g pro.* **Diabetic Exchanges:** *3 lean meat, 2 starch, 1 vegetable.*

MEAT LOAF FROM THE SLOW COOKER

I'm often asked for the recipe when I serve this easy-to-make meat loaf.

—LAURA BURGESS
MOUNT VERNON, SD

PREP: 25 MIN. • **COOK:** 3 HOURS
MAKES: 8 SERVINGS

- ½ cup tomato sauce
- 2 large eggs, lightly beaten
- ¼ cup ketchup
- 1 teaspoon Worcestershire sauce
- 1 small onion, chopped
- ⅓ cup crushed saltines (about 10 crackers)
- ¾ teaspoon minced garlic
- ¼ teaspoon seasoned salt
- ⅛ teaspoon seasoned pepper
- 1½ pounds lean ground beef (90% lean)
- ½ pound reduced-fat bulk pork sausage

SAUCE
- ½ cup ketchup
- 3 tablespoons brown sugar
- ¾ teaspoon ground mustard
- ¼ teaspoon ground nutmeg

1. Cut three 25x3-in. strips of heavy-duty foil; crisscross so they resemble spokes of a wheel. Place strips on the bottom and up the sides of a 4- or 5-qt. slow cooker. Coat strips with cooking spray.
2. In a large bowl, combine the first nine ingredients. Crumble beef and sausage over mixture and mix well (mixture will be moist). Shape into a loaf. Place meat loaf in the center of the strips.
3. In a small bowl, combine sauce ingredients. Spoon over meat loaf. Cover and cook on low 3-4 hours or until no pink remains and a thermometer reads 160°. Using foil strips as handles, remove the meat loaf to a platter.
PER SERVING *1 slice equals 284 cal., 14 g fat (5 g sat. fat), 119 mg chol., 681 mg sodium, 16 g carb., 1 g fiber, 24 g pro.* **Diabetic Exchanges:** *3 lean meat, 1 starch.*

FRENCH DIP SANDWICHES

I found this recipe in one of our local publications. The meat cooks for 10 to 12 hours, so come home to a dinner that's ready to go!

—DIANNE JOY RICHARDSON
COLORADO SPRINGS, CO

PREP: 15 MIN. • **COOK:** 10 HOURS
MAKES: 12 SANDWICHES

- 1 beef sirloin tip roast (3 to 4 pounds)
- ½ cup reduced-sodium soy sauce
- 1 teaspoon beef bouillon granules
- 1 bay leaf
- 3 to 4 whole peppercorns
- 1 teaspoon dried crushed rosemary
- 1 teaspoon dried thyme
- 1 teaspoon garlic powder
- 12 French rolls, split

1. Cut the roast in half. Place in a 5-qt. slow cooker. Combine the soy sauce, bouillon, seasonings; pour over roast. Add water to almost cover the roast, about 5 cups. Cover and cook on low 10-12 hours or until meat is tender.
2. Remove roast; cool slightly. Discard bay leaf. Shred the meat with two forks and return to slow cooker; heat through. Serve on rolls with broth.
PER SERVING *1 sandwich equals 318 cal., 8 g fat (2 g sat. fat), 72 mg chol., 792 mg sodium, 31 g carb., 1 g fiber, 29 g pro.* **Diabetic Exchanges:** *3 lean meat, 2 starch.*

TOP TIP

GET YOUR PROTEIN

Here's a hint for calculating your daily protein need: Multiply your body weight in pounds by .4 grams. For example, a 150-pound person needs about 60 grams of protein daily.

FRENCH DIP
SANDWICHES

ZESTY
BEEF STEW

ZESTY BEEF STEW

Preparation couldn't be simpler for this hearty stew. I created the dish when I didn't have some of my usual ingredients for vegetable beef soup. My husband told me it was the best stew I had ever made!

—**MARGARET TURZA** SOUTH BEND, IN

PREP: 10 MIN. • **COOK:** 3½ HOURS
MAKES: 6 SERVINGS

- 1 **pound beef stew meat, cut into 1-inch cubes**
- 1 **package (16 ounces) frozen mixed vegetables, thawed**
- 1 **can (15 ounces) pinto beans, rinsed and drained**
- 1½ **cups water**
- 1 **can (8 ounces) pizza sauce**
- 2 **tablespoons medium pearl barley**
- 1 **tablespoon dried minced onion**
- 2 **teaspoons beef bouillon granules**
- ¼ **teaspoon crushed red pepper flakes**

In a 3-qt. slow cooker, combine all ingredients. Cover and cook on low for 3½-4½ hours or until the meat is tender.

PER SERVING *1 serving (1 cup) equals 251 cal., 6 g fat (2 g sat. fat), 47 mg chol., 526 mg sodium, 28 g carb., 8 g fiber, 21 g pro.*

TOP TIP

MINCE IT YOURSELF

If you don't have or are out of dried minced onion, don't worry! Grab a raw onion and start chopping. A ¼ cup of minced raw onion equals 1 tablespoon of dried minced onion.

---

⑤INGREDIENTS

BRISKET WITH CRANBERRY GRAVY

With just a few minutes of work, this delectable beef brisket simmers into a comforting entree. The meat and gravy are great for sandwiches the next day.

—**NOELLE LABRECQUE**
ROUND ROCK, TX

PREP: 15 MIN. • **COOK:** 5½ HOURS
MAKES: 12 SERVINGS

- 1 **medium onion, sliced**
- 1 **fresh beef brisket (3 pounds), halved**
- 1 **can (14 ounces) jellied cranberry sauce**
- ½ **cup thawed cranberry juice concentrate**
- 2 **tablespoons cornstarch**
- ¼ **cup cold water**

1. Place the onion in a 5-qt. slow cooker; top with brisket. Combine the cranberry sauce and the juice concentrate; pour over beef. Cover and cook on low for 5½-6 hours or until meat is tender.

2. Remove the brisket and keep warm. Strain the cooking juices, discarding onion; skim fat. Place in a small saucepan and bring to a boil. Combine cornstarch and cold water until smooth; gradually stir into the pan. Cook and stir for 2 minutes or until thickened. Thinly slice brisket across the grain; serve with gravy.

NOTE *This is a fresh beef brisket, not corned beef.*

PER SERVING *3 ounces cooked beef with 3 tablespoons gravy equals 225 cal., 5 g fat (2 g sat. fat), 48 mg chol., 46 mg sodium, 21 g carb., 1 g fiber, 23 g pro.* **Diabetic Exchanges:** *3 lean meat, 1½ starch.*

BRISKET WITH CRANBERRY GRAVY

BEEF

SLOW-COOKED SIRLOIN

My family of five likes to eat beef, so this recipe is popular. I usually serve it with homemade bread or rolls to soak up the gravy.

—VICKI TORMASCHY DICKINSON, ND

PREP: 20 MIN. • **COOK:** 3½ HOURS
MAKES: 6 SERVINGS

- 1 beef top sirloin steak (1½ pounds)
- 1 medium onion, cut into 1-inch chunks
- 1 medium green pepper, cut into 1-inch chunks
- 1 can (14½ ounces) reduced-sodium beef broth
- ¼ cup Worcestershire sauce
- ¼ teaspoon dill weed
- ¼ teaspoon dried thyme
- ¼ teaspoon pepper
  Dash crushed red pepper flakes
- 2 tablespoons cornstarch
- 2 tablespoons cold water

1. In a large nonstick skillet coated with cooking spray, brown beef on both sides. Place onion and green pepper in a 3-qt. slow cooker. Top with beef. Combine the broth, Worcestershire sauce, dill, thyme, pepper and pepper flakes; pour over beef. Cover and cook on high for 3-4 hours or until meat reaches desired doneness and vegetables are crisp-tender.

2. Remove beef and keep warm. Combine cornstarch and water until smooth; gradually stir into cooking juices. Cover and cook on high for 30 minutes or until slightly thickened. Return beef to the slow cooker; heat through.

PER SERVING *1 serving equals 199 cal., 6 g fat (2 g sat. fat), 68 mg chol., 305 mg sodium, 8 g carb., 1 g fiber, 26 g pro.* **Diabetic Exchanges: 3 lean meat, 1 vegetable.**

BEEF AND BEANS

Serve this spicy steak and beans dish over rice. Family and friends will ask for more! It's a favorite in my recipe collection.

—MARIE LEAMON BETHESDA, MD

PREP: 10 MIN. • **COOK:** 1½ HOURS
MAKES: 8 SERVINGS

- 1½ pounds boneless round steak
- 1 tablespoon prepared mustard
- 1 tablespoon chili powder
- ½ teaspoon salt, optional
- ¼ teaspoon pepper
- 1 garlic clove, minced
- 2 cans (14½ ounces each) diced tomatoes, undrained
- 1 medium onion, chopped
- 1 beef bouillon cube, crushed
- 1 can (16 ounces) kidney beans, rinsed and drained
  Hot cooked rice

Cut steak into thin strips. Combine the mustard, chili powder, salt if desired, pepper and garlic in a bowl; add steak and toss to coat. Transfer to a 3-qt. slow cooker; add tomatoes, onion and bouillon. Cover and cook on low for 6-8 hours. Stir in beans; cook 30 minutes longer. Serve over the rice.

PER SERVING *1 cup (calculated without rice) equals 185 cal., 3 g fat (1 g sat. fat), 47 mg chol., 584 mg sodium, 16 g carb., 5 g fiber, 24 g pro.* **Diabetic Exchanges: 2 lean meat, 1 starch, 1 vegetable.**

TOP TIP

RINSE BEANS

Wondering why it says to rinse and drain canned beans before including them in a recipe? The answer: salt! Canned beans contain extra salt because of the canning process, so rinsing and draining will cut back on sodium.

SLOW-COOKED SIRLOIN

BEEF AND
BEANS

CHILI MAC

CHILI MAC

This recipe has regularly appeared on my family menus for more than 40 years, and it's never failed to please at potlucks and bring-a-dish gatherings. Sometimes I turn it into soup by adding a can of beef broth.

—**MARIE POSAVEC** BERWYN, IL

PREP: 15 MIN. • **COOK:** 6 HOURS
MAKES: 6 SERVINGS

- 1 pound lean ground beef (90% lean), cooked and drained
- 2 cans (16 ounces each) hot chili beans, undrained
- 2 large green peppers, chopped
- 1 large onion, chopped
- 4 celery ribs, chopped
- 1 can (8 ounces) no-salt-added tomato sauce
- 2 tablespoons chili seasoning mix
- 2 garlic cloves, minced
- 1 package (7 ounces) elbow macaroni, cooked and drained
  Salt and pepper to taste

In a 5-qt. slow cooker, combine the first eight ingredients. Cover and cook on low for 6 hours or until heated through. Stir in macaroni. Season with salt and pepper.

PER SERVING *1 serving equals 348 cal., 8 g fat (3 g sat. fat), 47 mg chol., 713 mg sodium, 49 g carb., 12 g fiber, 27 g pro.* **Diabetic Exchanges:** *3 starch, 3 lean meat.*

TERIYAKI BEEF STEW

In the spirit of the saying "Invention is the mother of necessity," I created this sweet-tangy beef stew because I had a package of stew meat that needed to be used. After spotting the ginger beer in the fridge, the rest is history.

—**LESLIE SIMMS** SHERMAN OAKS, CA

PREP: 20 MIN. • **COOK:** 6½ HOURS
MAKES: 8 SERVINGS

- 2 pounds beef stew meat
- 1 bottle (12 ounces) ginger beer or ginger ale
- ¼ cup teriyaki sauce
- 2 garlic cloves, minced
- 2 tablespoons sesame seeds
- 2 tablespoons cornstarch
- 2 tablespoons cold water
- 2 cups frozen peas, thawed
  Hot cooked rice, optional

1. In a large nonstick skillet, brown beef in batches. Transfer to a 3-qt. slow cooker.

2. In a small bowl, combine the ginger beer, teriyaki sauce, garlic and sesame seeds; pour over beef. Cover and cook on low for 6-8 hours or until meat is tender.

3. Combine the cornstarch and cold water until smooth; gradually stir into the stew. Stir in peas. Cover and cook on high for 30 minutes or until thickened. Serve with rice if desired.

PER SERVING *1 cup stew (calculated without rice) equals 310 cal., 12 g fat (4 g sat. fat), 94 mg chol., 528 mg sodium, 17 g carb., 2 g fiber, 33 g pro.* **Diabetic Exchanges:** *4 lean meat, 1 starch.*

SLOW COOKER FAJITAS

I love fajitas from Mexican restaurants, but when I tried to make them at home, the meat always seemed too chewy. Then I tried this recipe in my slow cooker, and my husband and I enjoyed every bite.

—**KATIE URSO** SENECA, IL

PREP: 25 MIN. • **COOK:** 8 HOURS
MAKES: 8 SERVINGS

- 1 each medium green, sweet red and yellow peppers, cut into ½-inch strips
- 1 sweet onion, cut into ½-inch strips
- 2 pounds beef top sirloin steaks, cut into thin strips
- ¾ cup water
- 2 tablespoons red wine vinegar
- 1 tablespoon lime juice
- 1 teaspoon ground cumin
- 1 teaspoon chili powder
- ½ teaspoon salt
- ½ teaspoon garlic powder
- ½ teaspoon pepper
- ½ teaspoon cayenne pepper
- 8 flour tortillas (8 inches), warmed
- ½ cup salsa
- ½ cup shredded reduced-fat cheddar cheese
- 8 teaspoons minced fresh cilantro

1. Place peppers and onion in a 5-qt. slow cooker. Top with beef. Combine the water, vinegar, lime juice and seasonings; pour over meat. Cover and cook on low for 8-10 hours or until meat is tender.

2. Using a slotted spoon, place about ¾ cup meat mixture down the center of each tortilla. Top with salsa, cheese and cilantro; roll up.

PER SERVING *1 fajita equals 335 cal., 10 g fat (3 g sat. fat), 69 mg chol., 564 mg sodium, 32 g carb., 2 g fiber, 29 g pro.* **Diabetic Exchanges:** *3 lean meat, 2 starch, 1 vegetable.*

ROUND STEAK SAUERBRATEN

My easy version of an old-world classic takes just minutes to prepare for the slow cooker. If you prefer, serve the meat with rice.
—**LINDA BLOOM** MCHENRY, IL

PREP: 20 MIN. • **COOK:** 6½ HOURS
MAKES: 10 SERVINGS

- 1 envelope brown gravy mix
- 2 tablespoons plus 1½ teaspoons brown sugar
- 2½ cups cold water, divided
- 1 cup chopped onion
- 2 teaspoons Worcestershire sauce
- 2 tablespoons white vinegar
- 2 bay leaves
- 2½ pounds beef top round steak, cut into 3x½-inch strips
- 2 teaspoons salt
- 1 teaspoon pepper
- ¼ cup cornstarch
- 10 cups hot cooked egg noodles

1. In a 5-qt. slow cooker, combine the gravy mix, brown sugar, 2 cups water, onion, Worcestershire sauce vinegar and bay leaves.
2. Sprinkle the beef with salt and pepper; stir into the gravy mixture. Cover and cook on low for 6-8 hours or until meat is tender.
3. Combine the cornstarch and remaining water until smooth; stir into beef mixture. Cover and cook on high for 30 minutes or until thickened. Discard bay leaves. Serve with noodles.
PER SERVING *¾ cup beef mixture with 1 cup noodles equals 331 cal., 6 g fat (2 g sat. fat), 96 mg chol., 741 mg sodium, 37 g carb., 2 g fiber, 32 g pro. Diabetic Exchanges: 3 lean meat, 2½ starch.*

SLOW COOKER VEGETABLE BEEF STEW

Here's a fun variation of beef stew that I came across. With some sweetness from apricots and butternut squash, the dish has a bit of a South American or Cuban flair.
—**RUTH RODRIGUEZ**
FORT MYERS BEACH, FL

PREP: 15 MIN. • **COOK:** 5½ HOURS
MAKES: 4 SERVINGS

- ¾ pound beef stew meat, cut into ½-inch cubes
- 2 teaspoons canola oil
- 1 can (14½ ounces) beef broth
- 1 can (14½ ounces) stewed tomatoes, cut up
- 1½ cups cubed peeled butternut squash
- 1 cup frozen corn, thawed
- 6 dried apricots or peaches, quartered
- ½ cup chopped carrot
- 1 teaspoon dried oregano
- ¼ teaspoon salt
- ¼ teaspoon pepper
- 2 tablespoons cornstarch
- ¼ cup cold water
- 2 tablespoons minced fresh parsley

1. In a nonstick skillet, brown beef in oil over medium heat. Transfer to a 3-qt. slow cooker. Add broth, tomatoes, squash, corn, apricots, carrot, oregano, salt and pepper.
2. Cover and cook on high for 5-6 hours or until vegetables and meat are tender.
3. Combine the cornstarch and water until smooth; gradually stir into stew. Cover and cook on high for 30 minutes or until thickened. Stir in parsley.
PER SERVING *1 serving (1½ cups) equals 278 cal., 9 g fat (3 g sat. fat), 53 mg chol., 717 mg sodium, 32 g carb., 5 g fiber, 21 g pro.*

STUFFED FLANK STEAK

This recipe came with my first slow cooker. Now on my fourth slow cooker, I still use the recipe!
—**KATHY CLARK** BYRON, MN

PREP: 20 MIN. • **COOK:** 8 HOURS + 10 MIN.
MAKES: 8 SERVINGS

- 1 beef flank steak (2 pounds)
- 1 medium onion, chopped
- 1 garlic clove, minced
- 1 tablespoon butter
- 1½ cups soft bread crumbs (about 3 slices)
- ½ cup chopped fresh mushrooms
- ¼ cup minced fresh parsley
- ¼ cup egg substitute
- ¾ teaspoon poultry seasoning
- ½ teaspoon salt
- ⅛ teaspoon pepper
- ½ cup beef broth
- 2 teaspoons cornstarch
- 4 teaspoons water

1. Flatten steak to ½-in. thickness; set aside.
2. In a skillet, saute the onion and garlic in butter until tender. Add bread crumbs, mushrooms, parsley, egg substitute, poultry seasoning, salt and pepper; mix well.
3. Spread over steak to within 1 in. of edge. Roll up jelly-roll style, starting with a long side; tie with kitchen string. Place in a 5-qt. slow cooker; add broth. Cover and cook on low for 8-10 hours.
4. Remove meat to a platter and keep warm. Skim fat from cooking juices; pour into a small saucepan.
5. Combine the cornstarch and water until smooth; stir into juices. Bring to a boil; cook and stir for 1-2 minutes or until thickened. Remove string before slicing the steak; serve with gravy.
PER SERVING *1 serving equals 230 cal., 11 g fat (5 g sat. fat), 62 mg chol., 348 mg sodium, 6 g carb., trace fiber, 26 g pro. Diabetic Exchanges: 3 lean meat, ½ starch, ½ fat.*

STUFFED
FLANK STEAK

PUMPKIN HARVEST
BEEF STEW

STEAK
BURRITOS

GERMAN-STYLE
SHORT RIBS

PUMPKIN HARVEST BEEF STEW

With this simmering and a batch of bread baking, your house will smell absolutely wonderful.

—MARCIA O'NEIL CEDAR CREST, NM

PREP: 25 MIN. • **COOK:** 6½ HOURS
MAKES: 6 SERVINGS

- 1 tablespoon canola oil
- 1 beef top round steak (1½ pounds), cut into 1-inch cubes
- 1½ cups cubed peeled pie pumpkin or sweet potatoes
- 3 small red potatoes, peeled and cubed
- 1 cup cubed acorn squash
- 1 medium onion, chopped
- 2 cans (14½ ounces each) reduced-sodium beef broth
- 1 can (14½ ounces) diced tomatoes, undrained
- 2 bay leaves
- 2 garlic cloves, minced
- 2 teaspoons reduced-sodium beef bouillon granules
- ½ teaspoon chili powder
- ½ teaspoon pepper
- ¼ teaspoon ground allspice
- ¼ teaspoon ground cloves
- ¼ cup water
- 3 tablespoons all-purpose flour

1. In a large skillet, heat oil over medium-high heat. Brown beef in batches; remove with a slotted spoon to a 4- or 5-qt. slow cooker. Add pumpkin, potatoes, squash and onion. Stir in broth, tomatoes and seasonings. Cover and cook on low for 6-8 hours or until meat is tender.
2. Remove bay leaves. In a small bowl, mix water and flour until smooth; gradually stir into stew. Cover and cook on high for 30 minutes or until liquid is thickened.
PER SERVING 1⅔ cups equals 258 cal., 6 g fat (1 g sat. fat), 67 mg chol., 479 mg sodium, 21 g carb., 4 g fiber, 29 g pro. **Diabetic Exchanges:** 3 lean meat, 1 starch, 1 vegetable, ½ fat.

STEAK BURRITOS

Your slow cooker does all the hard work, so just fill flour tortillas and add toppings for a tasty meal.

—VALERIE JONES PORTLAND, ME

PREP: 15 MIN. • **COOK:** 8 HOURS
MAKES: 10 SERVINGS

- 2 beef flank steaks (about 1 pound each)
- 2 envelopes reduced-sodium taco seasoning
- 1 medium onion, chopped
- 1 can (4 ounces) chopped green chilies
- 1 tablespoon white vinegar
- 10 flour tortillas (8 inches), warmed
- 1 cup (4 ounces) shredded Monterey Jack cheese
- 1½ cups chopped seeded plum tomatoes
- ¾ cup reduced-fat sour cream

1. Cut steaks in half; rub with taco seasoning. Place in a 3-qt. slow cooker coated with cooking spray. Top with onion, chilies and vinegar. Cover and cook on low for 8-9 hours or until meat is tender.
2. Remove steaks and cool slightly; shred meat with two forks. Return to slow cooker; heat through.
3. Spoon about ½ cup meat mixture near the center of each tortilla. Top with cheese, tomato and sour cream. Fold bottom and sides of tortilla over filling and roll up.
PER SERVING 1 burrito equals 339 cal., 12 g fat (6 g sat. fat), 59 mg chol., 816 mg sodium, 33 g carb., 2 g fiber, 25 g pro. **Diabetic Exchanges:** 3 lean meat, 2 starch.

GERMAN-STYLE SHORT RIBS

Our whole family is excited when I plug in the slow cooker to make these amazing ribs. We like them served over rice or egg noodles.

—BREGITTE RUGMAN SHANTY BAY, ON

PREP: 15 MIN. • **COOK:** 8 HOURS
MAKES: 8 SERVINGS

- ¾ cup dry red wine or beef broth
- ½ cup mango chutney
- 3 tablespoons quick-cooking tapioca
- ¼ cup water
- 3 tablespoons brown sugar
- 3 tablespoons cider vinegar
- 1 tablespoon Worcestershire sauce
- ½ teaspoon salt
- ½ teaspoon ground mustard
- ½ teaspoon chili powder
- ½ teaspoon pepper
- 4 pounds bone-in beef short ribs
- 2 medium onions, sliced
  Hot cooked egg noodles

1. In a 5-qt. slow cooker, combine the first 11 ingredients. Add ribs and turn to coat. Top with onions.
2. Cover and cook on low for 8-10 hours or until meat is tender. Remove ribs from slow cooker. Skim fat from cooking juices; serve with ribs and noodles.
PER SERVING 1 serving (calculated without noodles) equals 302 cal., 11 g fat (5 g sat. fat), 55 mg chol., 378 mg sodium, 28 g carb., 1 g fiber, 19 g pro.

SLOW-COOKED PEPPER STEAK

COFFEE BEEF ROAST

Coffee is the key to this tasty beef roast that cooks until it's fall-apart tender. Try it once, and I'm sure you'll make it again and again.

—**CHARLES TRAHAN** SAN DIMAS, CA

PREP: 15 MIN. • **COOK:** 8 HOURS
MAKES: 6 SERVINGS

- 1 **beef sirloin tip roast (2½ pounds), cut in half**
- 2 **teaspoons canola oil**
- 1½ **cups sliced fresh mushrooms**
- ⅓ **cup sliced green onions**
- 2 **garlic cloves, minced**
- 1½ **cups brewed coffee**
- 1 **teaspoon liquid smoke, optional**
- ½ **teaspoon salt**
- ½ **teaspoon chili powder**
- ¼ **teaspoon pepper**
- ¼ **cup cornstarch**
- ⅓ **cup cold water**

1. In a large nonstick skillet, brown roast on all sides in oil over medium-high heat. Place in a 5-qt. slow cooker. In the same skillet, saute mushrooms, onions and garlic until tender; stir in the coffee, liquid smoke if desired, salt, chili powder and pepper. Pour over roast.

2. Cover and cook on low for 8-10 hours or until the meat is tender. Remove roast and keep warm. Pour cooking juices into a 2-cup measuring cup; skim fat.

3. In a small saucepan, combine cornstarch and water until smooth. Gradually stir in 2 cups cooking juices. Bring to a boil; cook and stir for 2 minutes or until thickened. Serve with beef.

PER SERVING *1 serving (3 ounces cooked beef with ⅓ cup gravy) equals 209 cal., 7 g fat (2 g sat. fat), 82 mg chol., 244 mg sodium, 6 g carb., trace fiber, 28 g pro.* **Diabetic Exchanges:** *3 lean meat, ½ starch.*

FREEZE IT

SLOW-COOKED PEPPER STEAK

After a long day working in our greenhouse raising bedding plants, I enjoy coming in to this hearty beef dish for supper. It's one of my favorite meals.

—**SUE GRONHOLZ** BEAVER DAM, WI

PREP: 10 MIN. • **COOK:** 6½ HOURS
MAKES: 6 SERVINGS

- 1½ **pounds beef top round steak**
- 2 **tablespoons canola oil**
- 1 **cup chopped onion**
- ¼ **cup reduced-sodium soy sauce**
- 1 **garlic clove, minced**
- 1 **teaspoon sugar**
- ½ **teaspoon salt**
- ¼ **teaspoon ground ginger**
- ¼ **teaspoon pepper**
- 4 **medium tomatoes, cut into wedges or 1 can (14½ ounces) diced tomatoes, undrained**
- 1 **large green pepper, cut into strips**
- 1 **tablespoon cornstarch**
- ½ **cup cold water**
   Hot cooked noodles or rice

1. Cut beef into 3x1-in. strips. In a large skillet, brown beef in oil. Transfer to a 3-qt. slow cooker. Combine the onion, soy sauce, garlic, sugar, salt, ginger and pepper; pour over beef. Cover and cook on low for 5-6 hours or until meat is tender. Add tomatoes and green pepper; cook on low 1 hour longer or until vegetables are tender.

2. Combine cornstarch and cold water until smooth; gradually stir into slow cooker. Cover and cook on high for 20-30 minutes until thickened. Serve with noodles or rice.

FREEZE OPTION *Freeze cooled beef mixture in freezer containers. To use, partially thaw in the refrigerator overnight. Heat through in a covered saucepan, gently stirring and adding a little broth or water if necessary.*

PER SERVING *1 cup (calculated without noodles) equals 176 cal., 6 g fat (1 g sat. fat), 48 mg chol., 639 mg sodium, 8 g carb., 2 g fiber, 21 g pro.*

COFFEE BEEF
ROAST

BIG BATCH HUNGARIAN GOULASH

My grandmother used to make this goulash for my mother. Paprika and caraway add wonderful flavor, and the sour cream gives it a traditional creamy richness. It's scrumptious!

—**MARCIA DOYLE** POMPANO, FL

PREP: 20 MIN. • **COOK:** 7 HOURS
MAKES: 12 SERVINGS

- 3 medium onions, chopped
- 2 medium carrots, chopped
- 2 medium green peppers, chopped
- 3 pounds beef stew meat
- ¾ teaspoon salt, divided
- ¾ teaspoon pepper, divided
- 2 tablespoons olive oil
- 1½ cups reduced-sodium beef broth
- ¼ cup all-purpose flour
- 3 tablespoons paprika
- 2 tablespoons tomato paste
- 1 teaspoon caraway seeds
- 1 garlic clove, minced
  Dash sugar
- 12 cups uncooked whole wheat egg noodles
- 1 cup (8 ounces) reduced-fat sour cream

1. Place the onions, carrots and green peppers in a 5-qt. slow cooker. Sprinkle meat with ½ teaspoon salt and ½ teaspoon pepper. In a large skillet, brown meat in oil in batches. Transfer to slow cooker.

2. Add broth to skillet, stirring to loosen browned bits from the pan. Combine the flour, paprika, tomato paste, caraway seeds, garlic, sugar and remaining salt and pepper; stir into skillet. Bring to a boil; cook and stir for 2 minutes or until thickened. Pour over meat. Cover and cook on low for 7-9 hours or until meat is tender.

3. Cook noodles according to package directions. Stir sour cream into slow cooker. Drain noodles; serve with goulash.

BIG BATCH
HUNGARIAN
GOULASH

PER SERVING *⅔ cup goulash with 1 cup noodles equals 388 cal., 13 g fat (4 g sat. fat), 78 mg chol., 285 mg sodium, 41 g carb., 7 g fiber, 31 g pro.* **Diabetic Exchanges:** *3 lean meat, 2 starch, 1 vegetable, 1 fat.*

TOP TIP

GOULASH HISTORY
Goulash is actually a type of stew, with origins traced back to Hungary. And the key ingredient? Paprika!

BEEF ROAST DINNER

Because this healthy dish is slow-cooked, you can use less expensive beef roasts and have the same mouthwatering results you would get with more costly cuts. Change up the veggies for variety, nutrition or just to suit your tastes.

—SANDRA DUDLEY BEMIDJI, MN

PREP: 20 MIN. • **COOK:** 8 HOURS
MAKES: 10 SERVINGS

- 1 **pound red potatoes (about 4 medium), cubed**
- ¼ **pound small fresh mushrooms**
- 1½ **cups fresh baby carrots**
- 1 **medium green pepper, chopped**
- 1 **medium parsnip, chopped**
- 1 **small red onion, chopped**
- 1 **beef rump roast or bottom round roast (3 pounds)**
- 1 **can (14½ ounces) beef broth**
- ¾ **teaspoon salt**
- ¾ **teaspoon dried oregano**
- ¼ **teaspoon pepper**
- 3 **tablespoons cornstarch**
- ¼ **cup cold water**

1. Place vegetables in a 5-qt. slow cooker. Cut roast in half; place in slow cooker. Combine the broth, salt, oregano and pepper; pour over meat. Cover and cook on low for 8 hours or until meat is tender.
2. Remove meat and vegetables to a serving platter; keep warm. Skim the fat from cooking juices; transfer to a small saucepan. Bring liquid to a boil.
3. Combine cornstarch and water until smooth. Gradually stir into the pan. Bring to a boil; cook and stir for 2 minutes or until thickened. Serve with meat and vegetables.
PER SERVING *4 ounces cooked beef with ⅔ cup vegetables and ¼ cup gravy equals 245 cal., 7 g fat (2 g sat. fat), 82 mg chol., 427 mg sodium, 16 g carb., 2 g fiber, 29 g pro. Diabetic Exchanges: 4 lean meat, 1 starch.*

ALL-DAY BRISKET WITH POTATOES

ALL-DAY BRISKET WITH POTATOES

I think the slow cooker was invented with brisket in mind. This sweet and savory version just melts in your mouth. I always buy "first-cut" or "flat-cut" brisket, which has far less fat than other cuts.

—LANA GRYGA GLEN FLORA, WI

PREP: 30 MIN. • **COOK:** 8 HOURS
MAKES: 8 SERVINGS

- 2 **medium potatoes, peeled and cut into ¼-inch slices**
- 2 **celery ribs, sliced**
- 1 **fresh beef brisket (3 pounds)**
- 1 **tablespoon canola oil**
- 1 **large onion, sliced**
- 2 **garlic cloves, minced**
- 1 **can (12 ounces) beer**
- ½ **teaspoon beef bouillon granules**
- ¾ **cup stewed tomatoes**
- ⅓ **cup tomato paste**
- ¼ **cup red wine vinegar**
- 3 **tablespoons brown sugar**
- 3 **tablespoons Dijon mustard**
- 3 **tablespoons soy sauce**
- 2 **tablespoons molasses**
- ½ **teaspoon paprika**
- ¼ **teaspoon salt**
- ⅛ **teaspoon pepper**
- 1 **bay leaf**

1. Place potatoes and celery in a 5-qt. slow cooker. Cut brisket in half. In a large skillet, brown beef in oil on all sides; transfer to slow cooker. In the same pan, saute the onion until tender. Add garlic; cook 1 minute longer. Add to slow cooker.
2. Add beer and bouillon granules to skillet, stirring to loosen browned bits from pan; pour over meat. In a large bowl, combine remaining ingredients; add to slow cooker.
3. Cover and cook on low for 8-10 hours or until vegetables and meat are tender. Discard bay leaf. To serve, thinly slice across grain.
NOTE *This is a fresh beef brisket, not corned beef.*
PER SERVING *1 serving equals 352 cal., 9 g fat (3 g sat. fat), 72 mg chol., 722 mg sodium, 25 g carb., 2 g fiber, 38 g pro. Diabetic Exchanges: 5 lean meat, 1 starch, 1 vegetable, ½ fat.*

HEALTHY SLOW-COOKED MEAT LOAF

What could be easier than an Italian-inspired meat loaf made in the slow cooker? No fuss, easy cleanup and great taste; it's all right here!

—SHARON DELANEY-CHRONIS
SOUTH MILWAUKEE, WI

PREP: 15 MIN. • **COOK:** 3 HOURS
MAKES: 8 SERVINGS

- 1 cup soft bread crumbs
- 1½ cups spaghetti sauce, divided
- 1 large egg, lightly beaten
- 2 tablespoons dried minced onion
- 1 teaspoon salt
- ½ teaspoon garlic powder
- ½ teaspoon Italian seasoning
- ¼ teaspoon pepper
- 2 pounds lean ground beef (90% lean)

1. Cut four 20x3-in. strips of heavy-duty foil; crisscross so they resemble spokes of a wheel. Place strips on the bottom and up the sides of a 3-qt. slow cooker. Coat strips with cooking spray.
2. In a large bowl, combine bread crumbs, 1 cup spaghetti sauce, egg, onion, and seasonings. Crumble beef over mixture and mix well. Shape into a loaf; place in the center of the strips.
3. Spoon remaining spaghetti sauce over meat loaf. Cover and cook on low for 3-4 hours or until a thermometer reads 160°. Using foil strips as handles, remove meat loaf to a platter.
PER SERVING *1 slice equals 243 cal., 12 g fat (4 g sat. fat), 98 mg chol., 635 mg sodium, 8 g carb., 1 g fiber, 24 g pro. **Diabetic Exchanges:** 3 lean meat, 1 fat, ½ starch.*

SOUTHWEST BLACK BEAN & BEEF STEW

I made this stew for my ladies' group at church, and everyone loved it! Best of all, I started the dish before I left for work and had it ready to go when I got home.

—ANITA ROBERSON
WILLIAMSTON, NC

PREP: 30 MIN. • **COOK:** 7 HOURS
MAKES: 11 SERVINGS (2¾ QUARTS)

- 1½ pounds lean ground beef (90% lean)
- 1 large onion, chopped
- 2 cans (14½ ounces each) diced tomatoes, undrained
- 1 package (16 ounces) frozen corn
- 1 can (15 ounces) black beans, rinsed and drained
- 1 can (14½ ounces) chicken broth
- 1 can (10 ounces) diced tomatoes and green chilies, undrained
- 1 teaspoon garlic powder
- 1½ teaspoons salt-free Southwest chipotle seasoning blend
- 1½ cups cooked rice
- ¼ cup shredded cheddar cheese

1. In a large skillet, cook beef and onion over medium heat until meat is no longer pink; drain.
2. Transfer to a 5-qt. slow cooker. Stir in the tomatoes, corn, black beans, broth, tomatoes, garlic powder and seasoning blend. Cover and cook on low 6-8 hours or until heated through.
3. Stir in the rice; heat through. Sprinkle each serving with cheese.
PER SERVING *1 cup equals 228 cal., 6 g fat (3 g sat. fat), 42 mg chol., 482 mg sodium, 26 g carb., 4 g fiber, 17 g pro. **Diabetic Exchanges:** 2 lean meat, 1½ starch, 1 vegetable.*

⑤ INGREDIENTS
CIDER MUSHROOM BRISKET

Apple juice and gingersnaps give an autumn feel to this tender brisket. It's quick to prep, and the pleasing aroma will linger for hours.

—COLLEEN WESTON DENVER, CO

PREP: 10 MIN. • **COOK:** 6 HOURS
MAKES: 12 SERVINGS

- 1 fresh beef brisket (6 pounds)
- 2 jars (12 ounces each) mushroom gravy
- 1 cup apple cider or juice
- 1 envelope onion mushroom soup mix
- ⅓ cup crushed gingersnap cookies

1. Cut brisket into thirds; place in a 5- or 6-qt. slow cooker. In a large bowl, combine gravy, cider, soup mix and cookie crumbs; pour over the beef. Cover and cook on low for 6-8 hours or until meat is tender.
2. Thinly slice meat across grain. Skim the fat from cooking juices; thicken if desired.
NOTE *This is a fresh beef brisket, not corned beef.*
PER SERVING *6 ounces cooked meat with ½ cup cooking juices equals 336 cal., 11 g fat (4 g sat. fat), 101 mg chol., 566 mg sodium, 9 g carb., trace fiber, 47 g pro. **Diabetic Exchanges:** 6 lean meat, ½ starch, ½ fat.*

THE SKINNY

KEEP IT LEAN

Using lean ground beef in Healthy Slow-Cooked Meat Loaf instead of beef that's 80% lean saves 45 calories per 4-ounce serving of beef. Lean ground beef also is 29% lower in saturated fat.

HEALTHY SLOW-COOKED
MEAT LOAF

SOUTHWEST BLACK
BEAN & BEEF STEW

CIDER MUSHROOM
BRISKET

MEATBALL
CABBAGE ROLLS

MEATBALL CABBAGE ROLLS

My mother often would have these cabbage rolls waiting in her slow cooker when my family and I arrived home for visits. The mouthwatering meatballs tucked inside set the rolls apart from others.
—**BETTY BUCKMASTER** MUSKOGEE, OK

PREP: 25 MIN. • **COOK:** 8 HOURS
MAKES: 4 SERVINGS

- 1 **large head cabbage**
- 1 **can (8 ounces) no-salt-added tomato sauce**
- 1 **small onion, chopped**
- ⅓ **cup uncooked long grain rice**
- 2 **tablespoons chili powder**
- ¼ **teaspoon garlic powder**
- ⅛ **teaspoon salt**
- 1 **pound lean ground beef (90% lean)**
- 1 **can (15 ounces) tomato sauce**

1. In a Dutch oven, cook cabbage in boiling water just until the leaves fall off head. Set aside 12 large leaves for rolls. (Refrigerate the rest of the cabbage for another use.) Cut out thick vein from the bottom of each reserved leaf, making V-shaped cut.
2. In a large bowl, combine the no-salt-added tomato sauce, onion, rice, chili powder, garlic powder and salt. Crumble beef over mixture; mix well. Shape into 12 balls. Place one meatball on each cabbage leaf; overlap cut ends of leaf. Fold in sides, beginning from the cut end. Roll up completely to enclose meatball. Secure with toothpicks.
3. Place in a 5-qt. slow cooker. Pour the remaining tomato sauce over cabbage rolls. Cover and cook on low for 8 hours or until meat is no longer pink and the cabbage is tender. Discard toothpicks.
PER SERVING *3 rolls equals 323 cal., 11 g fat (4 g sat. fat), 71 mg chol., 762 mg sodium, 31 g carb., 7 g fiber, 28 g pro.* **Diabetic Exchanges:** *3 lean meat, 1½ starch, 1 vegetable.*

SATISFYING BEEF STEW

This stew is so hearty and tastes even better the next day—if there are leftovers! It goes great with corn bread or any bakery bread.
—**ABBEY MUELLER** ENID, OK

PREP: 30 MIN. • **COOK:** 6 HOURS
MAKES: 8 SERVINGS

- 2 **pounds beef stew meat**
- 1 **medium onion, chopped**
- 2 **tablespoons canola oil**
- 2 **cups water**
- ¼ **cup all-purpose flour**
- 3 **medium carrots, sliced**
- 3 **medium potatoes, peeled and cubed**
- 2 **cups frozen corn**
- 1½ **cups frozen cut green beans**
- 1 **can (15 ounces) Italian tomato sauce**
- 2 **teaspoons Worcestershire sauce**
- 1 **teaspoon salt**
- 1 **teaspoon paprika**
- 1 **teaspoon pepper**
  Dash ground cloves
- 2 **bay leaves**

1. In a large skillet, brown beef and onion in oil; drain. Transfer to a 5-qt. slow cooker. Combine water and flour; pour over beef. Stir in the remaining ingredients.
2. Cover and cook on low for 6-8 hours or until the meat and vegetables are tender. Discard bay leaves.
PER SERVING *1 cup equals 330 cal., 12 g fat (3 g sat. fat), 70 mg chol., 680 mg sodium, 32 g carb., 4 g fiber, 26 g pro.* **Diabetic Exchanges:** *3 lean meat, 1½ starch, 1 vegetable, 1 fat.*

BAVARIAN POT ROAST

I wasn't a fan of pot roast until I got this recipe at a church social and changed a few ingredients. My 7-year-old especially enjoys the seasoned apple gravy.
—**PATRICIA GASMUND** ROCKFORD, IL

PREP: 10 MIN. • **COOK:** 5 HOURS
MAKES: 12 SERVINGS

- 1 **beef top round roast (4 pounds), halved**
- 1½ **cups apple juice**
- 1 **can (8 ounces) tomato sauce**
- 1 **small onion, chopped**
- 2 **tablespoons white vinegar**
- 1 **tablespoon salt**
- 2 **to 3 teaspoons ground cinnamon**
- 1 **tablespoon minced fresh gingerroot**
- ¼ **cup cornstarch**
- ½ **cup water**

1. In a Dutch oven coated with cooking spray, brown the roast on all sides over medium-high heat. Transfer to a 5-qt. slow cooker. In a bowl, combine juice, tomato sauce, onion, vinegar, salt, cinnamon and ginger; pour over roast. Cover and cook on high for 5-7 hours.

2. In a small bowl, combine the cornstarch and water until smooth; stir into cooking juices until well combined. Cover and cook 1 hour longer or until the meat is tender and gravy begins to thicken.

PER SERVING *1 serving (4 ounces cooked beef with ½ cup gravy) equals 230 cal., 7 g fat (2 g sat. fat), 96 mg chol., 753 mg sodium, 8 g carb., 1 g fiber, 32 g pro.* **Diabetic Exchanges:** *4 lean meat, ½ fruit.*

BAVARIAN POT ROAST

BARBECUES FOR THE BUNCH

Serve a party-perfect meal right from your slow cooker. Just add chips and your best sides.

—LOUISE WATKINS LONG KEY, FL

PREP: 25 MIN. • **COOK:** 6 HOURS
MAKES: 16 SERVINGS

- 2 **pounds beef top sirloin steak, cubed**
- 1½ **pounds boneless pork loin roast, cubed**
- 2 **large onions, chopped**
- ¾ **cup chopped celery**
- 1 **can (6 ounces) tomato paste**
- ½ **cup packed brown sugar**
- ¼ **cup cider vinegar**
- ¼ **cup chili sauce**
- 2 **tablespoons Worcestershire sauce**
- 1 **tablespoon ground mustard**
- 16 **hamburger buns, split**

1. In a 5-qt. slow cooker, combine beef, pork, onions and celery. In a small bowl, combine the tomato paste, brown sugar, vinegar, chili sauce, Worcestershire sauce and mustard. Pour over meat mixture.

2. Cover and cook on high for 6-8 hours or until meat is very tender. Shred meat in the slow cooker with two forks. With a slotted spoon, serve ½ cup meat mixture on each bun.

PER SERVING *1 sandwich equals 297 cal., 7 g fat (2 g sat. fat), 53 mg chol., 336 mg sodium, 34 g carb., 2 g fiber, 24 g pro.* **Diabetic Exchanges:** *3 lean meat, 2 starch.*

TOP TIP

VINEGAR SWAP

Don't have cider vinegar on hand? Substitute balsamic vinegar or a mild red wine vinegar.

BARBECUES FOR THE BUNCH

SLOW-COOKED
STROGANOFF

SLOW-COOKED STROGANOFF

I've been preparing Stroganoff in the slow cooker for more than 30 years. Once you've done it this way, you'll never cook it on the stovetop again. It's great for family or company.
—**KAREN HERBERT** PLACERVILLE, CA

PREP: 20 MIN. • **COOK:** 5 HOURS
MAKES: 8-10 SERVINGS

- 3 pounds beef top round steaks
- ½ cup all-purpose flour
- 1½ teaspoons salt
- ½ teaspoon ground mustard
- ⅛ teaspoon pepper
- 1 medium onion, sliced and separated into rings
- 1 can (8 ounces) mushroom stems and pieces, drained
- 1 can (10½ ounces) condensed beef broth, undiluted
- 1½ cups (12 ounces) sour cream
  Hot cooked noodles

1. Cut beef into thin strips. In a shallow bowl, mix flour, salt, mustard and pepper. Add beef in batches; toss to coat.
2. In a 5-qt. slow cooker, layer the onion, mushrooms and beef. Pour the broth over top. Cook, covered, on low 5-7 hours or until meat is tender. Just before serving, stir in sour cream. Serve with noodles.
PER SERVING *4 ounces cooked beef (calculated without noodles) equals 275 cal., 10 g fat (5 g sat. fat), 99 mg chol., 680 mg sodium, 8 g carb., 1 g fiber, 34 g pro.*

HOW-TO

PREP MUSHROOMS
To clean mushrooms, gently remove the dirt by rubbing with a mushroom brush or a damp paper towel. Trim stems.

FREEZE IT
SWEET-AND-SOUR BEEF STEW

Combine meat and nutrient-packed vegetables into one delicious stew. Better yet, freeze some for later!
—**FRANCES CONKLIN** COTTONWOOD, ID

PREP: 25 MIN. • **COOK:** 8 HOURS
MAKES: 8 SERVINGS

- 2 pounds beef top round steak, cut into 1-inch cubes
- 2 tablespoons olive oil
- 1 can (15 ounces) tomato sauce
- 2 large onions, chopped
- 4 medium carrots, thinly sliced
- 1 large green pepper, cut into 1-inch pieces
- 1 cup canned pineapple chunks, drained
- ½ cup cider vinegar
- ¼ cup packed brown sugar
- ¼ cup light corn syrup
- 2 teaspoons chili powder
- 2 teaspoons paprika
- ½ teaspoon salt
  Hot cooked rice, optional

1. In a large skillet, brown beef in oil in batches; drain. Transfer to a 4- or 5-qt. slow cooker.
2. In a large bowl, combine the tomato sauce, onions, carrots, green pepper, pineapple, vinegar, brown sugar, corn syrup, chili powder, paprika and salt; pour over beef.
3. Cover and cook on low for 8-10 hours or until beef is tender. Serve with rice if desired.
FREEZE OPTION *Freeze cooled stew in freezer containers. To use, partially thaw in refrigerator overnight. Heat through in a saucepan, stirring occasionally and adding a little broth or water if necessary.*
PER SERVING *1 cup (calculated without rice) equals 290 cal., 7 g fat (2 g sat. fat), 64 mg chol., 465 mg sodium, 29 g carb., 3 g fiber, 28 g pro.* **Diabetic Exchanges:** *3 lean meat, 2 vegetable, 1 starch, ½ fat.*

SWISS STEAK SUPPER

Here is a satisfying dinner that is loaded with veggies. Save a step by seasoning the steak with peppered seasoned salt instead of using both pepper and seasoned salt.
—**KATHLEEN ROMANIUK** CHOMEDEY, QC

PREP: 20 MIN. • **COOK:** 5 HOURS
MAKES: 6 SERVINGS

- 1½ pounds beef top round steak
- ½ teaspoon seasoned salt
- ¼ teaspoon coarsely ground pepper
- 1 tablespoon canola oil
- 3 medium potatoes
- 1½ cups fresh baby carrots
- 1 medium onion, sliced
- 1 can (14½ ounces) Italian diced tomatoes
- 1 jar (12 ounces) home-style beef gravy
- 1 tablespoon minced fresh parsley

1. Cut steak into six serving-size pieces; flatten to ¼-in. thickness. Rub with seasoned salt and pepper. In a large skillet, brown beef in oil on both sides; drain.
2. Cut each potato into eight wedges. In a 5-qt. slow cooker, layer the potatoes, carrots, beef and onion. Combine tomatoes and gravy; pour over the top.
3. Cover and cook on low for 5-6 hours or until meat and vegetables are tender. Sprinkle with parsley.
PER SERVING *1 serving (1 each) equals 402 cal., 6 g fat (2 g sat. fat), 67 mg chol., 822 mg sodium, 53 g carb., 5 g fiber, 33 g pro.*

ROUND STEAK ITALIANO

My mom used to make this savory dish, and it's always been one that I've enjoyed. I especially like how the thick gravy drapes over the meat.

—DEANNE STEPHENS
MCMINNVILLE, OR

PREP: 15 MIN. • **COOK:** 7 HOURS
MAKES: 8 SERVINGS

- 2 pounds beef top round steak
- 1 can (8 ounces) tomato sauce
- 2 tablespoons onion soup mix
- 2 tablespoons canola oil
- 2 tablespoons red wine vinegar
- 1 teaspoon ground oregano
- ½ teaspoon garlic powder
- ¼ teaspoon pepper
- 8 medium potatoes (7 to 8 ounces each)
- 1 tablespoon cornstarch
- 1 tablespoon cold water

1. Cut steak into serving-size pieces; place in a 5-qt. slow cooker. In a large bowl, combine the tomato sauce, soup mix, oil, vinegar, oregano, garlic powder and pepper; pour over the meat. Scrub and pierce potatoes; place over meat. Cover and cook on low for 7 to 8 hours or until the meat and potatoes are tender.

2. Remove the meat and potatoes; keep warm. For gravy, pour cooking juices into a small saucepan; skim fat. Combine cornstarch and water until smooth; gradually stir into juices. Bring to a boil; cook and stir for 2 minutes or until thickened. Serve with meat and potatoes.

PER SERVING *1 serving equals 357 cal., 7 g fat (2 g sat. fat), 64 mg chol., 329 mg sodium, 42 g carb., 4 g fiber, 31 g pro.* **Diabetic Exchanges:** *3 lean meat, 2½ starch, ½ fat.*

CREAMY SWISS STEAK

When I was working, I would put this Swiss steak in the slow cooker before I left for the day. A creamy mushroom sauce made with canned soup nicely complements the round steak. It's so simple to make.

—GLORIA CARPENTER BANCROFT, MI

PREP: 15 MIN. • **COOK:** 8 HOURS
MAKES: 8 SERVINGS

- ¾ cup all-purpose flour
- 1 teaspoon salt
- ½ teaspoon pepper
- 2 pounds boneless beef round steak, cut into serving-size portions
- 2 tablespoons butter
- ½ cup chopped onion
- 2 cans (10¾ ounces each) condensed cream of mushroom soup, undiluted
- 1 cup water
  Hot cooked noodles

1. In a large resealable plastic bag, combine the flour, salt and pepper. Add beef, a few pieces at a time, and shake to coat.

2. In a large skillet, brown beef in butter on both sides. Transfer to a 3-qt. slow cooker; top with onion. Combine soup and water; pour over onion. Cover and cook on low for 8-10 hours or until meat is tender. Serve with noodles.

PER SERVING *1 serving (calculated without noodles) equals 243 cal., 8 g fat (4 g sat. fat), 73 mg chol., 624 mg sodium, 13 g carb., 1 g fiber, 28 g pro.*

SIRLOIN ROAST WITH GRAVY

My husband is a big fan of this recipe. The peppery fork-tender roast combines with rich gravy to create a tasty meal.

—RITA CLARK MONUMENT, CO

PREP: 15 MIN. • **COOK:** 5½ HOURS
MAKES: 10 SERVINGS

- 1 beef sirloin tip roast (3 pounds)
- 1 to 2 tablespoons coarsely ground pepper
- 1½ teaspoons minced garlic
- ¼ cup reduced-sodium soy sauce
- 3 tablespoons balsamic vinegar
- 1 tablespoon Worcestershire sauce
- 2 teaspoons ground mustard
- 2 tablespoons cornstarch
- ¼ cup cold water

1. Rub roast with pepper and garlic; cut in half and place in a 3-qt. slow cooker. Combine soy sauce, vinegar, Worcestershire sauce and mustard; pour over the beef. Cover and cook on low for 5½-6 hours or until meat is tender.

2. Remove roast and keep warm. Strain cooking juices into a small saucepan; skim fat. Combine the cornstarch and water until smooth; gradually stir into cooking juices. Bring to a boil; cook and stir for 2 minutes or until thickened. Serve with beef.

PER SERVING *4 ounces cooked beef with 3 tablespoons gravy equals 185 cal., 6 g fat (2 g sat. fat), 72 mg chol., 318 mg sodium, 4 g carb., trace fiber, 26 g pro.* **Diabetic Exchange:** *4 lean meat.*

SIRLOIN ROAST
WITH GRAVY

SAUCY ITALIAN ROAST

ROSEMARY POT ROAST

Come home to a comforting, ready-to-eat entree tonight. A neighbor shared this recipe with me. It always fills the house with a wonderful aroma.

—MARCIA SCHROEDER
RIVER EDGE, NJ

PREP: 15 MIN. • **COOK:** 8 HOURS
MAKES: 2 SERVINGS

- 1 boneless beef chuck steak (¾ inch thick and ¾ pound)
- 1 to 2 teaspoons canola oil
- ¼ cup beef broth
- ¼ cup tomato sauce
- ¼ cup dry red wine or additional beef broth
- 2 tablespoons chopped onion
- 1 garlic clove, minced
- 1½ teaspoons dried parsley flakes
- ¼ teaspoon minced fresh rosemary
- ⅛ teaspoon salt
- ⅛ teaspoon pepper
- 1½ teaspoons cornstarch
- 1 tablespoon water

1. In a large skillet, brown beef in oil on both sides. Transfer to a 1½-qt. slow cooker. In a small bowl, combine broth, tomato sauce, wine, onion, garlic, parsley, rosemary, salt and pepper; pour over beef. Cover and cook on low for 8 hours or until meat is tender.
2. Remove beef and keep warm. In a small saucepan, combine the cornstarch and water until smooth; stir in cooking juices. Bring to a boil; cook and stir for 2 minutes or until thickened. Serve with beef.
PER SERVING *1 serving (calculated with 1 teaspoon oil) equals 354 cal., 19 g fat (7 g sat. fat), 111 mg chol., 463 mg sodium, 6 g carb., 1 g fiber, 34 g pro.* **Diabetic Exchanges:** *5 lean meat, 2 fat, 1 vegetable.*

SAUCY ITALIAN ROAST

This roast is one of my favorite set-and-forget meals. I thicken the juices with a little flour and add ketchup, then serve the sauce and beef slices over pasta.

—JAN ROAT RED LODGE, MT

PREP: 10 MIN. • **COOK:** 8 HOURS
MAKES: 10 SERVINGS

- ½ to 1 teaspoon salt
- ½ teaspoon garlic powder
- ¼ teaspoon pepper
- 1 beef rump roast or bottom round roast (3 to 3½ pounds)
- 1 jar (4½ ounces) sliced mushrooms, drained
- 1 medium onion, diced
- 1 jar (14 ounces) spaghetti sauce
- ¼ to ½ cup red wine or beef broth
  Hot cooked pasta

1. Combine the salt, garlic powder and pepper; rub over roast. Place in a 5-qt. slow cooker. Top with mushrooms and onion. Combine the spaghetti sauce and wine; pour over meat and vegetables.
2. Cover and cook on low for 8-10 hours or until the meat is tender. Slice roast; serve with pasta and pan juices.
PER SERVING *4 ounces cooked beef (calculated without pasta) equals 218 cal., 8 g fat (3 g sat. fat), 82 mg chol., 415 mg sodium, 6 g carb., 1 g fiber, 28 g pro.*

GONE-ALL-DAY STEW

My whole family will dig into this healthy, hearty stew, but it's definitely one of my husband's favorites. I always use fresh mushrooms when possible.

—PATRICIA KILE ELIZABETHTOWN, PA

PREP: 25 MIN. • **COOK:** 4 HOURS
MAKES: 8 SERVINGS

- ¼ cup all-purpose flour
- 2 pounds boneless beef chuck roast, trimmed and cut into 1-inch cubes
- 2 tablespoons canola oil
- 1 can (10¾ ounces) condensed tomato soup, undiluted
- 1 cup water or red wine
- 2 teaspoons beef bouillon granules
- 3 teaspoons Italian seasoning
- 1 bay leaf
- ½ teaspoon coarsely ground pepper
- 6 white onions or yellow onions, quartered
- 4 medium potatoes, cut into 1½-inch slices
- 3 medium carrots, cut into 1-inch slices
- ½ cup sliced celery
- 12 large fresh mushrooms
  Hot cooked pasta or French bread, optional

1. Place flour in a large resealable plastic bag. Add beef, a few pieces at a time, and shake to coat.
2. In a large skillet, brown meat in oil in batches; drain. Transfer to a 5-qt. slow cooker. Combine the tomato soup, water or wine, bouillon and seasonings; pour over beef. Add onions, potatoes, carrots, celery and mushrooms.
3. Cover and cook on low for 4-5 hours or until meat is tender. Discard bay leaf. If desired, serve with pasta or French bread.
PER SERVING *1 serving equals 385 cal., 15 g fat (5 g sat. fat), 74 mg chol., 416 mg sodium, 36 g carb., 5 g fiber, 27 g pro.*

GONE-ALL-DAY STEW

HERBED BEEF WITH NOODLES

Just a handful of ingredients and a sprinkling of spices go into this down-home dish. Although it's very simple, it's full of subtle and creamy flavors.

—ROSLYN HURST BELMONT, CA

PREP: 25 MIN. • **COOK:** 5 HOURS
MAKES: 8 SERVINGS

- 2 **pounds beef top round steak**
- ½ **teaspoon salt**
- ½ **teaspoon pepper, divided**
- 2 **teaspoons canola oil**
- 1 **can (10¾ ounces) reduced-fat reduced-sodium condensed cream of celery soup, undiluted**
- 1 **medium onion, chopped**
- 1 **tablespoon fat-free milk**
- 1 **teaspoon dried oregano**
- ½ **teaspoon dried thyme**
- 6 **cups cooked wide egg noodles**
  Chopped celery leaves, optional

1. Cut steak into serving-size pieces; sprinkle with salt and ¼ teaspoon pepper. In a nonstick skillet coated with cooking spray, brown meat in oil on both sides. Transfer to a 3-qt. slow cooker.
2. In a small bowl, combine the soup, onion, milk, oregano, thyme and remaining pepper. Pour over meat. Cover and cook on low for 5-6 hours or until meat is tender.
3. Serve with noodles. Sprinkle with celery leaves if desired.

PER SERVING *3 ounces cooked beef with ¾ cup noodles equals 290 cal., 7 g fat (2 g sat. fat), 92 mg chol., 334 mg sodium, 26 g carb., 2 g fiber, 30 g pro.* **Diabetic Exchanges:** *3 lean meat, 1½ starch.*

CABBAGE PATCH STEW

I like to serve steaming helpings of this stew with slices of homemade bread. For a quicker prep, substitute coleslaw mix for the chopped cabbage.

—KAREN ANN BLAND GOVE, KS

PREP: 20 MIN. • **COOK:** 6 HOURS
MAKES: 8 SERVINGS (2 QUARTS)

- 1 **pound lean ground beef (90% lean)**
- 1 **cup chopped onions**
- 2 **celery ribs, chopped**
- 11 **cups coarsely chopped cabbage (about 2 pounds)**
- 2 **cans (14½ ounces each) stewed tomatoes, undrained**
- 1 **can (15 ounces) pinto beans, rinsed and drained**
- 1 **can (10 ounces) diced tomatoes with green chilies, undrained**
- ½ **cup ketchup**
- 1 **to 1½ teaspoons chili powder**
- ½ **teaspoon dried oregano**
- ½ **teaspoon pepper**
- ¼ **teaspoon salt**
  Sour cream and shredded cheddar cheese, optional

1. In a large skillet, cook the beef, onions and celery over medium heat until the meat is no longer pink; drain.
2. Transfer to a 5-qt. slow cooker. Stir in cabbage, stewed tomatoes, beans, diced tomatoes, ketchup, chili powder, oregano, pepper and the salt. Cover and cook on low for 6-8 hours or until cabbage is tender.
3. Serve with sour cream and cheese if desired.

PER SERVING *1½ cups (calculated without salt and optional toppings) equals 214 cal., 5 g fat (2 g sat. fat), 28 mg chol., 642 mg sodium, 29 g carb., 6 g fiber, 16 g pro.* **Diabetic Exchanges:** *2 lean meat, 2 vegetable, 1 starch.*

CABBAGE
PATCH STEW

SLOW COOKER BOEUF BOURGUIGNON

I've wanted to make boeuf bourguignon ever since I got one of Julia Child's cookbooks. My slow-cooked version of the popular beef stew equals the taste without the need to watch on the stovetop or in the oven.

—CRYSTAL JO BRUNS ILIFF, CO

PREP: 30 MIN. + MARINATING
COOK: 8 HOURS
MAKES: 12 SERVINGS (⅔ CUP EACH)

- 3 **pounds beef stew meat**
- 1¾ **cups dry red wine**
- 3 **tablespoons olive oil**
- 3 **tablespoons dried minced onion**
- 2 **tablespoons dried parsley flakes**
- 1 **bay leaf**
- 1 **teaspoon dried thyme**
- ¼ **teaspoon pepper**
- 8 **bacon strips, chopped**
- 1 **pound whole fresh mushrooms, quartered**
- 24 **pearl onions, peeled (about 2 cups)**
- 2 **garlic cloves, minced**
- ⅓ **cup all-purpose flour**
- 1 **teaspoon salt**
  Hot cooked whole wheat egg noodles, optional

1. Place beef in a large resealable plastic bag; add the wine, oil and seasonings. Seal bag and turn to coat. Refrigerate overnight.

2. In a large skillet, cook bacon over medium heat until crisp, stirring occasionally. Remove with a slotted spoon; drain on paper towels. Discard drippings, reserving 1 tablespoon in pan.

3. Add mushrooms and onions to drippings; cook and stir over medium-high heat until tender. Add garlic; cook 1 minute longer.

4. Drain beef, reserving marinade; transfer beef to a 4- or 5-qt. slow cooker. Sprinkle beef with flour and salt; toss to coat. Top with bacon and mushroom mixture. Add reserved marinade.

5. Cook, covered, on low for 8-10 hours or until the beef is tender. Remove the bay leaf. If desired, serve stew with noodles.
PER SERVING ⅔ *cup beef mixture (calculated without noodles) equals 289 cal., 15 g fat (5 g sat. fat), 77 mg chol., 350 mg sodium, 8 g carb., 1 g fiber, 25 g pro.* **Diabetic Exchanges:** *3 lean meat, 1½ fat, 1 vegetable.*

SLOW COOKER BOEUF BOURGUIGNON

TOP TIP

PASTA OPTIONS

Don't like whole wheat pasta? Try multigrain. It looks and tastes like white pasta, but is better for you.

SLOW-COOKED
ROUND STEAK

SLOW-COOKED ROUND STEAK

Quick and easy slow cooker recipes like this are a real plus, especially around the holidays. Serve these saucy steaks over mashed potatoes, rice or noodles.

—DONA MCPHERSON SPRING, TX

PREP: 15 MIN. • **COOK:** 7 HOURS
MAKES: 6-8 SERVINGS

- ¼ cup all-purpose flour
- ½ teaspoon salt
- ⅛ teaspoon pepper
- 2 pounds boneless beef round steak, cut into serving-size pieces
- 6 teaspoons canola oil, divided
- 1 medium onion, thinly sliced
- 1 can (10¾ ounces) condensed cream of mushroom soup, undiluted
- ½ teaspoon dried oregano
- ¼ teaspoon dried thyme

1. In a large resealable plastic bag, combine the flour, salt and pepper. Add the beef, a few pieces at a time, and shake to coat. In a large skillet, brown the meat on both sides in 4 teaspoons oil. Place in a 5-qt. slow cooker.

2. In the same skillet, saute onion in the remaining oil until lightly browned; place over beef. Combine the soup, oregano and thyme; pour over onion. Cover and cook on low for 7-8 hours or until meat is tender.

PER SERVING *1 serving equals 224 cal., 9 g fat (2 g sat. fat), 65 mg chol., 447 mg sodium, 8 g carb., 1 g fiber, 27 g pro.*

FREEZE IT
SIMPLE HUNGARIAN GOULASH

You'll love how simply this slow-cooked version of a beloved dish comes together. My son shared the recipe with me years ago.

—JACKIE KOHN DULUTH, MN

PREP: 15 MIN. • **COOK:** 8 HOURS
MAKES: 6-8 SERVINGS

- 2 pounds beef top round steak, cut into 1-inch cubes
- 1 cup chopped onion
- 2 tablespoons all-purpose flour
- 1½ teaspoons paprika
- 1 teaspoon garlic salt
- ½ teaspoon pepper
- 1 can (14½ ounces) diced tomatoes, undrained
- 1 bay leaf
- 1 cup (8 ounces) sour cream
  Hot cooked egg noodles

1. Place the beef and onion in a 3-qt. slow cooker. Combine flour, paprika, garlic salt and pepper; sprinkle over beef and stir to coat. Stir in tomatoes; add bay leaf. Cover and cook on low for 8-10 hours or until meat is tender.

2. Discard bay leaf. Just before serving, stir in sour cream; heat through. Serve with noodles.

FREEZE OPTION *Before adding sour cream, cool the stew. Freeze the stew in freezer containers. To use, partially thaw in refrigerator overnight. Heat through in a saucepan, stirring occasionally and adding a little broth if necessary. Remove from the heat; stir in the sour cream.*

PER SERVING *1 cup equals 224 cal., 8 g fat (5 g sat. fat), 83 mg chol., 339 mg sodium, 7 g carb., 1 g fiber, 27 g pro.*

SIMPLE HUNGARIAN GOULASH

SO-EASY SPAGHETTI SAUCE

Let the slow cooker do all the work for this filling spaghetti sauce. All you need to do is cook the pasta and bake up some crusty garlic bread.

—**CATHY JOHNSON** SOMERSET, PA

PREP: 30 MIN. • **COOK:** 5 HOURS
MAKES: ABOUT 2¼ QUARTS

- 1 **pound lean ground beef (90% lean)**
- 1 **medium onion, finely chopped**
- ¼ **cup finely chopped celery**
- 1 **can (29 ounces) tomato sauce**
- 2½ **cups tomato juice**
- 1 **can (14½ ounces) diced tomatoes, undrained**
- 1 **can (12 ounces) tomato paste**
- 2 **teaspoons sugar**
- 2 **teaspoons chili powder**
- 1 **teaspoon salt**
- 1 **teaspoon garlic powder**
- 1 **teaspoon dried basil**
- 1 **teaspoon dried oregano**
- ½ **teaspoon pepper**
- 4 **bay leaves**
  Hot cooked spaghetti
  Grated Parmesan cheese, optional

1. In a large skillet, cook the beef, onion and celery over medium heat until meat is no longer pink; drain. In a 4- or 5-qt. slow cooker, combine the tomato sauce, tomato juice, tomatoes, tomato paste, sugar, seasonings and beef mixture.

2. Cover and cook on low for 5-6 hours or until heated through. Discard bay leaves. Serve with spaghetti; sprinkle with cheese if desired.

PER SERVING *¾ cup (calculated without spaghetti and cheese) equals 125 cal., 3 g fat (1 g sat. fat), 19 mg chol., 744 mg sodium, 16 g carb., 4 g fiber, 10 g pro.* **Diabetic Exchanges:** *1 lean meat, 1 vegetable, ½ starch, ½ fat.*

SO-EASY SPAGHETTI SAUCE

HEARTY BEANS WITH BEEF

My husband raved about this sweet bean dish after tasting it at a party, so I knew I had to get the recipe. It's perfect for get-togethers because you can mix it up a day early and toss it into the slow cooker a few hours before guests arrive.

—**JAN BIEHL** LEESBURG, IN

PREP: 15 MIN. • **COOK:** 3 HOURS
MAKES: 8-10 SERVINGS

- 1 **pound ground beef**
- 1 **medium onion, chopped**
- 1 **can (16 ounces) baked beans, undrained**
- 1 **can (15½ ounces) butter beans, rinsed and drained**
- ½ **cup ketchup**
- ⅓ **cup packed brown sugar**
- 1 **tablespoon barbecue sauce**
- ¼ **teaspoon Worcestershire sauce**

1. In a large skillet, cook the beef and onion over medium heat until the meat is no longer pink; drain. Transfer to a 5-qt. slow cooker. Stir in the remaining ingredients.

2. Cover and cook on high for 3-4 hours or until heated through.

PER SERVING *1 serving (1 cup) equals 209 cal., 6 g fat (2 g sat. fat), 33 mg chol., 525 mg sodium, 27 g carb., 5 g fiber, 14 g pro.*

TOP TIP

CINNAMON TWIST

Want to add another flavor layer to Hearty Beans with Beef for only a few extra calories? Once finished, sprinkle a teaspoon or two of cinnamon on top.

HEARTY BEANS
WITH BEEF

SLOW-COOKED
SWISS STEAK

SLOW-COOKED SWISS STEAK

Everyone raves about how tender and rich this dish is. I make it about every two weeks during the winter! I modified my mom's Swiss steak to cook the recipe hands-free.

—KATHIE MORRIS REDMOND, OR

PREP: 15 MIN. • **COOK:** 8 HOURS
MAKES: 6 SERVINGS

- ¾ cup all-purpose flour
- 1 teaspoon pepper
- ¼ teaspoon salt
- 2 to 2½ pounds boneless beef top round steak
- 1 to 2 tablespoons butter
- 1 can (10¾ ounces) condensed cream of mushroom soup, undiluted
- 1⅓ cups water
- 1 cup sliced celery, optional
- ½ cup chopped onion
- 1 to 3 teaspoons beef bouillon granules
- ½ teaspoon minced garlic

1. In a shallow bowl, combine the flour, pepper and salt. Cut steak into six serving-size pieces; dredge in flour mixture.

2. In a large skillet, brown steak in butter. Transfer to a 3-qt. slow cooker. Combine the remaining ingredients; pour over steak. Cover and cook on low for 8-9 hours or until meat is tender.

PER SERVING *1 steak with about ½ cup gravy equals 313 cal., 9 g fat (4 g sat. fat), 92 mg chol., 666 mg sodium, 18 g carb., 2 g fiber, 37 g pro.*

FREEZE IT
CHIPOTLE SHREDDED BEEF

My slow cooker beef is irresistible when rolled up in a tortilla, burrito-style. We also like it over mashed potatoes or in buns. Leftovers make awesome quesadillas.

—DARCY WILLIAMS OMAHA, NE

PREP: 25 MIN. • **COOK:** 8 HOURS
MAKES: 10 SERVINGS

- 1 teaspoon canola oil
- 1 small onion, chopped
- 1 can (28 ounces) diced tomatoes, undrained
- ¼ cup cider vinegar
- ¼ cup chopped chipotle peppers in adobo sauce plus 2 teaspoons sauce
- 6 garlic cloves, minced
- 2 tablespoons brown sugar
- 2 bay leaves
- ½ teaspoon ground cumin
- ½ teaspoon paprika
- ½ teaspoon pepper
- ¼ teaspoon ground cinnamon
- 1 boneless beef chuck roast (2½ pounds)
- 5 cups cooked brown rice
  Shredded reduced-fat cheddar cheese and reduced-fat sour cream, optional

1. In a large skillet coated with cooking spray, heat the oil over medium-high heat. Add onion; cook and stir 2-3 minutes. Stir in tomatoes, vinegar, peppers with sauce, garlic, brown sugar, bay leaves and spices. Bring to a boil. Reduce heat; simmer, uncovered, 4-6 minutes or until thickened.

2. Place the roast in a 5-qt. slow cooker; add tomato mixture. Cook, covered, on low 8-10 hours or until meat is tender.

3. Discard bay leaves. Remove roast; cool slightly. Skim fat from cooking juices. Shred beef with two forks. Return the beef and cooking juices to slow cooker; heat through. Serve with rice. If desired, top with cheese and sour cream.

FREEZE OPTION *Freeze cooled meat mixture and juices in freezer containers. To use, partially thaw in refrigerator overnight. Heat through in a saucepan, stirring occasionally and adding a little water if necessary.*

PER SERVING *⅔ cup beef mixture with ½ cup cooked rice (calculated without optional ingredients) equals 345 cal., 13 g fat (4 g sat. fat), 74 mg chol., 194 mg sodium, 31 g carb., 3 g fiber, 26 g pro.* **Diabetic Exchanges:** *3 lean meat, 2 starch.*

CHIPOTLE
SHREDDED BEEF

SLOW COOKER BEEF TOSTADAS

I dedicate these slow-simmered tostadas to my husband, the only Italian man I know who can't get enough of Mexican flavors. Pile on your best toppings.
—TERESA DEVONO RED LION, PA

PREP: 20 MIN. • **COOK:** 6 HOURS
MAKES: 6 SERVINGS

- 1 large onion, chopped
- ¼ cup lime juice
- 1 jalapeno pepper, seeded and minced
- 1 serrano pepper, seeded and minced
- 1 tablespoon chili powder
- 3 garlic cloves, minced
- ½ teaspoon ground cumin
- 1 beef top round steak (about 1½ pounds)
- 1 teaspoon salt
- ½ teaspoon pepper
- ¼ cup chopped fresh cilantro
- 12 corn tortillas (6 inches)
  Cooking spray

TOPPINGS
- 1½ cups shredded lettuce
- 1 medium tomato, finely chopped
- ¾ cup shredded sharp cheddar cheese
- ¾ cup reduced-fat sour cream, optional

1. Place the first seven ingredients in a 3- or 4-qt. slow cooker. Cut the steak in half and sprinkle with salt and pepper; add to slow cooker. Cook, covered, on low 6-8 hours or until meat is tender.

2. Remove meat; cool slightly. Shred meat with two forks. Return beef to slow cooker and stir in the cilantro; heat through. Spritz both sides of tortillas with cooking spray. Place in a single layer on baking sheets; broil 1-2 minutes on each side or until crisp. Spoon beef mixture over tortillas; top with lettuce, tomato, cheese and, if desired, sour cream.

NOTE *Wear disposable gloves when cutting hot peppers; the oils can burn skin. Avoid touching your face.*
PER SERVING *2 tostadas equals 372 cal., 13 g fat (6 g sat. fat), 88 mg chol., 602 mg sodium, 30 g carb., 5 g fiber, 35 g pro.* **Diabetic Exchanges:** *4 lean meat, 2 starch, ½ fat.*

SLOW-COOKED CARIBBEAN POT ROAST

This dish is especially good in the fall and winter, but it's definitely an all-year-round recipe.
—JENN TIDWELL FAIR OAKS, CA

PREP: 30 MIN. • **COOK:** 6 HOURS
MAKES: 10 SERVINGS

- 2 medium sweet potatoes, cubed
- 2 large carrots, sliced
- ¼ cup chopped celery
- 1 boneless beef chuck roast (2½ pounds)
- 1 tablespoon canola oil
- 1 large onion, chopped
- 2 garlic cloves, minced
- 1 tablespoon all-purpose flour
- 1 tablespoon sugar
- 1 tablespoon brown sugar
- 1 teaspoon ground cumin
- ¾ teaspoon salt
- ¾ teaspoon ground coriander
- ¾ teaspoon chili powder
- ½ teaspoon dried oregano
- ⅛ teaspoon ground cinnamon
- ¾ teaspoon grated orange peel
- ¾ teaspoon baking cocoa
- 1 can (15 ounces) tomato sauce

1. Place the potatoes, carrots and the celery in a 5-qt. slow cooker. In a large skillet, brown meat in oil. Transfer meat to slow cooker.

2. In the same skillet, saute onion in the drippings until tender. Add the garlic; cook 1 minute longer. Combine the flour, sugar, brown sugar, seasonings, orange peel and cocoa. Stir in tomato sauce; add to skillet and heat through. Pour over the beef.

3. Cover and cook on low for 6-8 hours or until beef and vegetables are tender.

PER SERVING *3 ounces cooked beef with ½ cup vegetable mixture equals 278 cal., 12 g fat (4 g sat. fat), 74 mg chol., 453 mg sodium, 16 g carb., 3 g fiber, 25 g pro.* **Diabetic Exchanges:** *3 lean meat, 1 starch, 1 vegetable, ½ fat.*

MUSHROOM STEAK

When I knew in advance I wouldn't have time for this steak to bake one night, I let it simmer all day instead.
—SANDY PETTINGER LINCOLN, NE

PREP: 20 MIN. • **COOK:** 7 HOURS
MAKES: 6 SERVINGS

- ⅓ cup all-purpose flour
- ½ teaspoon salt
- ½ teaspoon pepper, divided
- 1 beef top round steak (2 pounds), cut into 1½-inch strips
- 2 cups sliced fresh mushrooms
- 1 small onion, cut into thin wedges
- 1 can (10¾ ounces) condensed golden mushroom soup, undiluted
- ¼ cup sherry or beef broth
- ½ teaspoon dried oregano
- ¼ teaspoon dried thyme
  Hot cooked egg noodles

1. In a large resealable plastic bag, combine flour, salt and ¼ teaspoon pepper. Add beef, a few pieces at a time, and shake to coat.

2. In a 3-qt. slow cooker, combine the mushrooms, onion and beef. Combine the soup, sherry, oregano, thyme and remaining pepper; pour over top. Cover and cook on low for 7-9 hours or until beef is tender. Serve with noodles.

PER SERVING *¾ cup (calculated without noodles) equals 265 cal., 6 g fat (2 g sat. fat), 87 mg chol., 612 mg sodium, 12 g carb., 1 g fiber, 36 g pro.* **Diabetic Exchanges:** *5 lean meat, 1 starch.*

SLOW COOKER
BEEF TOSTADAS

APPLE AND ONION
BEEF POT ROAST

reduced to 2 cups, about 15 minutes. Combine cornstarch and cold water until smooth; stir in the browning sauce. Stir into cooking liquid. Bring to a boil; cook and stir for 2 minutes or until thickened. Serve with beef and onion.

PER SERVING *1 serving (3 ounces cooked beef with 3 tablespoons gravy) equals 173 cal., 6 g fat (2 g sat. fat), 69 mg chol., 262 mg sodium, 4 g carb., trace fiber, 25 g pro.* **Diabetic Exchanges:** *3 lean meat.*

BEEF BURGUNDY

I trim the meat, cut up the veggies and store them separately the night before. The next day, I toss all the ingredients into the slow cooker. Shortly before dinnertime, I cook the noodles and sometimes bake some cheesy garlic toast.

—**MARY JO MILLER** MANSFIELD, OH

PREP: 10 MIN. • **COOK:** 5 HOURS
MAKES: 6 SERVINGS

- 1½ **pounds beef stew meat, cut into 1-inch cubes**
- ½ **pound whole fresh mushrooms, halved**
- 4 **medium carrots, chopped**
- 1 **can (10¾ ounces) condensed golden mushroom soup, undiluted**
- 1 **large onion, cut into thin wedges**
- ½ **cup Burgundy wine or beef broth**
- ¼ **cup quick-cooking tapioca**
- ½ **teaspoon salt**
- ¼ **teaspoon dried thyme**
- ¼ **teaspoon pepper**
  Hot cooked egg noodles

1. In a 5-qt. slow cooker, combine the first 10 ingredients.
2. Cover and cook on low for 5-6 hours or until meat is tender. Serve with noodles.

PER SERVING *1 cup (calculated without noodles) equals 273 cal., 9 g fat (3 g sat. fat), 73 mg chol., 642 mg sodium, 19 g carb., 3 g fiber, 24 g pro.*

APPLE AND ONION BEEF POT ROAST

I thicken the cooking juices from this roast to make an apple gravy that's wonderful over the beef and onions.
—**RACHEL KOISTINEN** HAYTI, SD

PREP: 30 MIN.
COOK: 5 HOURS + STANDING
MAKES: 8 SERVINGS WITH LEFTOVERS

- 1 **beef sirloin tip roast (3 pounds), cut in half**
- 1 **cup water**
- 1 **teaspoon seasoned salt**
- ½ **teaspoon reduced-sodium soy sauce**
- ½ **teaspoon Worcestershire sauce**
- ¼ **teaspoon garlic powder**
- 1 **large tart apple, quartered**
- 1 **large onion, sliced**
- 2 **tablespoons cornstarch**
- 2 **tablespoons cold water**
- ⅛ **teaspoon browning sauce**

1. In a large nonstick skillet coated with cooking spray, brown roast on all sides. Transfer to a 5-qt. slow cooker. Add water to skillet, stirring to loosen any browned bits; pour over roast. Sprinkle with seasoned salt, soy sauce, Worcestershire sauce and garlic powder. Top with apple and onion.
2. Cover and cook on low for 5-6 hours or until meat is tender.
3. Remove roast and onion; let stand for 15 minutes before slicing. Strain the cooking liquid into a saucepan, discarding the apple. Bring liquid to a boil; cook until

TRADITIONAL BEEF STEW

The aroma of this classic beef stew is irresistible, making it impossible not to dig in almost immediately the moment after you walk in the door.

—ROSANA PAPE HAMILTON, IN

PREP: 15 MIN. • **COOK:** 8 HOURS
MAKES: 4 SERVINGS

- 1 **pound beef stew meat, cut into 1-inch cubes**
- 1 **pound fresh baby carrots**
- 2 **medium potatoes, cut into chunks**
- 2 **medium onions, cut into wedges**
- 1 **cup drained diced tomatoes**
- 1 **cup beef broth**
- 1 **celery rib, cut into ½-inch pieces**
- 2 **tablespoons quick-cooking tapioca**
- 1 **teaspoon Worcestershire sauce**
- ¼ **teaspoon salt**
- ¼ **teaspoon pepper**

1. In a 3-qt. slow cooker, combine all ingredients.

2. Cover and cook on low for 8-10 hours or until meat and vegetables are tender.

PER SERVING *1½ cups equals 334 cal., 8 g fat (3 g sat. fat), 70 mg chol., 611 mg sodium, 39 g carb., 6 g fiber, 26 g pro.* **Diabetic Exchanges:** *3 lean meat, 2 starch, 2 vegetable.*

TRADITIONAL
BEEF STEW

SWEET 'N' TANGY
POT ROAST

SWEET 'N' TANGY POT ROAST

I fixed this roast the first time I cooked for my future husband more than 20 years ago. For the dessert, I made chocolate pudding spooned over marshmallows. He was absolutely impressed!

—CAROL MULLIGAN HONEOYE FALLS, NY

PREP: 10 MIN. • **COOK:** 9½ HOURS
MAKES: 8 SERVINGS

- 1 boneless beef chuck roast (3 pounds)
- ½ teaspoon salt
- ½ teaspoon pepper
- 1 cup water
- 1 cup ketchup
- ¼ cup red wine or beef broth
- 1 envelope brown gravy mix
- 2 teaspoons Dijon mustard
- 1 teaspoon Worcestershire sauce
- ⅛ teaspoon garlic powder
- 3 tablespoons cornstarch
- ¼ cup cold water

1. Cut the meat in half and place in a 5-qt. slow cooker. Sprinkle with salt and pepper. In a bowl, combine the water, ketchup, wine or broth, gravy mix, mustard, Worcestershire sauce and garlic powder; pour over the meat.
2. Cover and cook on low for 9-10 hours or until meat is tender.
3. Combine cornstarch and cold water until smooth. Stir into slow cooker. Cover and cook on high for 30 minutes or until gravy is thickened. Remove meat from slow cooker. Slice and serve with gravy.
PER SERVING *1 serving (3 ounces cooked beef with ½ cup gravy) equals 249 cal., 8 g fat (3 g sat. fat), 89 mg chol., 748 mg sodium, 13 g carb., 1 g fiber, 30 g pro.*

ITALIAN BEEF SANDWICHES

It takes very little effort to make these delicious sandwiches. Just set it and forget it for 8 hours!

—CHER SCHWARTZ ELLISVILLE, MO

PREP: 20 MIN. • **COOK:** 8 HOURS
MAKES: 12 SERVINGS

- 1 beef rump roast or bottom round roast (3 pounds)
- 3 cups reduced-sodium beef broth
- 1 envelope Italian salad dressing mix
- 1 teaspoon garlic powder
- 1 teaspoon onion powder
- 1 teaspoon dried parsley flakes
- 1 teaspoon dried basil
- 1 teaspoon dried oregano
- 1 teaspoon pepper
- 1 large onion, julienned
- 1 large green pepper, julienned
- 4½ teaspoons olive oil
- 12 hamburger buns, split
- 12 slices reduced-fat provolone cheese

1. Cut the roast in half; place in a 4-qt. slow cooker. Combine the broth, dressing mix and seasonings; pour over meat. Cover and cook on low for 8 hours or until tender.
2. Remove roast; cool slightly. Skim fat from cooking juices; reserve 1 cup juices. Shred the beef and return to slow cooker. Stir in reserved cooking juices; heat through.
3. Meanwhile, in a large skillet, saute onion and green pepper in oil until tender.
4. Using a slotted spoon, place beef on bun bottoms; layer with cheese and vegetables. Replace bun tops.
PER SERVING *1 sandwich equals 346 cal., 12 g fat (5 g sat. fat), 79 mg chol., 707 mg sodium, 25 g carb., 2 g fiber, 32 g pro. **Diabetic Exchanges:** 4 lean meat, 1½ starch, 1 fat.*

FLAVORFUL BEEF STEW

One way to enjoy the thick gravy in this stew? Dunk a slice of bread in it! I find it much easier to prepare the stew in the slow cooker than on the stove or in the oven.

—JACKITT TASTEOFHOME.COM

PREP: 25 MIN. • **COOK:** 6 HOURS
MAKES: 6 SERVINGS

- ½ pound medium fresh mushrooms, quartered
- 2 medium red potatoes, cubed
- 3 medium carrots, sliced
- 1 medium onion, chopped
- 1 celery rib, thinly sliced
- ¼ cup all-purpose flour
- 1 tablespoon paprika
- ¾ teaspoon salt
- ¼ teaspoon pepper
- 1 pound beef stew meat
- 1 can (14½ ounces) beef broth
- 4½ teaspoons reduced-sodium teriyaki sauce
- 2 garlic cloves, minced
- 1 bay leaf

1. Place mushrooms, potatoes, carrots, onion and celery in a 3-qt. slow cooker. In a large resealable plastic bag, combine flour, paprika, salt and pepper. Add beef, a few pieces at a time, and shake to coat. Add to slow cooker.
2. Combine the broth, teriyaki sauce, garlic and bay leaf; pour over beef. Cover and cook on low for 6-8 hours or until meat and vegetables are tender. Discard bay leaf.
PER SERVING *1 cup equals 202 cal., 6 g fat (2 g sat. fat), 47 mg chol., 745 mg sodium, 19 g carb., 3 g fiber, 19 g pro. **Diabetic Exchanges:** 2 lean meat, 1 starch, 1 vegetable.*

**TENDER
SALSA BEEF**

FREEZE IT
TENDER SALSA BEEF
This is my Mexican-style twist on comfort food. To keep it kid-friendly, use mild salsa.
—**STACIE STAMPER** NORTH WILKESBORO, NC

PREP: 15 MIN. • **COOK:** 8 HOURS
MAKES: 8 SERVINGS

- 1½ **pounds beef stew meat, cut into ¾-inch cubes**
- 2 **cups salsa**
- 1 **tablespoon brown sugar**
- 1 **tablespoon reduced-sodium soy sauce**
- 1 **garlic clove, minced**
- 4 **cups hot cooked brown rice**

In a 3-qt. slow cooker, combine the beef, salsa, brown sugar, soy sauce and garlic. Cover and cook on low for 8-10 hours or until the meat is tender. Using a slotted spoon, serve beef with rice.

FREEZE OPTION *Freeze individual portions of cooled stew in freezer containers. To use, partially thaw in refrigerator overnight. Heat through in a saucepan, stirring occasionally and adding water if necessary.*

PER SERVING *½ cup beef mixture with ½ cup rice equals 259 cal., 7 g fat (2 g sat. fat), 53 mg chol., 356 mg sodium, 28 g carb., 2 g fiber, 19 g pro.* **Diabetic Exchanges:** *2 starch, 2 lean meat.*

SUNDAY DINNER
BRISKET

SUNDAY DINNER BRISKET

We loved how tender this brisket turned out. The sauce has a robust taste with a slight tang from the balsamic vinegar, and caramelized onions complete the dish.

—TASTE OF HOME TEST KITCHEN

PREP: 45 MIN. • **COOK:** 8 HOURS
MAKES: 10 SERVINGS

- 3 **tablespoons olive oil, divided**
- 4 **cups sliced onions (about 4 medium)**
- 4 **garlic cloves, minced**
- 1 **tablespoon brown sugar**
- 1 **fresh beef brisket (4 to 5 pounds)**
- ⅓ **cup all-purpose flour**
- 1 **teaspoon salt**
- 1 **teaspoon coarsely ground pepper**
- ¼ **cup balsamic vinegar**
- 1 **can (14½ ounces) reduced-sodium beef broth**
- 2 **tablespoons tomato paste**
- 2 **teaspoons Italian seasoning**
- 1 **teaspoon Worcestershire sauce**
- ½ **teaspoon paprika**
- 1 **tablespoon cornstarch**
- 2 **tablespoons cold water**

1. In a skillet, heat 1 tablespoon oil over medium heat. Add the onions; cook and stir until softened. Sprinkle with the garlic and brown sugar. Reduce heat to medium-low; cook 10 minutes or until onions are golden brown, stirring occasionally. Transfer to an oval 6-qt. slow cooker.

2. If necessary to fit in the skillet, cut brisket in half. Sprinkle the brisket with flour and shake off excess. In skillet, heat remaining oil over medium heat. Brown both sides of brisket; sprinkle with salt and pepper. Place in slow cooker over onions.

3. Add vinegar to skillet; increase heat to medium-high. Cook, stirring to loosen browned bits from pan. Stir in broth, tomato paste, Italian seasoning, Worcestershire sauce and paprika until blended. Pour over brisket. Cook, covered, on low 8-10 hours or until meat is tender.

4. Remove brisket; keep warm. Transfer the cooking juices to a saucepan; skim fat and bring to a boil. In a small bowl, mix cornstarch and water until smooth; stir into cooking juices. Return to a boil; cook and stir 1-2 minutes or until thickened.

5. Cut brisket diagonally across the grain into thin slices. Serve with sauce.

NOTE *This is a fresh beef brisket, not corned beef.*

PER SERVING *5 ounces cooked beef with ⅓ cup sauce equals 319 cal., 12 g fat (4 g sat. fat), 78 mg chol., 381 mg sodium, 12 g carb., 1 g fiber, 39 g pro.* **Diabetic Exchanges:** *5 lean meat, 1 starch, 1 fat.*

TEXAS BEEF BARBECUE

We love these sandwiches! The beef simmers for hours in a slightly sweet sauce with plenty of spices.

—JENNIFER BAUER LANSING, MI

PREP: 15 MIN. • **COOK:** 8 HOURS
MAKES: 16 SERVINGS

- 1 **beef sirloin tip roast (4 pounds)**
- 1 **can (5½ ounces) spicy hot V8 juice**
- ½ **cup water**
- ¼ **cup white vinegar**
- ¼ **cup ketchup**
- 2 **tablespoons Worcestershire sauce**
- ½ **cup packed brown sugar**
- 1 **teaspoon salt**
- 1 **teaspoon ground mustard**
- 1 **teaspoon paprika**
- ¼ **teaspoon chili powder**
- ⅛ **teaspoon pepper**
- 16 **kaiser rolls, split**

1. Cut the roast in half; place in a 5-qt. slow cooker. Combine the V8 juice, water, vinegar, ketchup, Worcestershire sauce, brown sugar and seasonings; pour over roast. Cover and cook on low for 8-10 hours or until meat is tender.

2. Remove meat and shred with two forks; return to slow cooker and heat through. Spoon ½ cup meat mixture onto each roll.

PER SERVING *1 sandwich equals 339 cal., 8 g fat (2 g sat. fat), 60 mg chol., 606 mg sodium, 39 g carb., 1 g fiber, 27 g pro.* **Diabetic Exchanges:** *3 lean meat, 2½ starch.*

ITALIAN CHICKEN
CHARDONNAY, PAGE 105

CHICKEN & TURKEY

121

116

130

LEMON CHICKEN BREASTS

Dijon mustard, rosemary and lemon juice season the chicken breasts wonderfully in this fuss-free recipe. For an elegant finish, sprinkle on toasted almonds and fresh parsley.

—**KATHY EVANS** LACEY, WA

PREP: 20 MIN. • **COOK:** 4 HOURS
MAKES: 6 SERVINGS

- 6 **boneless skinless chicken breast halves (5 ounces each)**
- 1 **cup chicken broth, divided**
- ¼ **cup lemon juice**
- 3 **tablespoons Dijon mustard**
- 3 **garlic cloves, minced**
- 2 **tablespoons butter, melted**
- ¼ **teaspoon dried rosemary, crushed**
- 3 **tablespoons cornstarch**
  Hot cooked rice
- ½ **cup slivered almonds, toasted**
- 3 **tablespoons minced fresh parsley**

1. Place chicken in a 3-qt. slow cooker. In a small bowl, combine ¾ cup broth, lemon juice, mustard, garlic, butter and dried rosemary; pour over chicken. Cover and cook on low for 4-5 hours or until a thermometer reads 170°. Remove chicken; keep warm.

2. Skim fat from cooking juices; transfer to a small saucepan. Bring liquid to a boil. Combine cornstarch and remaining broth until smooth. Gradually stir into the pan. Bring to a boil; cook and stir for 2 minutes or until thickened.

3. Serve the chicken with rice and sauce. Sprinkle with the almonds and parsley.

PER SERVING *1 chicken breast half with ⅓ cup sauce equals 268 cal., 12 g fat (4 g sat. fat), 89 mg chol., 440 mg sodium, 9 g carb., 1 g fiber, 31 g pro.* **Diabetic Exchanges:** *4 lean meat, 2 fat, ½ starch.*

SWEET 'N' SOUR CURRY CHICKEN

A little mango chutney goes a long way in adding a zesty twist to this chicken. I also add some curry powder to give the dish flair.

—**CAROL CONRAD** EDMONTON, AB

PREP: 15 MIN. • **COOK:** 4½ HOURS
MAKES: 4 SERVINGS

- 1 **pound boneless skinless chicken breasts, cut into 1-inch pieces**
- 1 **can (14½ ounces) stewed tomatoes, cut up**
- 1 **large green pepper, cut into 1-inch pieces**
- 1 **large onion, sliced**
- ½ **cup mango chutney**
- 1½ **teaspoons curry powder**
- 2 **tablespoons cornstarch**
- ¼ **cup cold water**

1. In a 3-qt. slow cooker, combine chicken, tomatoes, green pepper, onion, chutney and curry powder. Cover and cook on low for 4-5 hours or until chicken is no longer pink.

2. Combine the cornstarch and water until smooth; stir into slow cooker. Cover and cook on high for 30 minutes or until thickened.

PER SERVING *1½ cups equals 314 cal., 3 g fat (1 g sat. fat), 63 mg chol., 583 mg sodium, 46 g carb., 3 g fiber, 25 g pro.*

LEMON CHICKEN BREASTS

SWEET 'N' SOUR
CURRY CHICKEN

CARIBBEAN
CHICKEN STEW

CARIBBEAN CHICKEN STEW

I lived with a family from the West Indies for a while and learned a lot from spending time in the kitchen with them. I lightened up this recipe by leaving out the oil and sugar, removing the skin from the chicken and using chicken sausage in place of pork.

—**JOANNE IOVINO** KINGS PARK, NY

PREP: 25 MIN. + MARINATING
COOK: 6 HOURS • **MAKES:** 8 SERVINGS

- ¼ cup ketchup
- 3 garlic cloves, minced
- 1 tablespoon sugar
- 1 tablespoon hot pepper sauce
- 1 teaspoon browning sauce, optional
- 1 teaspoon dried basil
- 1 teaspoon dried thyme
- 1 teaspoon paprika
- ½ teaspoon salt
- ½ teaspoon dried oregano
- ½ teaspoon ground allspice
- ½ teaspoon pepper
- 8 bone-in chicken thighs (about 3 pounds), skin removed
- 1 pound fully cooked andouille chicken sausage links, sliced
- 1 medium onion, finely chopped
- 2 medium carrots, finely chopped
- 2 celery ribs, finely chopped

1. In a large resealable plastic bag, combine ketchup, garlic, sugar, hot pepper sauce and, if desired, browning sauce; stir in seasonings. Add the chicken thighs, sausage and vegetables. Seal bag and turn to coat. Refrigerate 8 hours or overnight.

2. Transfer contents of bag to a 4- or 5-qt. slow cooker. Cook, covered, on low 6-8 hours or until chicken is tender.

PER SERVING *1 serving equals 309 cal., 14 g fat (4 g sat. fat), 131 mg chol., 666 mg sodium, 9 g carb., 1 g fiber, 35 g pro.* **Diabetic Exchanges:** *5 lean meat, ½ starch.*

ITALIAN CHICKEN CHARDONNAY

One day I needed to have dinner ready as soon as we walked in the door. So I altered a skillet dish that my family likes into this delicious slow cooker meal. It's perfect for just about any occasion.

—**JUDY ARMSTRONG** PRAIRIEVILLE, LA

PREP: 20 MIN. • **COOK:** 5 HOURS
MAKES: 6 SERVINGS

- 2 **teaspoons paprika**
- 1 **teaspoon salt**
- 1 **teaspoon pepper**
- ¼ **teaspoon cayenne pepper**
- 3 **pounds bone-in chicken breast halves, skin removed**
- ½ **pound baby portobello mushrooms, quartered**
- 1 **medium sweet red pepper, chopped**
- 1 **medium onion, chopped**
- 1 **can (14 ounces) water-packed artichoke hearts, rinsed and drained**
- 1½ **cups chardonnay**
- 1 **can (6 ounces) tomato paste**
- 3 **garlic cloves, minced**
- 2 **tablespoons minced fresh thyme or 2 teaspoons dried thyme**
- ¼ **cup minced fresh parsley**
  Hot cooked pasta
  Shredded Romano cheese

1. Combine the paprika, salt, pepper and cayenne; sprinkle over chicken. Place the chicken, mushrooms, red pepper, onion and artichokes in a 5-qt. slow cooker. In a small bowl, combine the chardonnay, tomato paste, garlic and thyme; pour over vegetables.

2. Cover and cook on low for 5-6 hours or until chicken is tender. Stir in parsley. Serve with pasta; sprinkle with cheese.

PER SERVING *1 serving (calculated without pasta and cheese) equals 282 cal., 5 g fat (2 g sat. fat), 103 mg chol., 550 mg sodium, 16 g carb., 5 g fiber, 43 g pro.* **Diabetic Exchanges:** *5 lean meat, 3 vegetable.*

ITALIAN CHICKEN
CHARDONNAY

**MOIST & TENDER
TURKEY BREAST**

MOIST & TENDER TURKEY BREAST

The first time I slow-cooked turkey was on vacation. It simmered while we were out, and we came back to a spectacularly juicy finished meal.
—**HEIDI VAWDREY** RIVERTON, UT

PREP: 10 MIN. • **COOK:** 4 HOURS
MAKES: 12 SERVINGS

- 1 **bone-in turkey breast (6 to 7 pounds)**
- 4 **fresh rosemary sprigs**
- 4 **garlic cloves, peeled**
- ½ **cup water**
- 1 **tablespoon brown sugar**
- ½ **teaspoon coarsely ground pepper**
- ¼ **teaspoon salt**

Place turkey breast, rosemary, garlic and water in a 6-qt. slow cooker. Mix the brown sugar, pepper and salt; sprinkle over turkey. Cook, covered, on low 4-6 hours or until turkey is tender and a thermometer inserted in turkey reads at least 170°.
PER SERVING *5 ounces cooked turkey equals 318 cal., 12 g fat (3 g sat. fat), 122 mg chol., 154 mg sodium, 2 g carb., trace fiber, 47 g pro.*

TOP TIP

PEEL IN A FLASH
To quickly peel fresh garlic, gently crush the clove with the flat side of a large knife blade to loosen the peel. If you don't have a large knife, you can crush the garlic with a small can.

TANGY TROPICAL CHICKEN

Pineapple and mango complement the chicken beautifully in this colorful dish. They lend a pleasant hint of sweetness that's balanced by the salty zip of soy sauce.
—**CHRISTINA AHO** NAPLES, FL

PREP: 20 MIN. • **COOK:** 4 HOURS
MAKES: 4 SERVINGS

- 1 **pound boneless skinless chicken breasts, cut into 1-inch strips**
- 2 **cups chopped peeled mangoes**
- 1 **medium onion, chopped**
- 1 **medium green pepper, sliced**
- 1 **garlic clove, minced**
- 1 **cup unsweetened pineapple juice**
- 1 **cup orange juice**
- ¼ **cup reduced-sodium soy sauce**
- 2 **tablespoons Thai chili sauce**
- ¼ **teaspoon pepper**
- 2 **tablespoons cornstarch**
- 2 **tablespoons cold water**
  Hot cooked rice

1. Place chicken in a 3-qt. slow cooker. Top with mangoes, onion, green pepper and garlic. In a small bowl, combine the pineapple juice, orange juice, soy sauce, chili sauce and pepper; pour over the chicken. Cover and cook on low for 4-5 hours or until chicken is tender.
2. Remove the chicken mixture to a serving platter; keep warm. Transfer cooking juices to a small saucepan. Bring juices to a boil. Combine cornstarch and water until smooth; gradually stir into the pan. Bring to a boil; cook and stir for 2 minutes or until thickened. Serve with chicken mixture and rice.
PER SERVING *1 cup (calculated without rice) equals 299 cal., 3 g fat (1 g sat. fat), 63 mg chol., 760 mg sodium, 42 g carb., 3 g fiber, 26 g pro.*

TANGY ORANGE CHICKEN THIGHS

It takes only 20 minutes to get this recipe ready. You can easily double or triple the ingredients, depending on the size of your slow cooker and expected crowd.

—**DAHLIA ABRAMS** DETROIT, MI

PREP: 20 MIN. • **COOK:** 5 HOURS
MAKES: 8 SERVINGS

- 2 cups sliced fresh carrots
- 1 can (14½ ounces) diced tomatoes, undrained
- 1 medium onion, chopped
- 1 can (6 ounces) tomato paste
- ½ cup orange juice
- 2 garlic cloves, minced
- 2 teaspoons dried basil
- 1½ teaspoons sugar
- ½ teaspoon dried oregano
- ½ teaspoon dried thyme
- ½ teaspoon dried rosemary, crushed
- ½ teaspoon pepper
- 2 teaspoons grated orange peel, divided
- 8 boneless skinless chicken thighs (about 2 pounds)
- 2 tablespoons lemon juice
- 4 bacon strips, cooked and crumbled

1. In a 3-qt. slow cooker, combine the first 12 ingredients. Stir in 1 teaspoon orange peel. Add the chicken; spoon sauce over top. Cover and cook on low for 5-6 hours or until chicken is tender.

2. Remove to a serving platter. Stir lemon juice and remaining orange peel into sauce; pour over chicken. Sprinkle with bacon.

PER SERVING *1 chicken thigh with ½ cup sauce equals 248 cal., 10 g fat (3 g sat. fat), 80 mg chol., 236 mg sodium, 15 g carb., 3 g fiber, 25 g pro.* **Diabetic Exchanges:** *3 lean meat, 1 starch.*

CHICKEN WITH BEANS AND POTATOES

This all-in-one entree is ideal for when you know your day is going to be busy. The onion soup mix and veggies give the broth lots of flavor.

—**TASTE OF HOME** TEST KITCHEN

PREP: 20 MIN. • **COOK:** 4 HOURS
MAKES: 10 SERVINGS

- 2 pounds boneless skinless chicken breasts, cut into 1-inch cubes
- ½ teaspoon lemon-pepper seasoning
- 1 tablespoon canola oil
- 1 pound fresh green beans, trimmed
- 1 pound small red potatoes, quartered
- ½ pound medium fresh mushrooms, halved
- ½ cup thinly sliced sweet onion
- 2 cans (14½ ounces each) chicken broth
- 2 tablespoons onion soup mix
- 2 teaspoons Worcestershire sauce
- 1 teaspoon grated lemon peel
- ½ teaspoon salt
- ½ teaspoon pepper
- ¼ teaspoon garlic powder

1. Sprinkle chicken with lemon-pepper. In a large skillet, saute chicken in oil over medium heat for 4-5 minutes or until lightly browned.

2. In a 5- or 6-qt. slow cooker, layer the green beans, potatoes, mushrooms and onion. In a small bowl, combine the remaining ingredients; pour over vegetables. Top with chicken.

3. Cover and cook on low for 4-5 hours or until vegetables are tender. Serve with a slotted spoon.

PER SERVING *1¼ cups equals 209 cal., 5 g fat (1 g sat. fat), 63 mg chol., 324 mg sodium, 15 g carb., 3 g fiber, 26 g pro.* **Diabetic Exchanges:** *3 lean meat, 1 vegetable, ½ starch.*

FREEZE IT

SLOW-COOKED SOUTHWEST CHICKEN

This savory low-fat chicken gets even more delicious with a garnish of reduced-fat sour cream and some fresh cilantro. With just 15 minutes of prep to this dish, you'll be out of the kitchen in no time.

—**BRANDI CASTILLO** SANTA MARIA, CA

PREP: 15 MIN. • **COOK:** 6 HOURS
MAKES: 6 SERVINGS

- 2 cans (15 ounces each) black beans, rinsed and drained
- 1 can (14½ ounces) reduced-sodium chicken broth
- 1 can (14½ ounces) diced tomatoes with mild green chilies, undrained
- ½ pound boneless skinless chicken breast
- 1 jar (8 ounces) chunky salsa
- 1 cup frozen corn
- 1 tablespoon dried parsley flakes
- 1 teaspoon ground cumin
- ¼ teaspoon pepper
- 3 cups hot cooked rice

1. In a 2- or 3-qt. slow cooker, combine beans, broth, tomatoes, chicken, salsa, corn and seasonings. Cover and cook on low for 6-8 hours or until a thermometer reads 170°.

2. Shred chicken with two forks and return to the slow cooker; heat through. Serve with rice.

FREEZE OPTION *After shredding chicken, freeze cooled mixture in freezer containers. To use, partially thaw in refrigerator overnight. Heat the mixture through in a saucepan, stirring occasionally and adding a little broth or water if necessary.*

PER SERVING *1 cup chicken mixture with ½ cup rice equals 320 cal., 1 g fat (trace sat. fat), 21 mg chol., 873 mg sodium, 56 g carb., 8 g fiber, 19 g pro.*

TANGY ORANGE
CHICKEN THIGHS

CHICKEN WITH BEANS
AND POTATOES

SLOW-COOKED
SOUTHWEST CHICKEN

CINCINNATI-STYLE
CHILI

CINCINNATI-STYLE CHILI

My husband had this type of chili when visiting a friend in Ohio and he was super thrilled when I made it at home. We like to plate it with spaghetti, cheese, onions and kidney beans.

—TARI AMBLER SHOREWOOD, IL

PREP: 35 MIN. • **COOK:** 6 HOURS
MAKES: 10 SERVINGS

- 2 **pounds extra-lean ground turkey**
- 2 **medium onions, finely chopped**
- 4 **garlic cloves, minced**
- 2 **cans (8 ounces each) no-salt-added tomato sauce**
- 1 **can (14½ ounces) reduced-sodium beef broth**
- 2 **tablespoons cider vinegar**
- ½ **ounce unsweetened chocolate, chopped**
- 3 **tablespoons chili powder**
- 1 **bay leaf**
- 2 **teaspoons Worcestershire sauce**
- 1 **teaspoon ground cumin**
- ¾ **teaspoon salt**
- ¾ **teaspoon ground cinnamon**
- ¼ **teaspoon ground allspice**
- ⅛ **teaspoon ground cloves**
- ⅛ **teaspoon cayenne pepper**
- 1 **package (16 ounces) whole wheat spaghetti**

TOPPINGS

- 1 **can (16 ounces) kidney beans, rinsed and drained**
- 1¼ **cups (5 ounces) shredded reduced-fat cheddar cheese**
- 1 **medium onion, chopped**

1. In a nonstick Dutch oven coated with cooking spray, cook turkey, onions and garlic until the turkey is no longer pink. Transfer to a 3-qt. slow cooker.
2. In a large bowl, combine tomato sauce, broth, vinegar, chocolate and seasonings; pour over turkey mixture. Cook, covered, on low 6-8 hours.

3. Cook the spaghetti according to package directions; drain. Remove the bay leaf from chili. For each serving, place ¾ cup spaghetti in a bowl. Top with about ⅔ cup chili, 3 tablespoons kidney beans, 2 tablespoons cheese and 1 tablespoon chopped onion.
PER SERVING *1 serving equals 388 cal., 6 g fat (3 g sat. fat), 47 mg chol., 523 mg sodium, 52 g carb., 10 g fiber, 37 g pro.*

TURKEY SLOPPY JOES

These tangy sandwiches go over well at gatherings large and small. I frequently take them to potlucks, and I'm always asked if there's a secret ingredient.

—MARYLOU LARUE FREELAND, MI

PREP: 15 MIN. • **COOK:** 4 HOURS
MAKES: 8 SERVINGS

- 1 **pound lean ground turkey**
- 1 **small onion, chopped**
- ½ **cup chopped celery**
- ¼ **cup chopped green pepper**
- 1 **can (10¾ ounces) reduced-sodium condensed tomato soup, undiluted**
- ½ **cup ketchup**
- 2 **tablespoons prepared mustard**
- 1 **tablespoon brown sugar**
- ¼ **teaspoon pepper**
- 8 **hamburger buns, split**

1. In a large skillet coated with cooking spray, cook the turkey, onion, celery and green pepper over medium heat until the meat is no longer pink; drain. Stir in the soup, ketchup, mustard, brown sugar and pepper.
2. Transfer to a 3-qt. slow cooker. Cover and cook on low for 4 hours. Serve on buns.
PER SERVING *1 serving equals 247 cal., 7 g fat (2 g sat. fat), 45 mg chol., 553 mg sodium, 32 g carb., 2 g fiber, 14 g pro.* **Diabetic Exchanges:** *2 starch, 1½ lean meat.*

ITALIAN SAUSAGE AND VEGETABLES

A complete meal in a pot is even better when it's also healthy and delicious! I found this recipe in a magazine and then made a few adjustments. I usually serve it with hot garlic bread.

—GINNY STUBY ALTOONA, PA

PREP: 20 MIN. • **COOK:** 5½ HOURS
MAKES: 6 SERVINGS

- 1¼ **pounds sweet or hot Italian turkey sausage links**
- 1 **can (28 ounces) diced tomatoes, undrained**
- 2 **medium potatoes, cut into 1-inch pieces**
- 4 **small zucchini, cut into 1-inch slices**
- 1 **medium onion, cut into wedges**
- ½ **teaspoon garlic powder**
- ¼ **teaspoon crushed red pepper flakes**
- ¼ **teaspoon dried oregano**
- ¼ **teaspoon dried basil**
- 1 **tablespoon dry bread crumbs**
- ¾ **cup shredded pepper jack cheese**

1. In a nonstick skillet, brown sausages over medium heat. Place in a 5-qt. slow cooker. Add the vegetables and seasonings. Cover and cook on low for 5½-6½ hours or until a thermometer reads 165°.
2. Remove sausages and cut into 1-in. pieces; return to slow cooker. Stir in bread crumbs. Serve in bowls; sprinkle with cheese.
PER SERVING *1 serving equals 304 cal., 13 g fat (4 g sat. fat), 71 mg chol., 838 mg sodium, 26 g carb., 5 g fiber, 22 g pro.*

CURRY
CHICKEN

SLOW-COOKED LEMON CHICKEN

A hint of lemon and fresh parsley brighten up everyday chicken. This is the perfect midwinter recipe for when you need a taste of spring.
—**WALTER POWELL** WILMINGTON, DE

PREP: 20 MIN. • **COOK:** 5¼ HOURS
MAKES: 6 SERVINGS

- 6 **bone-in chicken breast halves (12 ounces each), skin removed**
- 1 **teaspoon dried oregano**
- ½ **teaspoon seasoned salt**
- ¼ **teaspoon pepper**
- 2 **tablespoons butter**
- ¼ **cup water**
- 3 **tablespoons lemon juice**
- 2 **garlic cloves, minced**
- 1 **teaspoon chicken bouillon granules**
- 2 **teaspoons minced fresh parsley Hot cooked rice**

1. Pat chicken dry with paper towels. Combine the oregano, seasoned salt and pepper; rub over chicken. In a skillet over medium heat, brown the chicken in butter; transfer to a 5-qt. slow cooker. Add the water, lemon juice, garlic and bouillon to the skillet; bring to a boil, stirring to loosen browned bits. Pour over chicken.

2. Cover and cook on low for 5-6 hours. Baste chicken with cooking juices. Add parsley. Cover and cook 15-30 minutes longer or until meat juices run clear. Remove chicken to a platter and keep warm; if desired, thicken cooking juices. Serve over chicken and rice.

PER SERVING *1 chicken breast half equals 336 cal., 10 g fat (4 g sat. fat), 164 mg chol., 431 mg sodium, 1 g carb., 0 fiber, 56 g pro.*

CURRY CHICKEN

Our three children all love the spicy flavors found in this recipe. Add more or less curry depending on your preferences.
—**HELEN TOULANTIS** WANTAGH, NY

PREP: 25 MIN. • **COOK:** 4½ HOURS
MAKES: 6 SERVINGS

- 6 **boneless skinless chicken breast halves (6 ounces each)**
- 1¼ **teaspoons salt**
- 1 **can (13.66 ounces) light coconut milk**
- 1 **teaspoon curry powder**
- ½ **teaspoon ground turmeric**
- ½ **teaspoon cayenne pepper**
- 3 **green onions, sliced, divided**
- 2 **tablespoons cornstarch**
- 2 **tablespoons cold water**
- 1 **to 2 tablespoons lime juice**
- 3 **cups hot cooked rice**

1. Sprinkle the chicken with salt. In a large nonstick skillet coated with cooking spray, brown the chicken on both sides. Place in a 5-qt. slow cooker.

2. Combine coconut milk, curry, turmeric and cayenne; pour over chicken. Sprinkle with half of the onions. Cover and cook on low for 4-5 hours or until chicken is tender.

3. Combine cornstarch and water until smooth; stir into the slow cooker. Cover and cook on high for 30 minutes or until the sauce is thickened. Stir in the lime juice. Serve chicken with rice and sauce; sprinkle with remaining onions.

PER SERVING *1 serving equals 353 cal., 9 g fat (5 g sat. fat), 94 mg chol., 576 mg sodium, 27 g carb., 1 g fiber, 37 g pro.* **Diabetic Exchanges:** *5 lean meat, 1½ starch, 1 fat.*

SLOW-COOKED
LEMON CHICKEN

CHICKEN & TURKEY

SOUTHWEST TURKEY STEW

SOUTHWEST TURKEY STEW

I prefer main dishes that let me stay on my diet but still eat what the rest of the family is having. This stew is a constant hit with my husband and our young children.

—STEPHANIE HUTCHINSON
HELIX, OR

PREP: 15 MIN. • **COOK:** 5 HOURS
MAKES: 6 SERVINGS

- 1½ **pounds turkey breast tenderloins, cubed**
- 2 **teaspoons canola oil**
- 1 **can (15 ounces) turkey chili with beans, undrained**
- 1 **can (14½ ounces) diced tomatoes, undrained**
- 1 **medium sweet red pepper, chopped**
- 1 **medium green pepper, chopped**
- ¾ **cup chopped onion**
- ¾ **cup salsa**
- 3 **garlic cloves, minced**
- 1½ **teaspoons chili powder**
- ½ **teaspoon salt**
- ½ **teaspoon ground cumin**
- 1 **tablespoon minced fresh cilantro, optional**

1. In a nonstick skillet, brown turkey in oil; transfer to a 3-qt. slow cooker. Stir in the chili, tomatoes, peppers, onion, salsa, garlic, chili powder, salt and cumin.

2. Cover and cook on low 5-6 hours or until turkey is no longer pink and vegetables are tender. Garnish with cilantro if desired.

PER SERVING *1¼ cups equals 238 cal., 4 g fat (1 g sat. fat), 65 mg chol., 837 mg sodium, 17 g carb., 5 g fiber, 33 g pro.* **Diabetic Exchanges:** *4 lean meat, 1 vegetable, ½ starch.*

SLOW-COOKED CHICKEN CACCIATORE

Here's an all-time-favorite Italian dish made easy in the slow cooker! The herbs and garlic give it such a wonderful aroma as it cooks.

—DENISE HOLLEBEKE PENHOLD, AB

PREP: 20 MIN. • **COOK:** 4 HOURS
MAKES: 6 SERVINGS

- ⅓ **cup all-purpose flour**
- 1 **broiler/fryer chicken (3 to 4 pounds), cut up**
- 2 **tablespoons canola oil**
- 2 **medium onions, cut into wedges**
- 1 **medium green pepper, cut into strips**
- 1 **jar (6 ounces) sliced mushrooms, drained**
- 1 **can (14½ ounces) diced tomatoes, undrained**
- 2 **garlic cloves, minced**
- ½ **teaspoon salt**
- ½ **teaspoon dried oregano**
- ¼ **teaspoon dried basil**
- ½ **cup shredded Parmesan cheese**

1. Place flour in a large resealable plastic bag. Add the chicken, a few pieces at a time, and shake to coat. In a large skillet, brown chicken in oil on all sides.

2. Transfer to a 5-qt. slow cooker. Top with the onions, green pepper and mushrooms. In a small bowl, combine the tomatoes, garlic, salt, oregano and basil; pour over the vegetables. Cover and cook on low for 4-5 hours or until chicken juices run clear and vegetables are tender. Serve with cheese.

PER SERVING *1 serving (calculated without skin) equals 296 cal., 12 g fat (3 g sat. fat), 78 mg chol., 582 mg sodium, 16 g carb., 3 g fiber, 29 g pro.* **Diabetic Exchanges:** *3 lean meat, 2 vegetable, 1 fat, ½ starch.*

⑤ INGREDIENTS
SIMPLE SOUTHWEST CHICKEN

Chicken is cooked until tender and combined with corn, beans, cheese and salsa for a Southwestern-style meal. The garnishes really pull everything together.

—MADDYMOO TASTEOFHOME.COM

PREP: 15 MIN. • **COOK:** 4 HOURS
MAKES: 6 SERVINGS

- 1 **can (15¼ ounces) whole kernel corn, drained**
- 1 **can (15 ounces) black beans, rinsed and drained**
- 1 **jar (16 ounces) mild salsa**
- 4 **boneless skinless chicken breast halves (5 ounces each)**
  Sweet red and yellow pepper strips, sour cream, shredded cheddar cheese and sliced green onions, optional

1. In a 3-qt. slow cooker, layer three-fourths each of the corn and beans and half of the salsa. Arrange the chicken over the salsa; top with remaining corn, beans and salsa. Cover and cook on low for 4-5 hours or until chicken is tender.

2. Shred chicken with two forks and return to slow cooker; heat through. Top with the peppers, sour cream, cheese and onions if desired.

PER SERVING *1 cup (calculated without optional ingredients) equals 234 cal., 3 g fat (1 g sat. fat), 52 mg chol., 678 mg sodium, 23 g carb., 4 g fiber, 24 g pro.* **Diabetic Exchanges:** *3 lean meat, 1 starch, 1 vegetable.*

SIMPLE SOUTHWEST CHICKEN

FREEZE IT
SIMPLE CHICKEN TAGINE

Flavored with cinnamon and a touch of sweetness from the apricots, this stew tastes as if you spent all day in the kitchen! I like to sprinkle it with toasted almonds or cashews and serve it with hot couscous.

—ANGELA BUCHANAN
LONGMONT, CO

PREP: 15 MIN. • **COOK:** 6 HOURS
MAKES: 6 SERVINGS

- 2¼ **pounds bone-in chicken thighs, skin removed**
- 1 **large onion, chopped**
- 2 **medium carrots, sliced**
- ¾ **cup unsweetened apple juice**
- 1 **garlic clove, minced**
- 1 **teaspoon salt**
- ½ **teaspoon ground cinnamon**
- ½ **teaspoon pepper**
- 1 **cup chopped dried apricots**
  Hot cooked couscous

1. Place the chicken, onion and carrots in a 3- or 4-qt. slow cooker coated with cooking spray. In a small bowl, combine the apple juice, garlic, salt, cinnamon and pepper; pour over vegetables.
2. Cover and cook on low for 6-8 hours or until chicken is tender.
3. Remove chicken from slow cooker; shred meat with two forks. Skim fat from cooking juices; stir in apricots. Return shredded chicken to slow cooker; heat though. Serve with couscous.

FREEZE OPTION *Freeze cooled stew in freezer containers. To use, partially thaw in the refrigerator overnight. Heat the stew through in a saucepan, stirring occasionally and, if necessary, adding a little water. Serve with couscous.*
PER SERVING *1⅓ cups (calculated without couscous) equals 279 cal., 10 g fat (3 g sat. fat), 87 mg chol., 497 mg sodium, 23 g carb., 3 g fiber, 25 g pro.* **Diabetic Exchanges:** *3 lean meat, 1 vegetable, 1 fruit.*

FREEZE IT
ITALIAN TURKEY SANDWICHES

I hope you enjoy these tasty turkey sandwiches as much as our family does. The recipe makes plenty, so it's great for potlucks. Leftovers are just as good reheated the next day.

—CAROL RILEY OSSIAN, IN

PREP: 10 MIN. • **COOK:** 5 HOURS
MAKES: 12 SERVINGS

- 1 **bone-in turkey breast (6 pounds), skin removed**
- 1 **medium onion, chopped**
- 1 **small green pepper, chopped**
- ¼ **cup chili sauce**
- 3 **tablespoons white vinegar**
- 2 **tablespoons dried oregano or Italian seasoning**
- 4 **teaspoons beef bouillon granules**
- 12 **kaiser or hard rolls, split**

1. Place turkey breast in a greased 5-qt. slow cooker. Add onion and green pepper.
2. Combine chili sauce, vinegar, oregano and bouillon; pour over turkey and vegetables. Cover and cook on low for 5-6 hours or until turkey is tender.
3. Shred turkey with two forks and return to slow cooker; heat through. Spoon ½ cup onto each roll.

FREEZE OPTION *Place the cooled meat and juice mixture in freezer containers. To use, partially thaw in refrigerator overnight. Microwave, covered, on high in a microwave-safe dish until heated through, gently stirring and adding a little water if necessary.*
PER SERVING *1 sandwich equals 374 cal., 4 g fat (1 g sat. fat), 118 mg chol., 724 mg sodium, 34 g carb., 2 g fiber, 49 g pro.* **Diabetic Exchanges:** *6 lean meat, 2 starch.*

SIMPLE CHICKEN TAGINE

ITALIAN TURKEY
SANDWICHES

ONE-DISH
MOROCCAN CHICKEN

ONE-DISH MOROCCAN CHICKEN

Spices really work their magic on the chicken here. Dried fruit and couscous add an exotic touch.

—**KATHY MORGAN** RIDGEFIELD, WA

PREP: 20 MIN. • **COOK:** 6 HOURS
MAKES: 4 SERVINGS

- 4   medium carrots, sliced
- 2   large onions, halved and sliced
- 1   broiler/fryer chicken (3 to 4 pounds), cut up, skin removed
- ½   teaspoon salt
- ½   cup chopped dried apricots
- ½   cup raisins
- 1   can (14½ ounces) reduced-sodium chicken broth
- ¼   cup tomato paste
- 2   tablespoons all-purpose flour
- 2   tablespoons lemon juice
- 2   garlic cloves, minced
- 1½   teaspoons ground ginger
- 1½   teaspoons ground cumin
- 1   teaspoon ground cinnamon
- ¾   teaspoon pepper
      Hot cooked couscous

1. Place carrots and onions in a greased 5-qt. slow cooker. Sprinkle chicken with salt; add to the slow cooker. Top with the apricots and raisins. In a small bowl, whisk the broth, tomato paste, flour, lemon juice, garlic and seasonings until blended; add to slow cooker.

2. Cook, covered, on low 6-7 hours or until chicken is tender. Serve with couscous.

PER SERVING *1 serving (calculated without couscous) equals 435 cal., 9 g fat (3 g sat. fat), 110 mg chol., 755 mg sodium, 47 g carb., 6 g fiber, 42 g pro.*

THE SKINNY

REDUCE SODIUM

Using reduced-sodium chicken broth in this recipe saves you about 145 mg sodium per serving.

CONTEST-WINNING CHICKEN CACCIATORE

My husband and I operate a very busy farm. There are days when there's just no time left for cooking, so it's really nice to be able to come into the house and smell this chicken cacciatore meal. Then I just have to cook the pasta for dinner to be set.

—AGGIE ARNOLD-NORMAN
LIBERTY, PA

PREP: 15 MIN. • **COOK:** 6 HOURS
MAKES: 6 SERVINGS

- 2 medium onions, thinly sliced
- 1 broiler/fryer chicken (3 to 4 pounds), cut up and skin removed
- 2 garlic cloves, minced
- 1 to 2 teaspoons dried oregano
- 1 teaspoon salt
- ½ teaspoon dried basil
- ¼ teaspoon pepper
- 1 bay leaf
- 1 can (14½ ounces) diced tomatoes, undrained
- 1 can (8 ounces) tomato sauce
- 1 can (4 ounces) mushroom stems and pieces, drained, or 1 cup sliced fresh mushrooms
- ¼ cup white wine or water
  Hot cooked pasta

1. Place onions in a 5-qt. slow cooker. Add the chicken, seasonings, tomatoes, tomato sauce, mushrooms and wine.

2. Cover and cook on low for 6-8 hours or until chicken is tender. Discard bay leaf. Serve chicken with sauce over pasta.

PER SERVING *1 serving (calculated without pasta) equals 207 calories, 6 g fat (2 g saturated fat), 73 mg cholesterol, 787 mg sodium, 11 g carbohydrate, 3 g fiber, 27 g protein. Diabetic Exchanges: 4 lean meat, 2 vegetable.*

CONTEST-WINNING
CHICKEN CACCIATORE

SLOW COOKER
BBQ CHICKEN

SLOW COOKER BBQ CHICKEN

Of all the recipes I make in a slow cooker, this is my favorite. If you like your barbecue sweet with a little spice, this'll be your new go-to, too.

—YVONNE MCKIM VANCOUVER, WA

PREP: 15 MIN. • **COOK:** 5 HOURS
MAKES: 12 SERVINGS

- 6 chicken leg quarters, skin removed
- ¾ cup ketchup
- ½ cup orange juice
- ¼ cup packed brown sugar
- ¼ cup red wine vinegar
- ¼ cup olive oil
- 4 teaspoons minced fresh parsley
- 2 teaspoons Worcestershire sauce
- 1 teaspoon garlic salt
- ½ teaspoon pepper
- 2 tablespoons plus 2 teaspoons cornstarch
- ¼ cup water

1. Using a sharp knife, cut through the joint of each leg quarter to separate into two pieces. Place the chicken in a 4-qt. slow cooker.
2. In a small bowl, mix ketchup, orange juice, brown sugar, vinegar, oil, parsley, Worcestershire sauce, garlic salt and pepper; pour over chicken. Cook, covered, on low for 5-6 hours or until meat is tender.
3. Remove chicken to a serving platter; keep warm. Skim the fat from cooking juices; pour juices into a measuring cup to measure 2 cups. Transfer to a saucepan; bring to a boil. In a small bowl, mix the cornstarch and water until smooth; stir into cooking juices. Return to a boil, stirring constantly; cook and stir 1-2 minutes or until thickened. Serve with chicken.
PER SERVING *1 serving equals 179 cal., 9 g fat (2 g sat. fat), 45 mg chol., 392 mg sodium, 12 g carb., trace fiber, 13 g pro.* **Diabetic Exchanges:** *2 lean meat, 1 starch, 1 fat.*

NACHO CHICKEN & RICE

Simmer up a delicious low-fat meal with just a few basic ingredients. Your family is sure to love this medley of tender chicken, veggies and a zippy cheese sauce.

—LINDA FOREMAN
LOCUST GROVE, OK

PREP: 20 MIN. • **COOK:** 5 HOURS
MAKES: 6 SERVINGS

- 2½ pounds boneless skinless chicken breast halves, cubed
- 1 each small green, sweet red and orange peppers, cut into thin strips
- 1 can (10¾ ounces) condensed nacho cheese soup, undiluted
- ½ cup chunky salsa
- ⅛ teaspoon chili powder
- 4½ cups hot cooked rice

In a 3-qt. slow cooker, combine the chicken, peppers, soup, salsa and chili powder. Cover and cook on low for 5-6 hours or until chicken is tender. Serve with rice.
PER SERVING *1 cup chicken mixture with ¾ cup rice equals 360 cal., 7 g fat (2 g sat. fat), 84 mg chol., 553 mg sodium, 41 g carb., 2 g fiber, 34 g pro.* **Diabetic Exchanges:** *4 lean meat, 2½ starch, ½ fat.*

SOUTHWESTERN CHICKEN & LIMA BEAN STEW

When I make this for supper, my daughter, son-in-law and grandchildren make me happy by saying, "That was so good!" or just by quickly filling up their bowls.

—PAM CORDER MONROE, LA

PREP: 20 MIN. • **COOK:** 6 HOURS
MAKES: 6 SERVINGS

- 4 bone-in chicken thighs (1½ pounds), skin removed
- 2 cups frozen lima beans
- 2 cups frozen corn
- 1 large green pepper, chopped
- 1 large onion, chopped
- 2 cans (14 ounces each) fire-roasted diced tomatoes, undrained
- ¼ cup tomato paste
- 3 tablespoons Worcestershire sauce
- 3 garlic cloves, minced
- 1½ teaspoons ground cumin
- 1½ teaspoons dried oregano
- ¼ teaspoon salt
- ¼ teaspoon pepper
  Chopped fresh cilantro or parsley

1. Place the first five ingredients in a 5-qt. slow cooker. In a large bowl, combine tomatoes, tomato paste, Worcestershire sauce, garlic and dry seasonings; pour over top.
2. Cook, covered, on low 6-8 hours or until chicken is tender. Remove chicken from slow cooker. When cool enough to handle, remove meat from bones; discard bones. Shred meat with two forks; return to slow cooker and heat through. If desired, sprinkle with cilantro.
PER SERVING 1½ cups equals 312 cal., 7 g fat (2 g sat. fat), 58 mg chol., 614 mg sodium, 39 g carb., 8 g fiber, 24 g pro. *Diabetic Exchanges: 3 lean meat, 2 starch, 1 vegetable.*

SLOW-COOKED ORANGE CHICKEN

I decided I wanted to make a flavorful chicken dish that's lower in calories and fat. Everyone likes the taste, including my grandkids. It travels well, and I often take it to potluck suppers.

—NANCY WIT FREMONT, NE

PREP: 15 MIN. • **COOK:** 4½ HOURS
MAKES: 4 SERVINGS

- 1 broiler/fryer chicken (3 pounds), cut up and skin removed
- 3 cups orange juice
- 1 cup chopped celery
- 1 cup chopped green pepper
- 1 can (4 ounces) mushroom stems and pieces, drained
- 4 teaspoons dried minced onion
- 1 tablespoon minced fresh parsley or 1 teaspoon dried parsley flakes
- ½ teaspoon salt
- ¼ teaspoon pepper
- 3 tablespoons cornstarch
- 3 tablespoons cold water
  Hot cooked rice, optional
  Additional minced fresh parsley, optional

1. In a 3-qt. slow cooker, combine the first nine ingredients. Cover and cook on low for 4-5 hours or until chicken juices run clear.
2. Combine cornstarch and water until smooth; gradually stir into cooking liquid. Cover and cook on high for 30-45 minutes or until thickened. If desired, serve with rice and sprinkle with parsley.
PER SERVING 1 serving (calculated without rice) equals 364 cal., 9 g fat (2 g sat. fat), 110 mg chol., 515 mg sodium, 30 g carb., 2 g fiber, 39 g pro.

COCONUT CURRY CHICKEN

My husband and I love this yummy dish! It's a breeze to prepare in the slow cooker, and it tastes just like a meal you'd have at your favorite Indian or Thai restaurant.

—ANDI KAUFFMAN BEAVERCREEK, OR

PREP: 20 MIN. • **COOK:** 5 HOURS
MAKES: 4 SERVINGS

- 2 medium potatoes, peeled and cubed
- 1 small onion, chopped
- 4 boneless skinless chicken breast halves (4 ounces each)
- 1 cup light coconut milk
- 4 teaspoons curry powder
- 1 garlic clove, minced
- 1 teaspoon reduced-sodium chicken bouillon granules
- ¼ teaspoon salt
- ¼ teaspoon pepper
- 2 cups hot cooked rice
- ¼ cup thinly sliced green onions
  Raisins, flaked coconut and chopped unsalted peanuts, optional

1. Place potatoes and onion in a 3- or 4-qt. slow cooker. In a large nonstick skillet coated with cooking spray, brown chicken on both sides.
2. Transfer to slow cooker. In a small bowl, combine the coconut milk, curry, garlic, bouillon, salt and pepper; pour over chicken. Cover and cook on low for 5-6 hours or until meat is tender.
3. Serve chicken and sauce with rice; sprinkle with green onions. Garnish with raisins, coconut and peanuts if desired.
PER SERVING 1 serving (calculated without optional ingredients) equals 396 cal., 11 g fat (7 g sat. fat), 63 mg chol., 309 mg sodium, 43 g carb., 3 g fiber, 27 g pro. *Diabetic Exchanges: 3 lean meat, 2½ starch, 2 fat.*

SOUTHWESTERN CHICKEN
& LIMA BEAN STEW

SLOW-COOKED
ORANGE CHICKEN

COCONUT
CURRY CHICKEN

GARDEN CHICKEN
CACCIATORE

GARDEN CHICKEN CACCIATORE

Treat company to this perfect Italian meal. You'll have time to visit with your guests while it cooks, and it often earns me enthusiastic reviews. I like to present it with couscous, green beans and a dry red wine.
—**MARTHA SCHIRMACHER**
STERLING HEIGHTS, MI

PREP: 15 MIN. • **COOK:** 8½ HOURS
MAKES: 12 SERVINGS

- 12 **boneless skinless chicken thighs (about 3 pounds)**
- 2 **medium green peppers, chopped**
- 1 **can (14½ ounces) diced tomatoes with basil, oregano and garlic, undrained**
- 1 **can (6 ounces) tomato paste**
- 1 **medium onion, sliced**
- ½ **cup reduced-sodium chicken broth**
- ¼ **cup dry red wine or additional reduced-sodium chicken broth**
- 3 **garlic cloves, minced**
- ¾ **teaspoon salt**
- ⅛ **teaspoon pepper**
- 2 **tablespoons cornstarch**
- 2 **tablespoons cold water**

1. Place the chicken in a 4- or 5-qt. slow cooker. In a small bowl, combine green peppers, tomatoes, tomato paste, onion, broth, wine, garlic, salt and pepper; pour over chicken. Cook, covered, on low 8-10 hours or until the chicken is tender.
2. In a small bowl, mix cornstarch and water until smooth; gradually stir into slow cooker. Cook, covered, on high 30 minutes or until sauce is thickened.
PER SERVING *1 chicken thigh with scant ½ cup sauce equals 207 cal., 9 g fat (2 g sat. fat), 76 mg chol., 410 mg sodium, 8 g carb., 1 g fiber, 23 g pro.* **Diabetic Exchanges:** *3 lean meat, 1 vegetable, ½ fat.*

FREEZE IT
PULLED CHICKEN SANDWICHES

I was raised as a Southern girl with the love of barbecue built into my DNA. This recipe allows me to enjoy the flavors I grew up eating, while still following a healthy diet.
—**HEIDI MULHOLLAND** CUMMING, GA

PREP: 20 MIN. • **COOK:** 4 HOURS
MAKES: 6 SERVINGS

- 1 **medium onion, finely chopped**
- 1 **can (6 ounces) tomato paste**
- ¼ **cup reduced-sodium chicken broth**
- 2 **tablespoons brown sugar**
- 1 **tablespoon cider vinegar**
- 1 **tablespoon yellow mustard**
- 1 **tablespoon Worcestershire sauce**
- 2 **garlic cloves, minced**
- 2 **teaspoons chili powder**
- ¾ **teaspoon salt**
- ⅛ **teaspoon cayenne pepper**
- 1½ **pounds boneless skinless chicken breasts**
- 6 **whole wheat hamburger buns, split**

1. In a small bowl, mix the first 11 ingredients. Place chicken in a 3-qt. slow cooker. Pour sauce over the top.
2. Cook, covered, on low 4-5 hours or until chicken is tender. Remove chicken; cool slightly. Shred meat with two forks. Return to slow cooker; heat through. Serve in buns.
FREEZE OPTION *Freeze the cooled chicken mixture in freezer containers. To use, partially thaw in refrigerator overnight. Heat through in a saucepan, stirring occasionally and adding a little broth if necessary.*
PER SERVING *1 sandwich equals 296 cal., 5 g fat (1 g sat. fat), 63 mg chol., 698 mg sodium, 35 g carb., 5 g fiber, 29 g pro.* **Diabetic Exchanges:** *3 lean meat, 2 starch.*

---

⑤ INGREDIENTS
SAUCY RASPBERRY CHICKEN

I first had this dish as a teenage baby sitter—the mom prepared it for us before heading out. The kids loved it, and so did I! Now I make it for my own kids.
—**MELISSA WALES**
ELEPHANT BUTTE, NM

PREP: 15 MIN. • **COOK:** 5 HOURS
MAKES: 5 SERVINGS

- 5 **chicken leg quarters, skin removed**
- ⅓ **cup seedless raspberry spreadable fruit**
- 3 **tablespoons reduced-sodium soy sauce**
- 1 **teaspoon spicy brown mustard**
- ¼ **teaspoon pepper**
- 2 **tablespoons cornstarch**
- 2 **tablespoons cold water**

1. Place chicken in a 3-qt. slow cooker. In a small bowl, combine the spreadable fruit, soy sauce, mustard and pepper; pour over chicken. Cover and cook on low for 5-6 hours or until meat is tender.
2. Remove chicken to a serving platter; keep warm. Skim fat from cooking juices; transfer juices to a saucepan. Bring to a boil. Combine cornstarch and water until smooth; gradually stir into the pan. Bring to a boil; cook and stir for 2 minutes or until thickened. Serve with chicken.
PER SERVING *1 chicken leg quarter with ⅓ cup sauce equals 337 cal., 16 g fat (4 g sat. fat), 105 mg chol., 468 mg sodium, 14 g carb., trace fiber, 31 g pro.*

ITALIAN CHICKEN
AND PEPPERS

SAVORY LEMONADE CHICKEN

I don't know where this recipe originally came from, but my mother used to prepare it for our family when I was little. Now I love to make it! A sweet and tangy sauce nicely coats chicken that's ready to serve in just a few hours.

—JENNY COOK EAU CLAIRE, WI

PREP: 10 MIN. • **COOK:** 3 HOURS
MAKES: 6 SERVINGS

- 6 **boneless skinless chicken breast halves (4 ounces each)**
- ¾ **cup thawed lemonade concentrate**
- 3 **tablespoons ketchup**
- 2 **tablespoons brown sugar**
- 1 **tablespoon cider vinegar**
- 2 **tablespoons cornstarch**
- 2 **tablespoons cold water**

1. Place chicken in a 5-qt. slow cooker. In a small bowl, combine the lemonade concentrate, ketchup, brown sugar and vinegar; pour over chicken. Cover and cook on low for 2½ hours or until chicken is tender.
2. Remove chicken and keep warm. Combine cornstarch and water until smooth; gradually stir into cooking juices. Cover and cook on high for 30 minutes or until thickened. Return chicken to the slow cooker; heat through.
PER SERVING *1 chicken breast half with ¼ cup sauce equals 208 cal., 3 g fat (1 g sat. fat), 63 mg chol., 147 mg sodium, 22 g carb., trace fiber, 23 g pro.* **Diabetic Exchanges:** *3 lean meat, 1½ fruit.*

ITALIAN CHICKEN AND PEPPERS

I put this chicken recipe together one day when I had leftover peppers and wanted something easy. To my delight, the taste reminded me of pizza—something I love but can no longer eat! It pairs nicely with steamed broccoli.

—**BRENDA NOLEN** SIMPSONVILLE, SC

PREP: 20 MIN. • **COOK:** 4 HOURS
MAKES: 6 SERVINGS

- 6 **boneless skinless chicken breast halves (4 ounces each)**
- 1 **jar (24 ounces) garden-style spaghetti sauce**
- 1 **medium onion, sliced**
- ½ **each small green, sweet yellow and red peppers, julienned**
- ¼ **cup grated Parmesan cheese**
- 2 **garlic cloves, minced**
- 1 **teaspoon dried oregano**
- 1 **teaspoon dried basil**
- ½ **teaspoon salt**
- ¼ **teaspoon pepper**
- 4½ **cups uncooked spiral pasta Shaved Parmesan cheese, optional**

1. Place chicken in a 3-qt. slow cooker. In a large bowl, combine the spaghetti sauce, onion, peppers, cheese, garlic, oregano, basil, salt and pepper. Pour over the chicken. Cover and cook on low for 4-5 hours or until a thermometer reads 170°.
2. Cook the pasta according to package directions; drain. Serve with chicken and sauce. Top with shaved Parmesan cheese if desired.
PER SERVING *1 chicken breast half with ¾ cup pasta and ⅔ cup sauce (calculated without the Parmesan topping) equals 396 cal., 7 g fat (2 g sat. fat), 70 mg chol., 770 mg sodium, 50 g carb., 5 g fiber, 32 g pro.*

FREEZE IT

CHIPOTLE-MARMALADE CHICKEN

Big on flavor and simple to throw together, my chicken recipe is so appealing. The sweet-hot sauce gets its heat from chipotle pepper. I like to serve the chicken with a side of rice to use up every delectable drop of sauce.

—**CITTIE** TASTEOFHOME.COM

PREP: 15 MIN. • **COOK:** 4 HOURS
MAKES: 4 SERVINGS

- 4 **boneless skinless chicken breast halves (6 ounces each)**
- ¼ **teaspoon salt**
  Dash pepper
- ½ **cup chicken broth**
- ⅓ **cup orange marmalade**
- 1 **tablespoon canola oil**
- 1 **tablespoon balsamic vinegar**
- 1 **tablespoon minced chipotle pepper in adobo sauce**
- 1 **tablespoon honey**
- 1 **teaspoon chili powder**
- ¼ **teaspoon garlic powder**
- 4 **teaspoons cornstarch**
- 2 **tablespoons cold water**

1. Sprinkle chicken with salt and pepper. Transfer to a 3-qt. slow cooker. In a small bowl, combine the broth, marmalade, oil, vinegar, chipotle pepper, honey, chili powder and garlic powder; pour over the chicken. Cover and cook on low for 4-5 hours or until a thermometer reads 170°.

2. Remove chicken to a serving platter; keep warm. Place cooking juices in a small saucepan; bring to a boil. Combine cornstarch and water until smooth. Gradually stir into the pan. Bring to a boil; cook and stir for 2 minutes or until thickened. Serve with chicken.

FREEZE OPTION *Cool chicken mixture. Freeze in freezer containers. To use, partially thaw in refrigerator overnight. Heat through slowly in a covered skillet until a thermometer inserted in chicken reads 165°, stirring occasionally and adding a little broth or water if necessary.*
PER SERVING *1 chicken breast half with ⅓ cup sauce equals 315 cal., 8 g fat (1 g sat. fat), 95 mg chol., 400 mg sodium, 26 g carb., 1 g fiber, 35 g pro.* **Diabetic Exchanges:** *5 lean meat, 2 starch, ½ fat.*

INDONESIAN PEANUT CHICKEN

For this make-ahead recipe, I cut up fresh chicken, put it in a bag with the remaining slow cooker ingredients and freeze the bag. To cook, remove the bag a day ahead to thaw in the fridge, then pour all the contents into the slow cooker.

—**SARAH NEWMAN** MAHTOMEDI, MN

PREP: 15 MIN. • **COOK:** 4 HOURS
MAKES: 6 SERVINGS

- 1½ **pounds boneless skinless chicken breasts, cut into 1-inch cubes**
- ⅓ **cup chopped onion**
- ⅓ **cup water**
- ¼ **cup reduced-fat creamy peanut butter**
- 3 **tablespoons chili sauce**
- ¼ **teaspoon salt**
- ¼ **teaspoon cayenne pepper**
- ¼ **teaspoon pepper**
- 3 **cups hot cooked brown rice**
- 6 **tablespoons chopped salted peanuts**
- 6 **tablespoons chopped sweet red pepper**

1. Place chicken in a 4-qt. slow cooker. In a small bowl, combine the onion, water, peanut butter, chili sauce, salt, cayenne and pepper; pour over chicken. Cover and cook on low for 4-6 hours or until chicken is no longer pink.

2. Shred meat with two forks and return to slow cooker; heat through. Serve with rice and sprinkle with the peanuts and red pepper.
PER SERVING *½ cup chicken mixture with ½ cup rice equals 353 cal., 12 g fat (2 g sat. fat), 63 mg chol., 370 mg sodium, 31 g carb., 3 g fiber, 31 g pro.* **Diabetic Exchanges:** *3 lean meat, 2 starch, 2 fat.*

CHIPOTLE-MARMALADE CHICKEN

SOUTHERN BARBECUE SPAGHETTI SAUCE

SOUTHERN BARBECUE SPAGHETTI SAUCE

I revamped our favorite sloppy joe recipe into a thick spaghetti sauce that simmers in the slow cooker. The flavor is bold enough to interest adults, yet mild enough for the kids to enjoy.

—**RHONDA MELANSON** SARNIA, ON

PREP: 20 MIN. • **COOK:** 4 HOURS
MAKES: 12 SERVINGS

- 1 **pound lean ground turkey**
- 2 **medium onions, chopped**
- 1½ **cups sliced fresh mushrooms**
- 1 **medium green pepper, chopped**
- 2 **garlic cloves, minced**
- 1 **can (14½ ounces) diced tomatoes, undrained**
- 1 **can (12 ounces) tomato paste**
- 1 **can (8 ounces) tomato sauce**
- 1 **cup ketchup**
- ½ **cup beef broth**
- 2 **tablespoons Worcestershire sauce**
- 2 **tablespoons brown sugar**
- 1 **tablespoon ground cumin**
- 2 **teaspoons chili powder**
- 12 **cups hot cooked spaghetti**

1. In a large nonstick skillet, cook the turkey, onions, mushrooms and green pepper over medium heat until meat is no longer pink. Add garlic; cook 1 minute longer. Drain.
2. Transfer to a 3-qt. slow cooker. Stir in the tomatoes, tomato paste, tomato sauce, ketchup, beef broth, Worcestershire sauce, brown sugar, cumin and chili powder. Cover and cook on low for 4-5 hours or until vegetables are tender. Serve with spaghetti.

PER SERVING ⅔ cup sauce with 1 cup spaghetti equals 342 cal., 4 g fat (1 g sat. fat), 30 mg chol., 491 mg sodium, 60 g carb., 5 g fiber, 17 g pro.

SLOW-COOKED ITALIAN CHICKEN

With its seasoned tomato sauce, this enticing chicken entree is particularly good over pasta. My father especially loved this dish.

—**DEANNA D'AURIA** BANNING, CA

PREP: 20 MIN. • **COOK:** 4 HOURS
MAKES: 4 SERVINGS

- 4 **boneless skinless chicken breast halves (4 ounces each)**
- 1 **can (14½ ounces) reduced-sodium chicken broth**
- 1 **can (14½ ounces) stewed tomatoes, cut up**
- 1 **can (8 ounces) tomato sauce**
- 1 **medium green pepper, chopped**
- 1 **green onion, chopped**
- 1 **garlic clove, minced**
- 3 **teaspoons chili powder**
- 1 **teaspoon ground mustard**
- ½ **teaspoon pepper**
- ¼ **teaspoon garlic powder**
- ¼ **teaspoon onion powder**
- ⅓ **cup all-purpose flour**
- ½ **cup cold water**
  Hot cooked pasta

1. Place chicken in a 3-qt. slow cooker. In a bowl, combine the broth, tomatoes, tomato sauce, green pepper, onion, garlic and seasonings; pour over chicken. Cover and cook on low for 4-5 hours or until meat is tender. Remove the chicken and keep warm.

2. Pour cooking juices into a large saucepan; skim fat. Combine the flour and cold water until smooth; stir into juices. Bring to a boil; cook and stir for 2 minutes or until thickened. Serve with chicken and pasta.

PER SERVING *1 chicken breast half with ½ cup sauce (calculated without pasta) equals 231 cal., 3 g fat (1 g sat. fat), 63 mg chol., 818 mg sodium, 22 g carb., 3 g fiber, 28 g pro.* **Diabetic Exchanges:** *3 lean meat, 1 starch, 1 vegetable.*

SLOW-COOKED
ITALIAN CHICKEN

TENDER TURKEY BREAST WITH WHITE WINE GRAVY

I modified a well-loved dish for the slow cooker. The turkey comes out tender every time and is perfectly complemented by the white wine gravy. It's best to make with drinking wine, not cooking wine.

—TINA MACKISSOCK
MANCHESTER, NH

PREP: 20 MIN. • **COOK:** 6 HOURS
MAKES: 8 SERVINGS

- 1 cup white wine
- 1 medium apple, chopped
- ½ cup sliced fennel bulb
- ⅓ cup chopped celery
- ⅓ cup chopped carrot
- 3 garlic cloves, minced
- 1 teaspoon ground mustard
- 1 bay leaf
- ½ teaspoon dried rosemary, crushed
- ½ teaspoon dried thyme
- ½ teaspoon rubbed sage
- ¼ teaspoon pepper
- 1 package (3 pounds) frozen boneless turkey breast roast, thawed
- 2 tablespoons plus 1½ teaspoons cornstarch
- ½ cup half-and-half cream

1. In a 6-qt. slow cooker, combine wine, apple, fennel, celery, carrot, garlic, mustard and bay leaf. In a small bowl, combine the rosemary, thyme, sage and pepper; rub over turkey. Add turkey to slow cooker. Cover and cook on low for 6-8 hours or until meat is tender.

2. Remove the meat to a serving platter and keep warm. Strain the drippings into a measuring cup to measure 1 cup. Skim fat. In a small saucepan, combine cornstarch and cream; stir until smooth. Gradually add the drippings. Bring to a boil; cook and stir for 2 minutes or until thickened. Serve with turkey.

PER SERVING *5 ounces cooked turkey with 3 tablespoons gravy equals 238 cal., 3 g fat (1 g sat. fat), 113 mg chol., 102 mg sodium, 7 g carb., 1 g fiber, 43 g pro.* **Diabetic Exchanges:** *6 lean meat, ½ starch.*

SAUSAGE PASTA STEW

This delicious dish is packed with turkey sausage, beans and veggies. My family inhales it without even realizing it's healthy.

—SARA BOWEN UPLAND, CA

PREP: 20 MIN. • **COOK:** 7¼ HOURS
MAKES: 8 SERVINGS

- 1 pound turkey Italian sausage links, casings removed
- 4 cups water
- 1 jar (24 ounces) meatless spaghetti sauce
- 1 can (16 ounces) kidney beans, rinsed and drained
- 1 medium yellow summer squash, halved lengthwise and cut into 1-inch pieces
- 2 medium carrots, sliced
- 1 medium sweet red or green pepper, diced
- ⅓ cup chopped onion
- 1½ cups uncooked spiral pasta
- 1 cup frozen peas
- 1 teaspoon sugar
- ½ teaspoon salt
- ¼ teaspoon pepper

1. In a nonstick skillet, cook the sausage over medium heat until no longer pink; drain and place in a 5-qt. slow cooker. Stir in the water, spaghetti sauce, kidney beans, summer squash, carrots, red pepper and onion.

2. Cover; cook on low for 7-9 hours or until vegetables are tender.

3. Stir in the pasta, peas, sugar, salt and pepper. Cover and cook on high for 15-20 minutes or until the pasta is tender.

PER SERVING *1⅓ cups equals 276 cal., 6 g fat (2 g sat. fat), 30 mg chol., 1,111 mg sodium, 38 g carb., 6 g fiber, 18 g pro.*

TENDER TURKEY BREAST WITH WHITE WINE GRAVY

SAUSAGE
PASTA STEW

THAI CHICKEN
THIGHS

THAI CHICKEN THIGHS

Thanks to the slow cooker, a traditional Thai dish with peanut butter, jalapeno peppers and chili sauce becomes incredibly easy to make. If you want to crank up the heat, use more jalapeno.
—*TASTE OF HOME* TEST KITCHEN

PREP: 25 MIN. • **COOK:** 5 HOURS
MAKES: 8 SERVINGS

- 8 **bone-in chicken thighs (about 3 pounds), skin removed**
- ½ **cup salsa**
- ¼ **cup creamy peanut butter**
- 2 **tablespoons lemon juice**
- 2 **tablespoons reduced-sodium soy sauce**
- 1 **tablespoon chopped seeded jalapeno pepper**
- 2 **teaspoons Thai chili sauce**
- 1 **garlic clove, minced**
- 1 **teaspoon minced fresh gingerroot**
- 2 **green onions, sliced**
- 2 **tablespoons sesame seeds, toasted**
  Hot cooked basmati rice, optional

1. Place chicken in a 3-qt. slow cooker. In a small bowl, combine salsa, peanut butter, lemon juice, soy sauce, jalapeno, Thai chili sauce, garlic and ginger; pour over chicken.
2. Cover and cook on low 5-6 hours or until the chicken is tender. Sprinkle with green onions and sesame seeds. Serve with rice if desired.

NOTE *Wear disposable gloves when cutting hot peppers; the oils can burn skin. Avoid touching your face.*
PER SERVING *1 chicken thigh with ¼ cup sauce (calculated without rice) equals 261 cal., 15 g fat (4 g sat. fat), 87 mg chol., 350 mg sodium, 5 g carb., 1 g fiber, 27 g pro.* **Diabetic Exchanges:** *4 lean meat, 1 fat, ½ starch.*

(5)INGREDIENTS

CRANBERRY TURKEY BREAST WITH GRAVY

I'll often serve this for a holiday meal because it's so convenient and satisfying. You can use additional slow cookers to prepare side dishes such as homemade stuffing.

—**SHIRLEY WELCH** TULSA, OK

PREP: 15 MIN. • **COOK:** 5 HOURS
MAKES: 12 SERVINGS (3 CUPS GRAVY)

- **1 bone-in turkey breast (5 to 6 pounds)**
- **1 can (14 ounces) whole-berry cranberry sauce**
- **¼ cup orange juice**
- **1 envelope onion soup mix**
- **¼ teaspoon salt**
- **¼ teaspoon pepper**
- **3 to 4 teaspoons cornstarch**
- **1 tablespoon water**

1. Place turkey in a 5-qt. slow cooker. In a small bowl, combine the cranberry sauce, orange juice, onion soup mix, salt and pepper; pour over turkey. Cover and cook on low for 5-6 hours or until tender.

2. Remove turkey to a serving platter; keep warm. Skim the fat from cooking juices; transfer juices to a small saucepan. Bring to a boil. Combine cornstarch and water until smooth. Gradually stir into the pan. Bring to a boil; cook and stir for 2 minutes or until thickened. Serve with turkey.

PER SERVING *5 ounces cooked turkey with ¼ cup gravy equals 318 cal., 10 g fat (3 g sat. fat), 102 mg chol., 346 mg sodium, 15 g carb., 1 g fiber, 40 g pro.* **Diabetic Exchanges:** *5 lean meat, 1 starch.*

CRANBERRY TURKEY BREAST WITH GRAVY

**CHICKEN THIGHS WITH
GINGER-PEACH SAUCE**

CHICKEN THIGHS WITH GINGER-PEACH SAUCE

We often enjoy this chicken on Sundays. It's a cinch to prepare and requires very little cleanup.
—**LISA RENSHAW** KANSAS CITY, MO

PREP: 15 MIN. • **COOK:** 4 HOURS
MAKES: 10 SERVINGS

- 10 **boneless skinless chicken thighs (about 2½ pounds)**
- 1 **cup sliced peeled fresh or frozen peaches**
- 1 **cup golden raisins**
- 1 **cup peach preserves**
- ⅓ **cup chili sauce**
- 2 **tablespoons minced crystallized ginger**
- 1 **tablespoon reduced-sodium soy sauce**
- 1 **tablespoon minced garlic**
  Hot cooked rice, optional

1. Place chicken in a 4-qt. slow cooker coated with cooking spray. Top with peaches and raisins. In a small bowl, combine the preserves, chili sauce, ginger, soy sauce and garlic. Spoon over top.
2. Cover and cook on low for 4-5 hours or until the chicken is tender. Serve with rice if desired.
PER SERVING *1 serving (calculated without rice) equals 314 cal., 8 g fat (2 g sat. fat), 76 mg chol., 250 mg sodium, 39 g carb., 1 g fiber, 22 g pro.*

TOP TIP

PEACH SEASON

The peak season for fresh peaches is June through September. However, you can always substitute frozen peaches (thawed and drained) or well-drained canned peaches in equal amounts.

TURKEY IN CREAM SAUCE

I've relied on this recipe for tender turkey since I first moved out on my own. I serve it whenever I invite new guests to the house, and I'm always asked to share the recipe.
—**KATHY-JO WINTERBOTTOM** POTTSTOWN, PA

PREP: 20 MIN. • **COOK:** 7 HOURS
MAKES: 8 SERVINGS

- 1¼ **cups white wine or chicken broth**
- 1 **medium onion, chopped**
- 2 **garlic cloves, minced**
- 2 **bay leaves**
- 2 **teaspoons dried rosemary, crushed**
- ½ **teaspoon pepper**
- 3 **turkey breast tenderloins (¾ pound each)**
- 3 **tablespoons cornstarch**
- ½ **cup half-and-half cream or whole milk**
- ½ **teaspoon salt**

1. In a 3-qt. slow cooker, combine wine, onion, garlic and bay leaves. Combine rosemary and pepper; rub over turkey. Place in slow cooker. Cover and cook on low for 7-9 hours or until turkey is tender.
2. Remove the turkey to a serving platter; keep warm. Strain and skim fat from cooking juices; transfer juices to a small saucepan. Bring to a boil. Combine cornstarch, cream and salt until smooth. Gradually stir into the pan. Bring to a boil; cook and stir for 2 minutes or until thickened. Serve with turkey.
PER SERVING *1 serving equals 205 cal., 3 g fat (1 g sat. fat), 58 mg chol., 231 mg sodium, 6 g carb., trace fiber, 32 g pro.* **Diabetic Exchanges:** *4 lean meat, ½ starch, ½ fat.*

SPICY CHICKEN AND RICE

As a working mom with two kids, I have little time to prepare dinner during the week. This recipe is quick to toss together and fabulous to eat later. Both of my picky eaters love it!
—**JESSICA COSTELLO** FITCHBURG, MA

PREP: 20 MIN. • **COOK:** 5½ HOURS
MAKES: 8 SERVINGS

- 1½ **pounds boneless skinless chicken breast halves**
- 2 **cans (14½ ounces each) diced tomatoes with mild green chilies, undrained**
- 2 **medium green peppers, chopped**
- 1 **medium onion, chopped**
- 1 **garlic clove, minced**
- 1 **teaspoon smoked paprika**
- ¾ **teaspoon salt**
- ½ **teaspoon ground cumin**
- ½ **teaspoon ground chipotle pepper**
- 6 **cups cooked brown rice**
- 1 **can (15 ounces) black beans, rinsed and drained**
- ½ **cup shredded cheddar cheese**
- ½ **cup reduced-fat sour cream**

1. Place chicken in a 4- or 5-qt. slow cooker. In a bowl, combine tomatoes, green peppers, onion, garlic, paprika, salt, cumin and chipotle pepper; pour over chicken. Cover and cook on low for 5-6 hours or until chicken is tender.
2. Remove chicken; cool slightly. Shred with two forks and return to the slow cooker. Stir in rice and beans; heat through. Garnish with cheese and sour cream.
PER SERVING *1⅓ cups chicken mixture with 1 tablespoon cheese and 1 tablespoon sour cream equals 389 cal., 7 g fat (3 g sat. fat), 59 mg chol., 817 mg sodium, 53 g carb., 7 g fiber, 27 g pro.*

TURKEY THIGH SUPPER

This family-pleasing meal has it all—tender turkey thighs, tasty vegetables and a scrumptious sauce. You can substitute chicken breasts for the turkey or honey barbecue sauce for the soup mix.

—**BETTY GINGRICH** OXFORD, AR

PREP: 10 MIN. • **COOK:** 6 HOURS
MAKES: 4 SERVINGS

- 3 **medium red potatoes, cut into chunks**
- ½ **pound fresh baby carrots**
- 2 **medium onions, cut into chunks**
- 4 **turkey thighs, skin removed**
- 1 **can (10¾ ounces) condensed tomato soup, undiluted**
- ⅓ **cup water**
- 1 **teaspoon minced garlic**
- 1 **teaspoon Italian seasoning**
- ½ **to 1 teaspoon salt**

In a 5-qt. slow cooker, layer the potatoes, carrots and onions. Top with turkey. Combine the soup, water, garlic, Italian seasoning and salt; pour over turkey. Cover and cook on low for 6-8 hours or until a thermometer reads 170°-175° and vegetables are tender.
PER SERVING *1 serving equals 173 cal., 2 g fat (trace sat. fat), 6 mg chol., 773 mg sodium, 36 g carb., 4 g fiber, 6 g pro.*

TOP TIP

MIX IT UP

If you don't have Italian seasoning, you can mix up your own with equal amounts of basil, thyme, rosemary and oregano. You can also add parsley flakes, marjoram, sage, savory or garlic powder.

FREEZE IT
MUSHROOM MEAT LOAF

I'm a beginner cook, but this recipe is one I'm really proud of. The mushrooms and ground turkey are a nice combination, and it's a cool twist on regular meat loaf.

—**TYLER SHERMAN** WILLIAMSBURG, VA

PREP: 30 MIN. • **COOK:** 3¼ HOURS
MAKES: 6 SERVINGS

- 2 **large eggs, lightly beaten**
- 1⅓ **cups soft bread crumbs**
- ½ **pound large portobello mushrooms, stems removed, finely chopped**
- 1 **small onion, finely chopped**
- 2 **garlic cloves, minced**
- ¾ **teaspoon salt**
- ½ **teaspoon dried thyme**
- ¼ **teaspoon pepper**
- 1 **pound lean ground turkey**
- ¼ **cup chili sauce**
- 2 **teaspoons stone-ground mustard**
- ⅛ **teaspoon cayenne pepper**

1. Cut three 20x3-in. strips of heavy-duty foil; crisscross them so they resemble spokes of a wheel. Place strips on the bottom and up the sides of a 3-qt. slow cooker. Coat strips with cooking spray.
2. In a large bowl, combine eggs, bread crumbs, mushrooms, onion, garlic, salt, thyme and pepper. Crumble the ground turkey over this mixture and mix well. Shape into a 7½x4-in. loaf. Cook loaf immediately or wrap and freeze for up to 3 months.
3. Place meat loaf in the center of the strips. Cover and cook on low for 3-4 hours or until no pink remains and a thermometer reads 160°. Combine the chili sauce, mustard and cayenne; pour over meat. Cover and cook 15 minutes longer or until heated through. Using foil strips as handles, remove the meat loaf to a platter.

TO USE FROZEN MEAT LOAF
Thaw in the refrigerator overnight. Unwrap and cook as directed.
PER SERVING *1 slice equals 194 cal., 8 g fat (2 g sat. fat), 130 mg chol., 648 mg sodium, 12 g carb., 1 g fiber, 17 g pro.* **Diabetic Exchanges:** *2 lean meat, 1 starch, 1 vegetable.*

FREEZE IT **⑤ INGREDIENTS**
MAPLE MUSTARD CHICKEN

My husband loves this chicken dish. It calls for only five ingredients, and we try to have them all on hand for a delicious and cozy dinner anytime!

—**JENNIFER SEIDEL** MIDLAND, MI

PREP: 5 MIN. • **COOK:** 3 HOURS
MAKES: 6 SERVINGS

- 6 **boneless skinless chicken breast halves (6 ounces each)**
- ½ **cup maple syrup**
- ⅓ **cup stone-ground mustard**
- 2 **tablespoons quick-cooking tapioca**
   Hot cooked brown rice

Place chicken in a 3-qt. slow cooker. In a small bowl, combine the syrup, mustard and tapioca; pour over chicken. Cover and cook on low for 3-4 hours or until tender. Serve with rice.
FREEZE OPTION *Cool chicken in sauce. Freeze in freezer containers. To use, partially thaw in the refrigerator overnight. Heat through slowly in a covered skillet until a thermometer inserted in chicken reads 165°, stirring occasionally and adding a little broth or water if necessary.*
PER SERVING *1 chicken breast half with 3 tablespoons sauce (calculated without rice) equals 289 cal., 4 g fat (1 g sat. fat), 94 mg chol., 296 mg sodium, 24 g carb., 2 g fiber, 35 g pro.* **Diabetic Exchanges:** *5 lean meat, 1½ starch.*

TURKEY THIGH
SUPPER

MUSHROOM
MEAT LOAF

MAPLE MUSTARD
CHICKEN

SAGE TURKEY
THIGHS

SAGE TURKEY THIGHS

I created this for my boys, who love dark meat. It reminds me of our traditional Thanksgiving turkey, but it's more convenient than cooking a whole bird.

—**NATALIE SWANSON** BALTIMORE, MD

PREP: 15 MIN. • **COOK:** 6 HOURS
MAKES: 4 SERVINGS

- 4 medium carrots, halved
- 1 medium onion, chopped
- ½ cup water
- 2 garlic cloves, minced
- 1½ teaspoons rubbed sage, divided
- 2 turkey thighs or turkey drumsticks (2 pounds total), skin removed
- 1 tablespoon cornstarch
- ¼ cup cold water
- ¼ teaspoon salt
- ⅛ teaspoon pepper
- 1 teaspoon browning sauce, optional

1. In a 3-qt. slow cooker, combine the carrots, onion, water, garlic and 1 teaspoon sage. Top with turkey. Sprinkle with the remaining sage. Cover and cook on low for 6-8 hours or until a thermometer reads 170°-175°.
2. Remove turkey to a serving platter; keep warm. Strain broth, reserving vegetables. Skim fat from cooking juices; transfer juices to a small saucepan.
3. Place the vegetables in a food processor; cover and process until smooth. Add to the cooking juices. Bring to a boil. Combine cornstarch and water until smooth. Gradually stir into the pan. Add salt, pepper and, if desired, browning sauce. Bring to a boil; cook and stir for 2 minutes or until thickened. Serve with turkey.
PER SERVING *4 ounces cooked turkey with ¼ cup gravy equals 277 cal., 8 g fat (3 g sat. fat), 96 mg chol., 280 mg sodium, 15 g carb., 3 g fiber, 34 g pro.* **Diabetic Exchanges:** *4 lean meat, 3 vegetable.*

TURKEY MEATBALLS AND SAUCE

In an effort to eat healthier, I came up with a lighter take on meatballs. They're easy!

—**JANE WHITTAKER** PENSACOLA, FL

PREP: 40 MIN. • **COOK:** 6 HOURS
MAKES: 8 SERVINGS

- ¼ cup egg substitute
- ½ cup seasoned bread crumbs
- ⅓ cup chopped onion
- ½ teaspoon pepper
- ¼ teaspoon salt-free seasoning blend
- 1½ pounds lean ground turkey

SAUCE
- 1 can (15 ounces) tomato sauce
- 1 can (14½ ounces) diced tomatoes, undrained
- 1 small zucchini, chopped
- 1 medium green pepper, chopped
- 1 medium onion, chopped
- 1 can (6 ounces) tomato paste
- 2 bay leaves
- 2 garlic cloves, minced
- 1 teaspoon dried oregano
- 1 teaspoon dried basil
- 1 teaspoon dried parsley flakes
- ¼ teaspoon crushed red pepper flakes
- ¼ teaspoon pepper
- 1 package (16 ounces) whole wheat spaghetti

1. In a large bowl, combine the egg substitute, bread crumbs, onion, pepper and seasoning blend. Crumble turkey over mixture and mix well. Shape into 1-in. balls; place on a rack coated with cooking spray in a shallow baking pan. Bake at 400° for 15 minutes or until no longer pink.
2. Meanwhile, in a 4- or 5-qt. slow cooker, combine the tomato sauce, tomatoes, zucchini, green pepper, onion, tomato paste, bay leaves, garlic and seasonings. Stir in the meatballs. Cover and cook on low for 6 hours. Cook the spaghetti according to package directions; serve with meatballs and sauce.

PER SERVING *4 meatballs with ¾ cup sauce and 1 cup spaghetti equals 416 cal., 8 g fat (2 g sat. fat), 67 mg chol., 533 mg sodium, 61 g carb., 10 g fiber, 28 g pro.*

CHICKEN MUSHROOM STEW

The flavors blend beautifully in this pot of chicken, vegetables and herbs. It's perfect for busy days when you still want to enjoy a comforting meal.

—**KIM VAN RHEENEN** MENDOTA, IL

PREP: 20 MIN. • **COOK:** 4 HOURS
MAKES: 6 SERVINGS

- 6 boneless skinless chicken breast halves (4 ounces each)
- 2 tablespoons canola oil, divided
- 8 ounces fresh mushrooms, sliced
- 1 medium onion, diced
- 3 cups diced zucchini
- 1 cup chopped green pepper
- 4 garlic cloves, minced
- 3 medium tomatoes, chopped
- 1 can (6 ounces) tomato paste
- ¾ cup water
- 2 teaspoons each dried thyme, oregano, marjoram, and basil

1. Cut chicken into 1-in. cubes; brown in 1 tablespoon oil in a large skillet. Transfer to a 3-qt. slow cooker. In the same skillet, saute the mushrooms, onion, zucchini and green pepper in the remaining oil until crisp-tender; add garlic; cook 1 minute longer.
2. Place in slow cooker. Add the tomatoes, tomato paste, water and seasonings. Cover and cook on low for 4-5 hours or until the meat is no longer pink and the vegetables are tender.
PER SERVING *1⅓ cups equals 237 cal., 8 g fat (1 g sat. fat), 63 mg chol., 82 mg sodium, 15 g carb., 3 g fiber, 27 g pro.* **Diabetic Exchanges:** *3 lean meat, 1 starch, 1 fat.*

SESAME PULLED PORK
SANDWICHES, PAGE 145

PORK

147

168

154

CRANBERRY PORK TENDERLOIN

Canned cranberry sauce creates a sweet accompaniment for tender pork. I dress up the cranberries with orange juice, mustard, brown sugar and cloves.

—BETTY HELTON MELBOURNE, FL

PREP: 10 MIN. • **COOK:** 5¼ HOURS
MAKES: 4 SERVINGS

- 1 **pork tenderloin (1 pound)**
- 1 **can (14 ounces) whole-berry cranberry sauce**
- ½ **cup orange juice**
- ¼ **cup sugar**
- 1 **tablespoon brown sugar**
- 1 **teaspoon ground mustard**
- ¼ **to ½ teaspoon ground cloves**
- 2 **tablespoons cornstarch**
- 3 **tablespoons cold water**

1. Place pork in a 3-qt. slow cooker. In a small bowl, combine cranberry sauce, orange juice, sugars, mustard and cloves; pour over pork. Cover and cook on low for 5-6 hours or until meat is tender.
2. Remove pork and keep warm. Combine cornstarch and cold water until smooth; gradually stir into the cranberry mixture. Cover and cook on high for 15 minutes or until thickened. Serve with pork.
PER SERVING *3 ounces cooked pork equals 388 cal., 4 g fat (1 g sat. fat), 63 mg chol., 71 mg sodium, 65 g carb., 2 g fiber, 23 g pro.*

TOP TIP

MAKE IT SAUCY

Cornstarch needs just a few minutes of boiling or stirring to thicken a sauce or gravy. If it cooks too long, the cornstarch begins to lose its thickening power. Carefully follow the recipe for the best results.

---

⑤ INGREDIENTS

CIDER PORK ROAST

Apple cider, dried cherries and fresh rosemary put the pizzazz in this pleasing pork roast. It's even more flavorful when drizzled with the sweet pan juices.

—TERRY DANNER ROCHELLE, IL

PREP: 20 MIN. • **COOK:** 5 HOURS 10 MIN.
MAKES: 6 SERVINGS

- 1 **boneless pork loin roast (2 pounds)**
- ¾ **teaspoon salt**
- ¼ **teaspoon pepper**
- 2 **cups apple cider or unsweetened apple juice, divided**
- 3 **sprigs fresh rosemary**
- ½ **cup dried cherries**
- 5 **teaspoons cornstarch**

1. Sprinkle the pork with salt and pepper. In a nonstick skillet coated with cooking spray, brown pork for about 4 minutes on each side. Pour 1 cup apple cider in a 3-qt. slow cooker. Place two sprigs rosemary in slow cooker; top with meat and remaining rosemary. Place cherries around roast. Cover and cook on low for 5-6 hours or until meat is tender. Remove meat; keep warm.
2. Strain cooking liquid; reserve the liquid and transfer to a small saucepan. Stir in ¾ cup cider; bring to a boil. Combine the cornstarch and remaining cider until smooth. Gradually whisk into cider mixture. Bring to a boil; cook and stir for 1-2 minutes or until thickened. Serve with meat.
PER SERVING *1 serving (4 ounces cooked pork with ¼ cup gravy) equals 298 cal., 9 g fat (3 g sat. fat), 89 mg chol., 368 mg sodium, 20 g carb., 1 g fiber, 32 g pro.* **Diabetic Exchanges:** *4 lean meat, 1½ fruit.*

GRANDMA EDNA'S CAJUN PORK

My grandma used to make this every year as part of our Christmas dinner. These days I make it for my family at the holidays. We love to carry on the delicious tradition of Grandma's Cajun pork.

—TONYA CLINE GREENVILLE, OH

PREP: 35 MIN. • **COOK:** 6 HOURS
MAKES: 12 SERVINGS (2¼ CUPS SAUCE)

- 1 **small onion**
- 1 **celery rib**
- 1 **small green pepper**
- 3 **tablespoons butter**
- 3 **garlic cloves, minced**
- 2 **teaspoons dried thyme**
- 1 **teaspoon paprika**
- ½ **teaspoon each salt, white pepper and pepper**
- ½ **teaspoon ground mustard**
- ½ **teaspoon hot pepper sauce**
- 1 **boneless pork loin roast (4 pounds)**
- 2 **tablespoons cornstarch**
- 2 **tablespoons cold water**

1. Finely chop vegetables. In a large skillet, saute the vegetables in butter until tender. Add garlic; cook 1 minute longer. Stir in seasonings and pepper sauce.
2. Cut several slits in the roast to within ½ in. of bottom. Place in a 5-qt. slow cooker. Spoon the onion mixture between slits and over the top of meat. Cover and cook on low for 6-8 hours or until pork is tender.
3. Transfer the roast to a serving platter; keep warm. Pour cooking juices into a saucepan. Combine cornstarch and water until smooth; stir into the pan. Bring to a boil; cook and stir for 2 minutes or until thickened. Serve with roast.
PER SERVING *4 ounces cooked pork with 3 tablespoons gravy equals 225 cal., 10 g fat (4 g sat. fat), 83 mg chol., 167 mg sodium, 3 g carb., 1 g fiber, 29 g pro.* **Diabetic Exchanges:** *4 lean meat, ½ fat.*

GRANDMA EDNA'S
CAJUN PORK

SESAME PULLED
PORK SANDWICHES

SESAME PULLED PORK SANDWICHES

I wanted to build a better pork sandwich, and this Asian-style filling was a huge hit with my husband and co-workers. Top with wasabi mayo if you'd like an extra kick.

—**JENNIFER BERRY** LEXINGTON, OH

PREP: 15 MIN. • **COOK:** 4½ HOURS
MAKES: 12 SERVINGS

- 3 **pork tenderloins (1 pound each)**
- 1¾ **cups reduced-fat sesame ginger salad dressing, divided**
- ¼ **cup packed brown sugar**

SLAW
- 1 **package (14 ounces) coleslaw mix**
- 4 **green onions, chopped**
- ¼ **cup minced fresh cilantro**
- 2 **tablespoons reduced-fat sesame ginger salad dressing**
- 2 **teaspoons sesame oil**
- 1 **teaspoon sugar**
- 1 **teaspoon reduced-sodium soy sauce**

TO SERVE
- 12 **multigrain hamburger buns, split**
  Wasabi mayonnaise, optional

1. Place the tenderloins in a 5-qt. slow cooker coated with cooking spray; pour ¾ cup salad dressing over pork, turning to coat. Cook, covered, on low 4-5 hours or until meat is tender.

2. Remove pork; cool slightly. Shred meat into bite-size pieces; return to slow cooker. Stir in brown sugar and remaining salad dressing. Cook, covered, for 30-45 minutes longer or until heated through.

3. Combine slaw ingredients. Serve pork on buns with slaw and, if desired, mayonnaise.

NOTE *This recipe was tested with Newman's Own Sesame Ginger Dressing.*

PER SERVING *1 sandwich (calculated without mayonnaise) equals 324 cal., 9 g fat (2 g sat. fat), 64 mg chol., 756 mg sodium, 33 g carb., 3 g fiber, 27 g pro.* **Diabetic Exchanges:** *3 lean meat, 2 starch.*

⑤INGREDIENTS
BBQ PORK & PEPPERS

My husband taught me how to make this dish. It was the first time I ever prepared something in a slow cooker, but now I turn to it often. I'll usually pair this entree with white rice or a salad.

—**RACHAEL HUGHES**
SOUTHAMPTON, PA

PREP: 10 MIN. • **COOK:** 8 HOURS
MAKES: 4 SERVINGS

- 4 **bone-in pork loin chops (7 ounces each)**
- 1 **large onion, chopped**
- 1 **large sweet red pepper, chopped**
- 1 **large green pepper, chopped**
- 1 **cup barbecue sauce**

Place chops in a 4-qt. slow cooker coated with cooking spray. Top with onion, peppers and barbecue sauce. Cover and cook on low 8-10 hours or until pork is tender.

PER SERVING *1 chop with ¾ cup sauce equals 291 cal., 10 g fat (3 g sat. fat), 86 mg chol., 638 mg sodium, 17 g carb., 3 g fiber, 33 g pro.* **Diabetic Exchanges:** *4 lean meat, 1 vegetable, ½ starch.*

PORK

SLOW-COOKED
PORK BURRITOS

SLOW-COOKED PORK BURRITOS

I've been making this recipe for 20 years, changing it here and there until this delectable version came together one day.

—**SHARON BELMONT** LINCOLN, NE

PREP: 20 MIN. • **COOK:** 8 HOURS
MAKES: 14 SERVINGS

- 1 boneless pork sirloin roast (3 pounds)
- ¼ cup reduced-sodium chicken broth
- 1 envelope reduced-sodium taco seasoning
- 1 tablespoon dried parsley flakes
- 2 garlic cloves, minced
- ½ teaspoon pepper
- ¼ teaspoon salt
- 1 can (16 ounces) refried beans
- 1 can (4 ounces) chopped green chilies
- 14 flour tortillas (8 inches), warmed
  Optional toppings: shredded lettuce, chopped tomatoes, chopped green pepper, guacamole, reduced-fat sour cream and shredded reduced-fat cheddar cheese

1. Cut roast in half; place in a 4- or 5-qt. slow cooker. In a small bowl, mix broth, taco seasoning, parsley, garlic, pepper and salt; pour over roast. Cover and cook on low 8-10 hours or until meat is very tender.
2. Remove pork from slow cooker; cool slightly. Shred meat with two forks. Skim fat from cooking juices. Return cooking juices and pork to slow cooker. Stir in the beans and chilies; heat through.
3. Spoon ½ cup pork mixture across center of each tortilla; add toppings as desired. Fold bottom and sides of tortilla over filling and roll up.

TO FREEZE BURRITOS *Roll up burritos without toppings. Wrap individually in paper towels, and then foil. Transfer to a resealable plastic bag. May be frozen for up to 2 months. To use frozen burritos, remove foil. Place paper towel-wrapped burritos on a microwave-safe plate. Microwave on high for 3-4 minutes or until heated through. Serve with toppings as desired.*

PER SERVING *1 burrito (calculated without optional toppings) equals 320 cal., 9 g fat (3 g sat. fat), 61 mg chol., 606 mg sodium, 33 g carb., 2 g fiber, 26 g pro.* **Diabetic Exchanges: 2 starch, 2 lean meat, 1 fat.**

FRUITY PORK ROAST

I like using the slow cooker because it frees up the oven for other dishes. This pork roast, which I created by adapting other recipes, shines with the fruit.

—**MARY JEPPESEN-DAVIS** ST. CLOUD, MN

PREP: 25 MIN.
COOK: 8 HOURS + STANDING
MAKES: 8 SERVINGS

- ½ medium lemon, sliced
- ½ cup dried cranberries
- ⅓ cup golden raisins
- ⅓ cup unsweetened apple juice
- 3 tablespoons sherry or additional unsweetened apple juice
- 1 teaspoon minced garlic
- ½ teaspoon ground mustard
- 1 boneless pork loin roast (3 pounds)
- ½ teaspoon salt
- ¼ teaspoon pepper
- ⅛ to ¼ teaspoon ground ginger
- 1 medium apple, peeled and sliced
- ½ cup packed fresh parsley sprigs

1. In a small bowl, combine the first seven ingredients; set aside. Cut roast in half; sprinkle with salt, pepper and ginger.
2. Transfer to a 3-qt. slow cooker. Pour the fruit mixture over roast. Place apple and parsley around roast. Cover and cook on low for 8-10 hours or until meat is tender.
3. Transfer meat to a serving platter. Let stand for 10-15 minutes before slicing.

PER SERVING *5 ounces cooked pork with ¼ cup fruit mixture equals 272 cal., 8 g fat (3 g sat. fat), 85 mg chol., 200 mg sodium, 15 g carb., 1 g fiber, 33 g pro.* **Diabetic Exchanges: 5 lean meat, 1 fruit.**

HAM TETRAZZINI

I modified a recipe that came with my slow cooker to reduce the fat without sacrificing the familiar taste. Family and friends are pleasantly surprised when they find out they're eating healthy.

—**SUSAN BLAIR** STERLING, MI

PREP: 15 MIN. • **COOK:** 4 HOURS
MAKES: 5 SERVINGS

- 1 can (10¾ ounces) reduced-fat reduced-sodium condensed cream of mushroom soup, undiluted
- 1 cup sliced fresh mushrooms
- 1 cup cubed fully cooked ham
- ½ cup fat-free evaporated milk
- 2 tablespoons white wine or water
- 1 teaspoon prepared horseradish
- 1 package (7 ounces) spaghetti
- ½ cup shredded Parmesan cheese

1. In a 3-qt. slow cooker, combine the soup, mushrooms, ham, milk, wine and horseradish. Cover and cook on low for 4 hours.
2. Cook spaghetti according to package directions; drain. Add the spaghetti and cheese to slow cooker; toss to coat.

PER SERVING *1 cup equals 290 cal., 6 g fat (3 g sat. fat), 24 mg chol., 759 mg sodium, 39 g carb., 2 g fiber, 16 g pro.* **Diabetic Exchanges: 2½ starch, 1 lean meat, ½ fat.**

HONEY-GLAZED HAM

The simple ham is perfect for family dinners where time in the kitchen is as valuable as space in the oven.
—**JACQUIE STOLZ** LITTLE SIOUX, IA

PREP: 10 MIN. • **COOK:** 4½ HOURS
MAKES: 14 SERVINGS

- 1 **boneless fully cooked ham (4 pounds)**
- 1½ **cups ginger ale**
- ¼ **cup honey**
- ½ **teaspoon ground mustard**
- ½ **teaspoon ground cloves**
- ¼ **teaspoon ground cinnamon**

1. Cut ham in half; place in a 5-qt. slow cooker. Pour ginger ale over ham. Cover and cook on low for 4-5 hours or until heated through.
2. Combine the honey, mustard, cloves and cinnamon; stir until smooth. Spread over ham; cook 30 minutes longer.

PER SERVING *4 ounces cooked ham equals 166 cal., 5 g fat (2 g sat. fat), 66 mg chol., 1,347 mg sodium, 8 g carb., trace fiber, 24 g pro.*

CITRUS-HERB PORK ROAST

The genius combo of seasonings and citrus in this tender roast is exactly what you're looking for.
—**LAURA BRODINE**
COLORADO SPRINGS, CO

PREP: 25 MIN. • **COOK:** 8 HOURS
MAKES: 8 SERVINGS

- 1 **boneless pork sirloin roast (3 to 4 pounds)**
- 1 **teaspoon dried oregano**
- ½ **teaspoon ground ginger**
- ½ **teaspoon pepper**
- 2 **medium onions, cut into thin wedges**
- 1 **cup plus 3 tablespoons orange juice, divided**
- 1 **tablespoon sugar**
- 1 **tablespoon white grapefruit juice**
- 1 **tablespoon steak sauce**
- 1 **tablespoon reduced-sodium soy sauce**
- 1 **teaspoon grated orange peel**
- ½ **teaspoon salt**
- 3 **tablespoons cornstarch**
  Hot cooked egg noodles

1. Cut the roast in half. In a small bowl, combine the oregano, ginger and pepper; rub over pork. In a large nonstick skillet coated with cooking spray, brown the roast on all sides. Transfer to a 4-qt. slow cooker and add the onions.
2. In a small bowl, combine 1 cup orange juice, sugar, grapefruit juice, steak sauce and soy sauce; pour over roast. Cover and cook on low for 8-10 hours or until meat is tender. Remove the meat and onions to a serving platter; keep warm.
3. Skim fat from cooking juices; transfer to a small saucepan. Add the orange peel and salt. Bring to a boil. Combine the cornstarch and remaining orange juice until smooth. Gradually stir into the pan. Bring to a boil; cook and stir for 2 minutes or until thickened. Serve with pork and noodles.

PER SERVING *5 ounces cooked pork with 2 tablespoons gravy (calculated without egg noodles) equals 289 cal., 10 g fat (4 g sat. fat), 102 mg chol., 326 mg sodium, 13 g carb., 1 g fiber, 35 g pro.* **Diabetic Exchanges:** *5 lean meat, 1 starch.*

HONEY-GLAZED HAM

CITRUS-HERB
PORK ROAST

GLAZED ROSEMARY PORK ROAST

For a change of pace, I'll serve this pork roast at holiday gatherings. It's a welcome break from traditional turkey or ham, and when dressed with an herb-infused glaze featuring rosemary, thyme and sage, the flavor is unbeatable.

—**JOYCE MANIER** BEECH GROVE, IN

PREP: 20 MIN. • **COOK:** 4 HOURS
MAKES: 8 SERVINGS

- 1 **boneless pork loin roast (3 pounds)**
- 1 **tablespoon butter**
- 1 **teaspoon olive oil**
- 1 **large onion, sliced**
- 1 **tablespoon brown sugar**
- 1 **tablespoon minced fresh rosemary**
- 1 **teaspoon dried thyme**
- 1 **teaspoon rubbed sage**
- 1 **teaspoon grated orange peel**
- ½ **teaspoon pepper**
- ¼ **teaspoon salt**
- ⅔ **cup apricot jam**
- ½ **cup orange juice**
- 1 **bay leaf**

1. Cut the roast in half. In a large skillet, brown the roast in butter and oil on all sides. Transfer to a 4- or 5-qt. slow cooker.

2. Add onion to the same skillet; cook and stir until tender. Stir in the brown sugar, herbs, orange peel, pepper and salt. Spread over pork. Combine the jam and orange juice; pour over top. Add bay leaf.

3. Cover and cook on low for 4 hours or until a thermometer reads 160°. Discard bay leaf.

PER SERVING *5 ounces cooked pork equals 314 cal., 10 g fat (4 g sat. fat), 88 mg chol., 145 mg sodium, 22 g carb., 1 g fiber, 33 g pro.*

GLAZED ROSEMARY PORK ROAST

SLOW-COOKED SWEET 'N' SOUR PORK

A co-worker gave me this recipe more than 20 years ago, and my family still enjoys it today. No need to order takeout tonight when you can come home to this meal.

—MARTHA NICKERSON
HANCOCK, ME

PREP: 20 MIN. • **COOK:** 6½ HOURS
MAKES: 6 SERVINGS

- 2 **tablespoons plus 1½ teaspoons paprika**
- 1½ **pounds boneless pork loin roast, cut into 1-inch strips**
- 1 **tablespoon canola oil**
- 1 **can (20 ounces) unsweetened pineapple chunks**
- 1 **medium onion, chopped**
- 1 **medium green pepper, chopped**
- ¼ **cup cider vinegar**
- 3 **tablespoons brown sugar**
- 3 **tablespoons reduced-sodium soy sauce**
- 1 **tablespoon Worcestershire sauce**
- ½ **teaspoon salt**
- 2 **tablespoons cornstarch**
- ¼ **cup cold water**
  Hot cooked rice, optional

1. Place paprika in a large resealable plastic bag. Add pork, a few pieces at a time, and shake to coat. In a nonstick skillet, brown pork in oil in batches over medium-high heat. Transfer to a 3-qt. slow cooker.

2. Drain pineapple, reserving juice; refrigerate the pineapple. Add the pineapple juice, onion, green pepper, vinegar, brown sugar, soy sauce, Worcestershire sauce and salt to slow cooker. Cover and cook on low for 6-8 hours or until meat is tender.

3. Combine cornstarch and water until smooth; stir into pork mixture. Add pineapple. Cover and cook 30 minutes longer or until sauce is thickened. Serve over rice if desired.
PER SERVING *1 cup pork mixture (calculated without rice) equals 312 cal., 10 g fat (3 g sat. fat), 73 mg chol., 592 mg sodium, 28 g carb., 2 g fiber, 27 g pro.* **Diabetic Exchanges:** *3 lean meat, 1 fruit, ½ starch, ½ fat.*

(5)INGREDIENTS
LEMON PORK CHOPS

These pork chops can simmer all day on low and be ready to serve by dinnertime. I serve them with a crisp salad or mac and cheese on the side.

—BARBARA DE FRANG HAZEN, ND

PREP: 5 MIN. • **COOK:** 6 HOURS
MAKES: 4 SERVINGS

- 4 **bone-in pork chops (7 ounces each)**
- ½ **teaspoon salt**
- ¼ **teaspoon pepper**
- 1 **medium onion, thinly sliced**
- 1 **medium lemon, thinly sliced**
- ¼ **cup packed brown sugar**
- ¼ **cup ketchup**

1. Place the pork chops in a 3-qt. slow cooker. Sprinkle with salt and pepper. Top with onion and lemon. Sprinkle with brown sugar; drizzle with ketchup.

2. Cover and cook on low for 6-8 hours or until meat is tender.
PER SERVING *1 serving equals 290 cal., 8 g fat (3 g sat. fat), 86 mg chol., 543 mg sodium, 22 g carb., 1 g fiber, 31 g pro.*

SLOW-COOKED
SWEET 'N' SOUR PORK

CANADIAN PORK
ROAST WITH GRAVY

ASIAN PORK
ROAST

SLOW-COOKED
PORK AND BEANS

CANADIAN PORK ROAST WITH GRAVY

My son asked if I had a slow cooker meal he could make to impress his girlfriend. They loved this!

—**MARILYN MCCRORY** CRESTON, BC

PREP: 20 MIN. • **COOK:** 5 HOURS
MAKES: 10 SERVINGS

- 1 **boneless pork loin roast (3 pounds)**
- ⅓ **cup maple syrup**
- 1 **tablespoon lemon juice**
- 1 **tablespoon Dijon mustard**
- 1 **garlic clove, minced**
- 2 **tablespoons cornstarch**
- ¼ **cup cold water**

1. Cut roast in half. Transfer to a 5-qt. slow cooker. Combine the maple syrup, lemon juice, mustard and garlic; pour over pork. Cover and cook on low for 5-6 hours or until meat is tender.

2. Remove the meat to a serving platter; keep warm. Strain cooking juices; transfer 1 cup to a saucepan. Combine the cornstarch and water until smooth; stir into the cooking juices. Bring to a boil; cook and stir for 2 minutes or until thickened. Slice roast; serve with gravy.

PER SERVING *1 serving equals 205 cal., 6 g fat (2 g sat. fat), 68 mg chol., 76 mg sodium, 9 g carb., trace fiber, 26 g pro.* **Diabetic Exchanges: 4 lean meat, ½ starch.**

HOW-TO

SAVE LEMON JUICE

When a recipe calls for lemon juice, you can either use fresh, frozen or bottled lemon juice in equal amounts. You can also freeze fresh lemon juice in ice cube trays for later.

ASIAN PORK ROAST

We can't get enough of this pork roast with honey, soy and spices. It's particularly perfect on chilly nights. The aroma will draw everyone to the kitchen.

—**SHEREE SHOWN** JUNCTION CITY, OR

PREP: 25 MIN. • **COOK:** 4 HOURS
MAKES: 12 SERVINGS

- 2 **large onions, thinly sliced**
- 3 **garlic cloves, minced**
- ½ **teaspoon salt**
- ½ **teaspoon pepper**
- 1 **boneless pork loin roast (3 pounds)**
- 1 **tablespoon canola oil**
- 3 **bay leaves**
- ¼ **cup hot water**
- ¼ **cup honey**
- ¼ **cup reduced-sodium soy sauce**
- 2 **tablespoons rice vinegar**
- 1 **teaspoon ground ginger**
- ½ **teaspoon ground cloves**
- 3 **tablespoons cornstarch**
- ¼ **cup cold water**
- 2 **tablespoons sesame seeds, toasted**
     Hot cooked rice and sliced green onion tops, optional

1. Place onions in a 5-qt. slow cooker. In a small bowl, combine the garlic, salt and pepper. Cut roast in half; rub with garlic mixture. In a large nonstick skillet coated with cooking spray, brown pork in oil on all sides. Transfer to slow cooker; add bay leaves.

2. In a small bowl, combine hot water and honey; stir in soy sauce, vinegar, ginger and cloves. Pour over pork. Cover and cook on low for 4-5 hours or until meat is tender.

3. Remove meat and onions from slow cooker; keep warm. Discard bay leaves. Combine cornstarch and cold water until smooth; gradually stir into slow cooker.

4. Cover and cook on high for 30 minutes or until thickened, stirring twice. Slice the pork; top with sauce and sprinkle with sesame seeds. Serve with rice and garnish with green onion tops if desired.

PER SERVING *3 ounces cooked pork with 3 tablespoons onions and 3 tablespoons sauce (calculated without optional ingredients) equals 203 cal., 7 g fat (2 g sat. fat), 56 mg chol., 342 mg sodium, 11 g carb., 1 g fiber, 23 g pro.* **Diabetic Exchanges: 3 lean meat, 1 starch.**

SLOW-COOKED PORK AND BEANS

I like to get this dish started before leaving for work in the morning. Then when I get home, my supper is ready. It's a hearty meal that's also good for a potluck. Place a generous helping of the pork and beans next to a slice of warm corn bread.

—**PATRICIA HAGER**
NICHOLASVILLE, KY

PREP: 15 MIN. • **COOK:** 6 HOURS
MAKES: 12 SERVINGS

- 1 **boneless pork loin roast (3 pounds)**
- 1 **medium onion, sliced**
- 3 **cans (15 ounces each) pork and beans**
- 1½ **cups barbecue sauce**
- ¼ **cup packed brown sugar**
- 1 **teaspoon garlic powder**

1. Cut the roast in half; place in a 5-qt. slow cooker. Top with onion. In a large bowl, combine the beans, barbecue sauce, brown sugar and garlic powder; pour over the meat. Cover and cook on low for 6-8 hours or until meat is tender.

2. Remove roast; shred with two forks. Return meat to slow cooker; heat through.

PER SERVING *1 serving (1 cup) equals 217 cal., 6 g fat (2 g sat. fat), 56 mg chol., 404 mg sodium, 16 g carb., 2 g fiber, 24 g pro.*

THAI-STYLE PORK

A creamy Thai peanut sauce coats tender pork in this delectable dish. The recipe comes from a friend in my cooking club and it's always a crowd favorite.

—AMY VAN ORMAN ROCKFORD, MI

PREP: 15 MIN. • **COOK:** 6¼ HOURS
MAKES: 6 SERVINGS

- 2 **pounds boneless pork loin chops**
- ¼ **cup teriyaki sauce**
- 2 **tablespoons rice vinegar**
- 1 **teaspoon crushed red pepper flakes**
- 1 **teaspoon minced garlic**
- 1 **tablespoon cornstarch**
- ¼ **cup cold water**
- ¼ **cup creamy peanut butter**
   Hot cooked rice
- ½ **cup chopped green onions**
- ½ **cup dry roasted peanuts**
   Lime juice, optional

1. Place pork chops in a 3-qt. slow cooker. In a small bowl, combine the teriyaki sauce, vinegar, pepper flakes and garlic; pour over meat. Cover and cook on low for 6-8 hours or until meat is tender.

2. Remove the pork and cut into bite-size pieces; keep warm. Place cooking juices in a small saucepan; bring to a boil. Combine cornstarch and water until smooth. Gradually stir into the pan. Bring to a boil; cook and stir for 2 minutes or until thickened. Stir in peanut butter; add meat.

3. Serve with rice and sprinkle with onions and peanuts. Drizzle with lime juice if desired.

PER SERVING *⅔ cup (calculated without rice) equals 357 cal., 20 g fat (5 g sat. fat), 73 mg chol., 598 mg sodium, 9 g carb., 2 g fiber, 35 g pro.* **Diabetic Exchanges:** *5 lean meat, 2 fat, ½ starch.*

THAI-STYLE
PORK

SLOW-COOKED PORK ROAST DINNER

You can cut this roast with a fork, and it's just as moist and tender later—if there are any leftovers.

—JANE MONTGOMERY PIQUA, OH

PREP: 25 MIN. • **COOK:** 6 HOURS
MAKES: 8 SERVINGS

- 1 **cup hot water**
- ¼ **cup sugar**
- 3 **tablespoons cider vinegar**
- 2 **tablespoons reduced-sodium soy sauce**
- 1 **tablespoon ketchup**
- ½ **teaspoon salt**
- ½ **teaspoon pepper**
- ¼ **teaspoon garlic powder**
- ¼ **teaspoon chili powder**
- 1 **large onion, halved and sliced**
- 1 **boneless pork loin roast (2½ pounds), halved**
- 4 **medium potatoes (about 1¾ pounds), peeled and cut into 1-inch pieces**
- 1 **package (16 ounces) frozen sliced carrots, thawed**
- 2 **tablespoons cornstarch**
- 2 **tablespoons cold water**

1. In a small bowl, whisk first nine ingredients until blended. Place onion in a 5-qt. slow cooker. Place roast, potatoes and carrots over the onion. Pour sauce mixture over top. Cook, covered, on low 6-8 hours or until pork and potatoes are tender.

2. Remove roast and vegetables from the slow cooker; keep warm. Transfer cooking juices to a small saucepan; skim fat. Bring juices to a boil. In a bowl, mix the cornstarch and water until smooth; stir into juices. Bring to a boil; cook and stir 1-2 minutes or until thickened. Serve with roast and vegetables.

PER SERVING *4 ounces cooked pork with ⅔ cup vegetables and ⅓ cup sauce equals 304 cal., 7 g fat (2 g sat. fat), 70 mg chol., 401 mg sodium, 30 g carb., 3 g fiber, 29 g pro.* **Diabetic Exchanges:** *4 lean meat, 1½ starch, 1 vegetable.*

SLOW-COOKED
PORK ROAST DINNER

**LIGHT GLAZED
PORK ROAST**

LIGHT GLAZED PORK ROAST

My roast with a hint of orange is popular with adults and children alike. It's an excellent take-along meal for potlucks.

—RADELLE KNAPPENBERGER
OVIEDO, FL

PREP: 30 MIN. • **COOK:** 4 HOURS
MAKES: 16 SERVINGS

- 1 **boneless pork loin roast (4 pounds), trimmed**
- 1 **tablespoon olive oil**
- 1 **tablespoon butter, melted**
- ⅔ **cup thawed orange juice concentrate**
- ⅓ **cup water**
- 3 **garlic cloves, minced**
- 1½ **teaspoons salt**
- ½ **teaspoon pepper**

GLAZE
- ¼ **cup packed brown sugar**
- 2 **tablespoons balsamic vinegar**
- 1 **tablespoon thawed orange juice concentrate**
- 1 **garlic clove, minced**
- 1 **can (11 ounces) mandarin oranges, drained, optional**

1. Cut the roast in half. In a large skillet, brown roast in oil and butter on all sides.

2. Transfer to a 5-qt. slow cooker. Add the orange juice concentrate, water, garlic, salt and pepper. Cover and cook on low for 4-6 hours or until meat is tender.

3. For glaze, in a small saucepan, combine the brown sugar, vinegar, orange juice concentrate and garlic. Bring to a boil. Reduce the heat and simmer, uncovered, for 3-5 minutes or until reduced to about ¼ cup. Brush over roast. Garnish with oranges if desired.

PER SERVING *3 ounces cooked pork (calculated without oranges) equals 190 cal., 7 g fat (2 g sat. fat), 58 mg chol., 263 mg sodium, 9 g carb., trace fiber, 22 g pro.* **Diabetic Exchanges:** *3 lean meat, ½ starch.*

PORK CHOP CACCIATORE

It's hard to believe that so much flavor can come from such an easy recipe. Serve it with noodles and a simple green salad.

—TRACY HIATT GRICE SOMERSET, WI

PREP: 30 MIN. • **COOK:** 8 HOURS
MAKES: 6 SERVINGS

- 6 **bone-in pork loin chops (7 ounces each)**
- ¾ **teaspoon salt, divided**
- ¼ **teaspoon pepper**
- 1 **tablespoon olive oil**
- 1 **cup sliced fresh mushrooms**
- 1 **small onion, chopped**
- 1 **celery rib, chopped**
- 1 **small green pepper, chopped**
- 2 **garlic cloves, minced**
- 1 **can (14½ ounces) diced tomatoes**
- ½ **cup water, divided**
- ½ **teaspoon dried basil**
- 2 **tablespoons cornstarch**
- 4½ **cups cooked egg noodles**

1. Sprinkle chops with ½ teaspoon salt and pepper. In a large skillet, brown the chops in oil in batches. Transfer to a 4-or 5-qt. slow cooker coated with cooking spray. Saute the mushrooms, onion, celery and green pepper in drippings until tender. Add garlic; cook 1 minute longer. Stir in the tomatoes, ¼ cup water, basil and remaining salt; pour over chops.

2. Cover and cook on low for 8-10 hours or until pork is tender. Remove meat to a serving platter; keep warm. Skim fat from cooking juices if necessary; transfer juices to a small saucepan. Bring liquid to a boil. Combine the cornstarch and remaining water until smooth. Gradually stir into the pan. Bring to a boil; cook and stir for 2 minutes or until thickened. Serve with meat and noodles.

PER SERVING *1 pork chop with ¾ cup noodles and ½ cup sauce equals 371 cal., 12 g fat (4 g sat. fat), 110 mg chol., 458 mg sodium, 29 g carb., 3 g fiber, 35 g pro.* **Diabetic Exchanges:** *4 lean meat, 1½ starch, 1 vegetable, ½ fat.*

SOUTHERN PULLED PORK

Here's my New England take on a Southern favorite. The sweet and tangy pork takes just a few minutes to get going in the slow cooker. It's irresistible piled high on cooked sweet potatoes.

—KATIE GRADY WEST BOYLSTON, MA

PREP: 20 MIN. • **COOK:** 6½ HOURS
MAKES: 10 SERVINGS

- 1 **boneless pork shoulder butt roast (3 pounds)**
- ⅓ **cup spicy brown mustard**
- ⅓ **cup molasses**
- ¼ **cup packed brown sugar**
- 1½ **teaspoons soy sauce**
- 1 **tablespoon cornstarch**
- ¼ **cup cold water**
     Baked sweet potatoes, optional

1. Place pork in a 3- or 4-qt. slow cooker. Combine the mustard, molasses, brown sugar and soy sauce; pour over roast. Cover and cook on low for 6-8 hours or until meat is tender.

2. Remove meat; cool slightly. Skim the fat from cooking juices; transfer juices to a large saucepan. Bring to a boil. Combine cornstarch and water until smooth; gradually stir into the juices. Return to a boil; cook and stir for 2 minutes or until the sauce has thickened.

3. Shred the meat with two forks; return to slow cooker. Stir in sauce. Cover and cook 15 minutes longer or until heated through. Serve with sweet potatoes if desired.

PER SERVING *½ cup (calculated without potatoes) equals 282 cal., 14 g fat (5 g sat. fat), 81 mg chol., 240 mg sodium, 14 g carb., trace fiber, 23 g pro.* **Diabetic Exchanges:** *3 medium-fat meat, 1 starch.*

PORK CHOP CACCIATORE

SWEETENED PORK ROAST

Need to keep cool during the summer? Try this entree that doesn't need the oven to cook. It's sure to become a favorite.

—**MARION LOWERY** MEDFORD, OR

PREP: 20 MIN.
COOK: 6 HOURS + STANDING
MAKES: 12 SERVINGS

- 2 cans (8 ounces each) unsweetened crushed pineapple, undrained
- 1 cup barbecue sauce
- 2 tablespoons unsweetened apple juice
- 1 tablespoon minced fresh rosemary or 1 teaspoon dried rosemary, crushed
- 1 teaspoon minced garlic
- 2 teaspoons grated lemon peel
- 1 teaspoon liquid smoke, optional
- ½ teaspoon salt
- ¼ teaspoon pepper
- 1 boneless pork loin roast (3 to 4 pounds)

1. In a large saucepan, combine the first nine ingredients. Bring to a boil. Reduce the heat and simmer, uncovered, for 3 minutes.
2. Meanwhile, cut roast in half. In a nonstick skillet coated with cooking spray, brown pork roast on all sides.
3. Place the roast in a 5-qt. slow cooker. Pour sauce over the roast and turn to coat. Cover and cook on low for 6-7 hours or until meat is tender. Let stand for 10 minutes before slicing.

PER SERVING *3 ounces cooked pork with ¼ cup sauce equals 202 cal., 7 g fat (2 g sat. fat), 66 mg chol., 306 mg sodium, 8 g carb., 1 g fiber, 26 g pro.* **Diabetic Exchanges:** *3 lean meat, ½ starch.*

PORK CHOPS WITH SCALLOPED POTATOES

My sister gave me this recipe to make as a casserole baked in the oven, but I've also fixed it on the stovetop and in the slow cooker. Everyone who has tasted it loves it.

—**ELIZABETH JOHNSTON** GLENDALE, AZ

PREP: 30 MIN. • **COOK:** 8 HOURS
MAKES: 6 SERVINGS

- 4 medium potatoes, peeled and thinly sliced
- 6 bone-in pork loin chops (7 ounces each)
- 1 tablespoon canola oil
- 2 large onions, sliced and separated into rings
- 2 teaspoons butter
- 3 tablespoons all-purpose flour
- ¼ teaspoon salt
- ¼ teaspoon pepper
- 1 can (14½ ounces) reduced-sodium chicken broth
- 1 cup fat-free milk

1. Place potatoes in a 5- or 6-qt. slow cooker coated with cooking spray. In a large nonstick skillet, brown pork chops in oil in batches.
2. Place chops over potatoes. Saute onions in drippings until tender; place over chops. Melt the butter in a skillet. Combine the flour, salt, pepper and broth until smooth; stir into pan. Add the milk. Bring to a boil; cook and stir for 2 minutes or until thickened.
3. Pour sauce over onions. Cover and cook on low for 8-10 hours or until pork is tender. Skim fat and thicken cooking juices if desired.

PER SERVING *1 pork chop with ¾ cup potatoes equals 372 cal., 12 g fat (4 g sat. fat), 90 mg chol., 389 mg sodium, 29 g carb., 2 g fiber, 35 g pro.* **Diabetic Exchanges:** *4 lean meat, 2 starch, 1 fat.*

SWEETENED PORK ROAST

FRUITED PORK CHOPS

Here's one of my best dishes. I often prepare these juicy pineapple pork chops with brown rice.

—CINDY RAGAN
NORTH HUNTINGDON, PA

PREP: 10 MIN. • **COOK:** 6¼ HOURS
MAKES: 6 SERVINGS

- 3 tablespoons all-purpose flour
- 1½ teaspoons dried oregano
- ¾ teaspoon salt
- ¼ teaspoon garlic powder
- ¼ teaspoon pepper
- 6 boneless pork loin chops (5 ounces each)
- 1 tablespoon olive oil
- 1 can (20 ounces) unsweetened pineapple chunks
- ¾ cup unsweetened pineapple juice
- ¼ cup water
- 2 tablespoons brown sugar
- 2 tablespoons dried minced onion
- 2 tablespoons tomato paste
- ¼ cup raisins

1. In a large resealable plastic bag, combine the flour, oregano, salt, garlic powder and pepper; add the pork chops, one at a time, and shake to coat. In a nonstick skillet, brown chops in oil on both sides. Transfer to a 5-qt. slow cooker.

2. Drain pineapple, reserving juice; set the pineapple aside. In a bowl, combine the ¾ cup pineapple juice with reserved pineapple juice. Stir in water, brown sugar, onion and tomato paste; pour over the chops. Sprinkle with raisins.

3. Cover and cook on low for 6-8 hours or until meat is tender. Stir in reserved pineapple. Cover and cook 15 minutes longer or until heated through.

PER SERVING *1 serving equals 366 cal., 12 g fat (4 g sat. fat), 79 mg chol., 353 mg sodium, 31 g carb., 2 g fiber, 32 g pro.* **Diabetic Exchanges:** *4 lean meat, 2 fruit.*

CRANBERRY-APRICOT PORK ROAST WITH POTATOES

I got this recipe from one of my dearest friends. Perfect for the chilly fall and winter months, the comfy entree features apricots, whole-berry cranberry sauce and a hint of cayenne to accent the pork.

—PAT BARNES PANAMA CITY, FL

PREP: 15 MIN. • **COOK:** 5 HOURS
MAKES: 8 SERVINGS

- 4 medium potatoes, peeled and quartered
- 1 boneless pork loin roast (3 pounds)
- 1 can (14 ounces) whole-berry cranberry sauce
- 1 can (15 ounces) apricot halves, drained
- 1 medium onion, quartered
- ½ cup chopped dried apricots
- 1 tablespoon sugar
- ½ teaspoon ground mustard
- ¼ teaspoon cayenne pepper

1. Place potatoes in a 5-qt. slow cooker. Add pork.

2. In a blender, combine the cranberry sauce, apricots, onion, dried apricots, sugar, mustard and cayenne. Cover and process for 30 seconds or until almost smooth. Pour over pork.

3. Cover and cook on low for 5-6 hours or until meat is tender. Serve meat and potatoes with cooking juices.

PER SERVING *1 serving equals 433 cal., 8 g fat (3 g sat. fat), 85 mg chol., 71 mg sodium, 56 g carb., 4 g fiber, 35 g pro.*

LIME-CHIPOTLE CARNITAS TOSTADAS

At your next party, set out various toppings and garnishes so guests can customize their own tostadas.

—JAN VALDEZ CHICAGO, IL

PREP: 20 MIN. • **COOK:** 8 HOURS
MAKES: 16 SERVINGS

- ½ cup chicken broth
- 4 teaspoons ground chipotle pepper
- 4 teaspoons ground cumin
- 1 teaspoon salt
- 1 boneless pork shoulder roast (4 to 5 pounds), halved
- 1 large onion, peeled and halved
- 8 garlic cloves, peeled
- 1 to 2 limes, halved
- 16 tostada shells
  Optional toppings: warmed refried beans, salsa, sour cream, shredded lettuce, chopped avocado, crumbled queso fresco and minced fresh cilantro
  Lime wedges

1. Add broth to a 5-qt. slow cooker. Mix the seasonings; rub over all sides of pork. Place in slow cooker. Add onion and garlic cloves. Cook, covered, on low 8-10 hours or until meat is tender.

2. Remove the pork; cool slightly. Strain cooking juices, reserving garlic cloves; discard onion. Skim fat from cooking juices. Mash the garlic with a fork. Shred the pork with two forks.

3. Return cooking juices, garlic and pork to slow cooker. Squeeze the lime juice over pork; heat through, stirring to combine. Layer tostada shells with the pork mixture and toppings as desired. Serve with the lime wedges.

PER SERVING *1 tostada (calculated without optional toppings) equals 269 cal., 15 g fat (5 g sat. fat), 76 mg chol., 279 mg sodium, 9 g carb., 1 g fiber, 23 g pro.* **Diabetic Exchanges:** *3 medium-fat meat, ½ starch.*

LIME-CHIPOTLE
CARNITAS TOSTADAS

PORK

PORK ROAST
DINNER

TUSCAN
PORK STEW

TANGY
PORK CHOPS

PORK ROAST DINNER

I love to cook, so I often make meals for friends. They love trying my new recipes, and this was one of their favorites. Use any leftover meat to create barbecue pork sandwiches the next day.

—**LISA CHAMBERLAIN** ST. CHARLES, IL

PREP: 30 MIN. + MARINATING
COOK: 8 HOURS • **MAKES:** 8 SERVINGS

- 2 teaspoons minced garlic
- 2 teaspoons fennel seed, crushed
- 1½ teaspoons dried rosemary, crushed
- 1 teaspoon dried oregano
- 1 teaspoon paprika
- ¾ teaspoon salt
- ¼ teaspoon pepper
- 1 boneless whole pork loin roast (3 to 4 pounds)
- 1½ pounds medium potatoes, peeled and cut into chunks
- 1½ pounds large sweet potatoes, peeled and cut into chunks
- 2 large sweet onions, cut into eighths
- ½ cup chicken broth

1. Combine the garlic, fennel, rosemary, oregano, paprika, salt and pepper; rub over pork. Cover and refrigerate for 8 hours.
2. Place potatoes and onions in a 5-qt. slow cooker. Top with pork. Pour broth over meat. Cover and cook on low for 8-10 hours or until meat and vegetables are tender.
3. Let meat stand 10-15 minutes before slicing.
PER SERVING *5 ounces cooked pork with 1 cup vegetables equals 369 cal., 9 g fat (3 g sat. fat), 99 mg chol., 349 mg sodium, 29 g carb., 3 g fiber, 41 g pro.* **Diabetic Exchanges:** *5 lean meat, 2 starch.*

TANGY PORK CHOPS

My husband and I discovered this convenient recipe after the birth of our first child. I could start it during nap time and we'd enjoy an easy, satisfying dinner that night.

—**KAROL HINES** KITTY HAWK, NC

PREP: 15 MIN. • **COOK:** 5½ HOURS
MAKES: 4 SERVINGS

- 4 bone-in pork loin chops
- ⅛ teaspoon pepper
- 2 medium onions, chopped
- 2 celery ribs, chopped
- 1 large green pepper, sliced
- 1 can (14½ ounces) no-salt-added stewed tomatoes
- ½ cup ketchup
- 2 tablespoons cider vinegar
- 2 tablespoons Worcestershire sauce
- 2 tablespoons brown sugar
- 1 tablespoon lemon juice
- 1 teaspoon beef bouillon granules
- 2 tablespoons cornstarch
- 2 tablespoons cold water
  Hot cooked rice, optional

1. Place the chops in a 3-qt. slow cooker; sprinkle with pepper. Add onions, celery, green pepper and tomatoes. Combine the ketchup, vinegar, Worcestershire sauce, brown sugar, lemon juice and bouillon; pour over the vegetables. Cover and cook on low for 5-6 hours or until meat is tender.
2. Mix cornstarch and water until smooth; stir into liquid in the slow cooker. Cover and cook on high for 30 minutes or until thickened. Serve with rice if desired.
PER SERVING *1 serving equals 349 cal., 9 g fat (3 g sat. fat), 86 mg chol., 757 mg sodium, 34 g carb., 4 g fiber, 32 g pro.*

TUSCAN PORK STEW

Tender chunks of pork cook slowly in a seasoned, wine-infused sauce. Add some crushed red pepper flakes for a little extra kick.

—**PENNY HAWKINS** MEBANE, NC

PREP: 15 MIN. • **COOK:** 8½ HOURS
MAKES: 8 SERVINGS

- 1½ pounds boneless pork loin roast, cut into 1-inch cubes
- 2 tablespoons olive oil
- 2 cans (14½ ounces each) Italian diced tomatoes, undrained
- 2 cups reduced-sodium chicken broth
- 2 cups frozen pepper stir-fry vegetable blend, thawed
- ½ cup dry red wine or additional reduced-sodium chicken broth
- ¼ cup orange marmalade
- 2 garlic cloves, minced
- 1 teaspoon dried oregano
- ½ teaspoon fennel seed
- ½ teaspoon pepper
- ⅛ teaspoon crushed red pepper flakes, optional
- 2 tablespoons cornstarch
- 2 tablespoons cold water
  Hot cooked fettuccine, optional

1. In a large skillet, brown the pork in oil; drain. Transfer to a 5-qt. slow cooker.
2. Stir in the tomatoes, broth, vegetable blend, wine, marmalade, garlic, oregano, fennel seed, pepper and, if desired, red pepper flakes. Cover and cook on low 8-10 hours or until meat is tender.
3. Combine cornstarch and water until smooth; gradually stir into stew. Cover and cook on high for 30 minutes or until thickened. Serve with fettuccine if desired.
PER SERVING *1 cup (calculated without fettuccine) equals 232 cal., 7 g fat (2 g sat. fat), 42 mg chol., 614 mg sodium, 19 g carb., 1 g fiber, 19 g pro.* **Diabetic Exchanges:** *2 lean meat, 1 starch, 1 vegetable, ½ fat.*

ALL-DAY RED BEANS & RICE

My family loves New Orleans-style cooking, so I make this authentic dish often. I appreciate how simple it is to throw together.

—CELINDA DAHLGREN NAPA, CA

PREP: 20 MIN. + SOAKING
COOK: 8½ HOURS • **MAKES:** 6 SERVINGS

- 1　cup dried red beans
- 7　cups water, divided
- 2　smoked ham hocks
- 1　medium onion, chopped
- 1½　teaspoons minced garlic
- 1　teaspoon ground cumin
- 1　medium tomato, chopped
- 1　medium green pepper, chopped
- 1　teaspoon salt
- 4　cups hot cooked rice

1. Sort beans and rinse in cold water. Place beans in a 3-qt. slow cooker. Add 4 cups water; cover and let stand overnight.

2. Drain and rinse the beans, discarding liquid. Return beans to slow cooker; add the ham hocks, onion, garlic, cumin and remaining water. Cover and cook on low for 8-10 hours or until beans are tender.

3. Remove the ham hocks; cool slightly. Remove meat from bones. Finely chop meat and return to slow cooker; discard bones. Stir in tomato, pepper and salt; cover and cook on high for 30 minutes or until pepper is tender. Serve with rice.

FREEZE OPTION *Freeze the cooled bean mixture in freezer containers. To use, partially thaw in the refrigerator overnight. Microwave, covered, on high in a microwave-safe dish until heated through, stirring and adding a little water if necessary.*

PER SERVING *⅔ cup beans with ⅔ cup rice equals 297 cal., 7 g fat (3 g sat. fat), 33 mg chol., 441 mg sodium, 50 g carb., 12 g fiber, 17 g pro.*

SHREDDED PORK WITH BEANS

A friend gave me this recipe, which my sons all say is a keeper. For a change of pace, spoon the pork into corn or whole wheat tortillas.

—SARAH JOHNSTON LINCOLN, NE

PREP: 20 MIN. • **COOK:** 8 HOURS
MAKES: 12 SERVINGS

- 3　pounds pork tenderloin, cut into 3-inch lengths
- 2　cans (15 ounces each) black beans, rinsed and drained
- 1　jar (24 ounces) picante sauce
　　Hot cooked rice, optional

Place the pork, beans and picante sauce in a 5-qt. slow cooker. Cover and cook on low for 8 hours or until pork is tender. Shred the pork; return to slow cooker. Serve with rice if desired.

PER SERVING *1 cup (calculated without rice) equals 207 cal., 4 g fat (1 g sat. fat), 64 mg chol., 595 mg sodium, 14 g carb., 3 g fiber, 26 g pro.* **Diabetic Exchanges:** *3 lean meat, 1 starch.*

ALL-DAY RED BEANS & RICE

TOP TIP

WHICH RICE?

When picking the most nutritious rice option, many point to brown rice. Brown rice has the husk removed but not the bran layer—the bran layer retains more vitamin, mineral and fiber content than white rice.

SHREDDED PORK
WITH BEANS

CRANBERRY PORK ROAST

PORK CHOP DINNER

Family and friends call me the Crock-Pot Queen. Of my many slow-cooked specialties, this fabulous dish gets a thumbs-up from my husband every time.

—**JANET PHILLIPS** MEADVILLE, PA

PREP: 10 MIN. • **COOK:** 4 HOURS
MAKES: 6 SERVINGS

- 6 **pork loin chops (¾ inch thick)**
- 1 **tablespoon canola oil**
- 1 **large onion, sliced**
- 1 **medium green pepper, chopped**
- 1 **can (4 ounces) mushroom stems and pieces, drained**
- 1 **can (8 ounces) tomato sauce**
- 1 **tablespoon brown sugar**
- 2 **teaspoons Worcestershire sauce**
- 1½ **teaspoons cider vinegar**
- ½ **teaspoon salt**
  Hot cooked rice, optional

In a skillet, brown pork chops on both sides in oil; drain. Place chops in a 3-qt. slow cooker. Add onion, green pepper and mushrooms. In a bowl, combine the tomato sauce, brown sugar, Worcestershire sauce, vinegar and salt. Pour over meat and vegetables. Cover and cook on low for 4-5 hours or until meat is tender. Serve with rice if desired.

PER SERVING *1 serving equals 199 cal., 8 g fat (2 g sat. fat), 59 mg chol., 507 mg sodium, 10 g carb., 1 g fiber, 22 g pro. **Diabetic Exchange:** 3 lean meat.*

CRANBERRY PORK ROAST

The colorful cranberry sauce in this recipe accompanies the juicy pork wonderfully. There's plenty of sauce for each serving.

—**JESSICA PHILLEO** CARMEL, IN

PREP: 25 MIN. • **COOK:** 8 HOURS
MAKES: 10 SERVINGS (5 CUPS SAUCE)

- 1 **package (12 ounces) fresh or frozen cranberries, thawed**
- 1 **package (12 ounces) frozen pitted dark sweet cherries, thawed**
- ¼ **cup packed brown sugar**
- ¼ **cup Marsala wine or unsweetened apple juice**
- ⅓ **cup raspberry vinaigrette**
- 1 **large red onion, sliced**
- 1 **large apple, peeled and sliced**
- 1 **boneless whole pork loin roast (4 pounds)**
- 1 **teaspoon minced fresh rosemary or ¼ teaspoon dried rosemary, crushed**
- 1 **teaspoon coarsely ground pepper**
- 2 **teaspoons cornstarch**
- 2 **teaspoons water**

1. In a large saucepan, combine the cranberries, cherries, brown sugar and wine. Cook over medium heat until berries pop, about 15 minutes. Stir in vinaigrette.
2. Place half of the onion and apple in a 4- or 5-qt. slow cooker. Cut the roast in half; add to slow cooker. Top with remaining onion and apple. Pour cranberry mixture over top. Sprinkle with the rosemary and pepper. Cover and cook on low for 8-10 hours or until meat is tender.
3. Remove meat to a serving platter; keep warm. Skim fat from cooking juices; transfer juices to a small saucepan. Bring liquid to a boil. Combine cornstarch and water until smooth. Gradually stir into the pan. Bring to a boil; cook and stir for 2 minutes or until thickened. Serve with meat.
PER SERVING *5 ounces cooked pork with ½ cup sauce equals 294 cal., 11 g fat (3 g sat. fat), 68 mg chol., 110 mg sodium, 21 g carb., 3 g fiber, 27 g pro. **Diabetic Exchanges:** 4 lean meat, 1 fruit, 1 fat, ½ starch.*

THE SKINNY

CHOOSE LEAN

If you want to eat lean protein, try pork (round, loin or tenderloin), or skinless chicken or turkey. All of these options will fill you up in a healthy way.

FREEZE IT
COUNTRY-STYLE PORK LOIN

This pork roast tops my son's list of favorite foods. The meat practically melts in your mouth. Good with a variety of sides, we enjoy it with mashed potatoes.

—CORINA FLANSBERG
CARSON CITY, NV

PREP: 20 MIN.
COOK: 5 HOURS + STANDING
MAKES: 8 SERVINGS

- 1 boneless pork loin roast (3 pounds)
- ½ cup all-purpose flour
- 1 teaspoon onion powder
- 1 teaspoon ground mustard
- 2 tablespoons canola oil
- 2 cups reduced-sodium chicken broth
- ¼ cup cornstarch
- ¼ cup cold water
  Hot mashed potatoes, optional

1. Cut the roast in half. In a large resealable plastic bag, combine the flour, onion powder and mustard. Add pork, one portion at a time, and shake to coat. In a large skillet, brown pork in oil on all sides.

2. Transfer to a 5-qt. slow cooker. Pour broth over pork. Cover and cook on low for 5-6 hours or until tender. Remove the pork and keep warm; let stand for 10-15 minutes before slicing.

3. Strain cooking juices, reserving 2½ cups; skim the fat from the reserved juices. Transfer to a small saucepan. Bring the liquid to a boil. Combine the cornstarch and water until smooth; gradually stir into the pan. Bring to a boil; cook and stir for 2 minutes or until thickened. Serve the pork and gravy with mashed potatoes if desired.

FREEZE OPTION *Cool pork and gravy. Freeze sliced pork and gravy in freezer containers. To use, partially thaw in the refrigerator overnight. Heat through slowly in a covered skillet, stirring occasionally and adding a little broth or water if necessary. Serve as directed.*

PER SERVING *5 ounces cooked pork with ¼ cup gravy (calculated without potatoes) equals 291 cal., 11 g fat (3 g sat. fat), 85 mg chol., 204 mg sodium, 10 g carb., trace fiber, 34 g pro.* **Diabetic Exchanges:** *5 lean meat, ½ starch, ½ fat.*

COUNTRY-STYLE
PORK LOIN

CARNE GUISADA

After temporarily moving out of state, my boyfriend and I really started to miss the spicy flavors of Texas, so we made this recipe often. We serve it with homemade flour tortillas or brown rice.

—**KELLY EVANS** DENTON, TX

PREP: 25 MIN. • **COOK:** 7 HOURS
MAKES: 12 SERVINGS
(ABOUT 2 QUARTS)

- 1 **bottle (12 ounces) beer**
- ¼ **cup all-purpose flour**
- 2 **tablespoons tomato paste**
- 1 **jalapeno pepper, seeded and chopped**
- 4 **teaspoons Worcestershire sauce**
- 1 **bay leaf**
- 2 **to 3 teaspoons crushed red pepper flakes**
- 2 **teaspoons chili powder**
- 1½ **teaspoons ground cumin**
- ½ **teaspoon salt**
- ½ **teaspoon paprika**
- 2 **garlic cloves, minced**
- ½ **teaspoon red wine vinegar Dash liquid smoke, optional**
- 1 **boneless pork shoulder butt roast (3 pounds), cut into 2-inch pieces**
- 2 **large unpeeled red potatoes, chopped**
- 1 **medium onion, chopped Whole wheat tortillas or hot cooked brown rice, lime wedges and chopped fresh cilantro, optional**

1. In a 4- or 5-qt. slow cooker, combine the first 13 ingredients. If desired, stir in liquid smoke. Add pork, potatoes and onion; toss to combine. Cook, covered, 7-9 hours or until pork is tender.
2. Discard bay leaf; skim fat from cooking juices. Shred pork slightly with two forks. If desired, serve with tortillas, lime and cilantro.
NOTE *Wear disposable gloves when cutting hot peppers; the oils can burn skin. Avoid touching your face.*

PER SERVING *⅔ cup (calculated without tortillas) equals 261 cal., 12 g fat (4 g sat. fat), 67 mg chol., 200 mg sodium, 16 g carb., 2 g fiber, 21 g pro.* **Diabetic Exchanges:** *3 medium-fat meat, 1 starch.*

PORK ROAST WITH PEACH SAUCE

My husband loves this roast with spiced peaches. Easy to make, it's ideal for special occasions or weeknight meals when it's chilly.

—**JANICE CHRISTOFFERSON**
EAGLE RIVER, WI

PREP: 20 MIN. • **COOK:** 6 HOURS
MAKES: 8 SERVINGS (2½ CUPS SAUCE)

- 1 **boneless pork loin roast (3 to 4 pounds)**
- 2 **teaspoons canola oil**
- ¼ **teaspoon onion salt**
- ¼ **teaspoon pepper**
- 1 **can (15¼ ounces) sliced peaches**
- ½ **cup chili sauce**
- ⅓ **cup packed brown sugar**
- 3 **tablespoons cider vinegar**
- 1 **teaspoon pumpkin pie spice**
- 2 **tablespoons cornstarch**
- 2 **tablespoons cold water**

1. Cut the roast in half. In a large skillet, brown the pork in oil on all sides. Transfer to a 4- or 5-qt. slow cooker. Sprinkle with the onion salt and pepper.
2. Drain peaches, reserving juice in a small bowl; stir chili sauce, brown sugar, vinegar and pie spice into the juice. Spoon peaches over the roast; top with juice mixture. Cover and cook on low for 6-8 hours or until meat is tender.
3. Remove meat and peaches to a serving platter; keep warm. Skim fat from cooking juices; transfer juices to a saucepan. Bring liquid to a boil. Combine the cornstarch and water until smooth; gradually stir into the pan. Bring to a boil; cook and stir for 2 minutes or until thickened. Serve with pork and peaches.

PER SERVING *5 ounces cooked pork with about ⅓ cup sauce equals 318 cal., 8 g fat (3 g sat. fat), 85 mg chol., 344 mg sodium, 25 g carb., trace fiber, 33 g pro.* **Diabetic Exchanges:** *4 lean meat, 1 starch, ½ fruit.*

PORK ROAST WITH PEACH SAUCE

CARNE
GUISADA

TOMATO-TOPPED
ITALIAN PORK CHOPS

TOMATO-TOPPED ITALIAN PORK CHOPS

When you're only seven ingredients away from a delicious meal, what's not to love?

—KRYSTLE CHASSE
RADIUM HOT SPRINGS, BC

PREP: 25 MIN. • **COOK:** 8 HOURS
MAKES: 6 SERVINGS

- 6 **bone-in pork loin chops (7 ounces each)**
- 1 **tablespoon canola oil**
- 1 **small onion, chopped**
- ½ **cup chopped carrot**
- 1 **can (14½ ounces) diced tomatoes, drained**
- ¼ **cup reduced-fat balsamic vinaigrette**
- 2 **teaspoons dried oregano**

1. In a large skillet, brown the chops in oil in batches. Transfer to a 4- or 5-qt. slow cooker coated with cooking spray. Saute the onion and carrot in drippings until tender. Stir in the tomatoes, vinaigrette and oregano; pour over chops.
2. Cover and cook on low for 8-10 hours or until meat is tender.
PER SERVING *1 pork chop equals 267 cal., 12 g fat (3 g sat. fat), 86 mg chol., 234 mg sodium, 7 g carb., 2 g fiber, 31 g pro.* **Diabetic Exchanges: 4 lean meat, 1 vegetable, 1 fat.**

TOP TIP

GETTING VITAMIN A

You probably heard that you should eat carrots because they're good for your eyes, right? Turns out it might be true! Carrots are an excellent source of vitamin A, which can promote good eyesight. In addition, carrots contain vitamin K, which helps blood clot properly.

CHOPS 'N' BEANS

Combine tender pork chops and two kinds of beans for a satisfying supper right from your slow cooker.

—DOROTHY PRITCHETT
WILLS POINT, TX

PREP: 15 MIN. • **COOK:** 5 HOURS
MAKES: 4 SERVINGS

- 4 **pork loin chops (½ inch thick)**
- ¼ **teaspoon salt**
- ¼ **teaspoon pepper**
- 1 **tablespoon canola oil**
- 2 **medium onions, chopped**
- 2 **garlic cloves, minced**
- ¼ **cup chili sauce**
- 1½ **teaspoons brown sugar**
- 1 **teaspoon prepared mustard**
- 1 **can (16 ounces) kidney beans, rinsed and drained**
- 1¾ **cups frozen lima beans, thawed**

1. Sprinkle pork chops with salt and pepper. In a large skillet, heat oil over medium-high heat. Brown chops on both sides. Transfer to a 3-qt. slow cooker. Discard the drippings, reserving 1 tablespoon drippings in skillet. Add onions; cook and stir until tender. Add garlic; cook and stir 1 minute. Stir in the chili sauce, brown sugar and mustard. Pour over chops.
2. Cook, covered, on low 4 hours or until meat is almost tender. Stir in beans. Cook, covered, 1 to 2 hours longer or until heated through.
PER SERVING *1 serving equals 297 cal., 5 g fat (1 g sat. fat), 14 mg chol., 607 mg sodium, 45 g carb., 11 g fiber, 19 g pro.* **Diabetic Exchanges: 3 starch, 3 lean meat.**

SLOW-COOKED PORK TACOS

Sometimes I'll substitute Bibb lettuce leaves for the tortillas to make crunchy lettuce wraps instead of tacos. It's good either way.

—**KATHLEEN WOLF** NAPERVILLE, IL

PREP: 20 MIN. • **COOK:** 4 HOURS
MAKES: 10 SERVINGS

- 2 **pounds boneless pork sirloin, cut into 1-inch pieces**
- 1½ **cups salsa verde**
- 1 **medium sweet red pepper, chopped**
- 1 **medium onion, chopped**
- ¼ **cup chopped dried apricots**
- 2 **tablespoons lime juice**
- 2 **garlic cloves, minced**
- 1 **teaspoon ground cumin**
- ½ **teaspoon salt**
- ¼ **teaspoon white pepper**
  Dash hot pepper sauce
- 10 **flour tortillas (8 inches), warmed**
  Reduced-fat sour cream, thinly sliced green onions, cubed avocado, shredded reduced-fat cheddar cheese and chopped tomato, optional

1. In a 3-qt. slow cooker, combine the first 11 ingredients. Cover and cook on high for 4-5 hours or until meat is tender.

2. Shred pork with two forks. Place about ½ cup pork mixture in the center of each tortilla. Serve with toppings if desired.

PER SERVING *1 taco (calculated without optional toppings) equals 301 cal., 8 g fat (2 g sat. fat), 54 mg chol., 616 mg sodium, 32 g carb., 1 g fiber, 24 g pro.* **Diabetic Exchanges:** *3 lean meat, 2 starch.*

SLOW-COOKED
PORK TACOS

HERBED PORK ROAST

A quick rub of butter and herbs adds awesome flavor to this roast. I like to serve the roast with parsley-tossed potatoes and a green salad.

—SHELIA LETCHWORTH
VERSAILLES, MO

PREP: 25 MIN.
COOK: 8 HOURS + STANDING
MAKES: 12 SERVINGS

- **1 boneless pork loin roast (4 pounds)**
- **1 cup water**
- **¼ cup butter, softened**

- **2 tablespoons rubbed sage**
- **2 tablespoons dried parsley flakes**
- **2 teaspoons pepper**
- **1 teaspoon minced garlic**
- **1 teaspoon dried oregano**
- **½ teaspoon salt**
- **1 small onion, thinly sliced**
- **1 teaspoon browning sauce, optional**

Cut roast in half. Place pork and water in a 4-qt. slow cooker. Spread butter over meat. Combine the sage, parsley, pepper, garlic, oregano and salt; sprinkle over meat. Top with onion. Cover and cook on low for 8-10 hours or until meat is tender. If desired, thicken cooking juices. Stir in browning sauce if desired. Let the meat stand 10 minutes before slicing.

PER SERVING *4 ounces cooked meat with about 2 tablespoons gravy (calculated without browning sauce) equals 227 cal., 11 g fat (5 g sat. fat), 85 mg chol., 171 mg sodium, 1 g carb., trace fiber, 29 g pro.* **Diabetic Exchanges:** *4 lean meat, 1 fat.*

HERBED PORK ROAST

VEGETARIAN STUFFED
PEPPERS, PAGE 181

OTHER ENTREES

LAMB WITH ORZO

Looking to switch up your slow-cooked staples? Consider this lamb entree with some traditional Greek flavors. A splash of lemon juice and zesty lemon peel complement the spinach and feta cheese.

—DAN KELMENSON
WEST BLOOMFIELD, MI

PREP: 30 MIN. • **COOK:** 8 HOURS
MAKES: 9 SERVINGS

- 1 boneless lamb shoulder roast (3 pounds)
- 3 tablespoons lemon juice
- 3 garlic cloves, minced
- 2 teaspoons dried oregano
- 2 teaspoons grated lemon peel
- ¼ teaspoon salt
- 1 package (16 ounces) orzo pasta
- 2 packages (9 ounces each) fresh spinach, torn divided
- 1 cup (4 ounces) crumbled feta cheese, divided

1. Cut the roast in half. Place in a 5-qt. slow cooker. Drizzle with lemon juice. Sprinkle with garlic, oregano, lemon peel and salt. Cover and cook on low for 8-10 hours or until meat is tender.

2. Cook orzo according to package directions. Remove lamb from slow cooker. Shred meat with two forks; set aside and keep warm.

3. Skim the fat from cooking juices if necessary; return 1 cup cooking juices to the slow cooker. Add a package of spinach. Cook on high for 5-10 minutes or until spinach is wilted. Drain orzo; add to spinach mixture. Stir in reserved meat and ½ cup feta cheese.

4. To serve, arrange remaining fresh spinach on nine individual plates. Top with lamb mixture. Sprinkle each with the remaining feta cheese.

PER SERVING *1 cup lamb mixture with ½ cup spinach equals 438 cal., 11 g fat (4 g sat. fat), 105 mg chol., 333 mg sodium, 41 g carb., 3 g fiber, 41 g pro.*

LAMB WITH ORZO

TANGY LAMB TAGINE

I love lamb stew but wanted to try something different, so I created this recipe that uses Moroccan spices. The stew tastes even better served a day or two later, when the flavors have had a chance to meld.

—BRIDGET KLUSMAN OTSEGO, MI

PREP: 40 MIN. • **COOK:** 8 HOURS
MAKES: 8 SERVINGS

- 3 pounds lamb stew meat, cut into 1½-inch cubes
- 1 teaspoon salt
- 1 teaspoon pepper
- 4 tablespoons olive oil, divided
- 6 medium carrots, sliced
- 2 medium onions, chopped
- 6 garlic cloves, minced
- 2 teaspoons grated lemon peel
- ¼ cup lemon juice
- 1 tablespoon minced fresh gingerroot
- 1½ teaspoons ground cinnamon
- 1½ teaspoons ground cumin
- 1½ teaspoons paprika
- 2½ cups reduced-sodium chicken broth
- ¼ cup sweet vermouth
- ¼ cup honey
- ½ cup pitted dates, chopped
- ½ cup sliced almonds, toasted

1. Sprinkle lamb with salt and pepper. In a Dutch oven, brown meat in 2 tablespoons oil in batches. Using a slotted spoon, transfer to a 4- or 5-qt. slow cooker.

2. In the Dutch oven, saute the carrots, onions, garlic and lemon peel in remaining oil until crisp-tender. Add the lemon juice, ginger, cinnamon, cumin and paprika; cook and stir 2 minutes longer. Add to slow cooker.

3. Stir in the broth, vermouth, honey and dates. Cover and cook on low for 8-10 hours or until lamb is tender. Sprinkle with almonds.

PER SERVING *1¼ cups equals 440 cal., 19 g fat (4 g sat. fat), 111 mg chol., 620 mg sodium, 28 g carb., 4 g fiber, 38 g pro.*

TANGY LAMB TAGINE

SWEET POTATO
LENTIL STEW

SWEET POTATO LENTIL STEW

Years ago, I first experienced the spiciness and wonderful aroma of this hearty dish. You can serve the stew alone or as a topper for meat or poultry. It's great either way!

—**HEATHER GRAY** LITTLE ROCK, AR

PREP: 15 MIN. • **COOK:** 5 HOURS
MAKES: 6 SERVINGS

- 1¼ **pounds sweet potatoes (about 2 medium), peeled and cut into 1-inch pieces**
- 1½ **cups dried lentils, rinsed**
- 3 **medium carrots, cut into 1-inch pieces**
- 1 **medium onion, chopped**
- 4 **garlic cloves, minced**
- ½ **teaspoon ground cumin**
- ¼ **teaspoon ground ginger**
- ¼ **teaspoon cayenne pepper**
- 1 **carton (32 ounces) vegetable broth**
- ¼ **cup minced fresh cilantro**

In a 3-qt. slow cooker, combine first nine ingredients. Cook, covered, on low 5-6 hours or until vegetables and lentils are tender. Stir in the cilantro.

PER SERVING *1⅓ cups equals 290 cal., 1 g fat (trace sat. fat), 0 chol., 662 mg sodium, 58 g carb., 15 g fiber, 15 g pro.*

SIMPLE POACHED SALMON

My kind of recipe is healthy and almost effortless. The salmon here always cooks to perfection!
—**ERIN CHILCOAT** CENTRAL ISLIP, NY

PREP: 10 MIN. • **COOK:** 1½ HOURS
MAKES: 4 SERVINGS

- 2 **cups water**
- 1 **cup white wine**
- 1 **medium onion, sliced**
- 1 **celery rib, sliced**
- 1 **medium carrot, sliced**
- 2 **tablespoons lemon juice**
- 3 **fresh thyme sprigs**
- 1 **fresh rosemary sprig**
- 1 **bay leaf**
- ½ **teaspoon salt**
- ¼ **teaspoon pepper**
- 4 **salmon fillets (1¼ inches thick and 6 ounces each)**
  Lemon wedges

1. In a 3-qt. slow cooker, combine first 11 ingredients. Cook, covered, on low 45 minutes.
2. Carefully place fillets in liquid; add additional warm water (120° to 130°) to cover if needed. Cook, covered, 45-55 minutes or just until fish flakes easily with a fork (a thermometer inserted in fish should read at least 145°). Remove the fish from cooking liquid. Serve warm or cold with lemon wedges.
PER SERVING *1 salmon fillet equals 272 cal., 16 g fat (3 g sat. fat), 85 mg chol., 115 mg sodium, 1 g carb., trace fiber, 29 g pro.* **Diabetic Exchange:** *4 lean meat.*

FREEZE IT
RED CLAM SAUCE

While this luscious sauce may taste like you've worked on it all day, it actually cooks hands-free! What a great way to jazz up pasta.
—**JOANN BROWN** LATROBE, PA

PREP: 25 MIN. • **COOK:** 3 HOURS
MAKES: 4 SERVINGS

- 1 **medium onion, chopped**
- 1 **tablespoon canola oil**
- 2 **garlic cloves, minced**
- 2 **cans (6½ ounces each) chopped clams, undrained**
- 1 **can (14½ ounces) diced tomatoes, undrained**
- 1 **can (6 ounces) tomato paste**
- ¼ **cup minced fresh parsley**
- 1 **bay leaf**
- 1 **teaspoon sugar**
- 1 **teaspoon dried basil**
- ½ **teaspoon dried thyme**
- 6 **ounces linguine, cooked and drained**

1. In a small skillet, saute the onion in oil until tender. Add garlic; cook 1 minute longer.
2. Transfer to a 1½- or 2-qt. slow cooker. Stir in the clams, tomatoes, tomato paste, parsley, bay leaf, sugar, basil and thyme.
3. Cover and cook on low for 3-4 hours or until heated through. Discard bay leaf. Serve with linguine.
FREEZE OPTION *Cool sauce before placing in a freezer container. Cover and freeze for up to 3 months. To use, thaw in refrigerator overnight. Place in a large saucepan; heat through, stirring occasionally. Serve with linguine.*
PER SERVING *1 cup sauce with ¾ cup cooked linguine equals 305 cal., 5 g fat (trace sat. fat), 15 mg chol., 553 mg sodium, 53 g carb., 7 g fiber, 15 g pro.*

RED CLAM SAUCE

ENCHILADA PIE

Stacked high with layers of beans, veggies and cheese, this mile-high pie makes for a fun fiesta night with the family. Who would have guessed it all comes together so easily in the slow cooker?

—**JACQUELINE CORREA** LANDING, NJ

PREP: 40 MIN. • **COOK:** 4 HOURS
MAKES: 8 SERVINGS

- 1 **package (12 ounces) frozen vegetarian meat crumbles**
- 1 **cup chopped onion**
- ½ **cup chopped green pepper**
- 2 **teaspoons canola oil**
- 1 **can (16 ounces) kidney beans, rinsed and drained**
- 1 **can (15 ounces) black beans, rinsed and drained**
- 1 **can (10 ounces) diced tomatoes and green chilies, undrained**
- ½ **cup water**
- 1½ **teaspoons chili powder**
- ½ **teaspoon ground cumin**
- ¼ **teaspoon pepper**
- 6 **whole wheat tortillas (8 inches)**
- 2 **cups (8 ounces) shredded reduced-fat cheddar cheese**

1. Cut three 25x3-in. strips of heavy-duty foil; crisscross so they resemble spokes of a wheel. Place strips on the bottom and up the sides of a 5-qt. slow cooker. Coat strips with cooking spray.
2. In a large saucepan, cook the meat crumbles, onion and green pepper in oil until vegetables are tender. Stir in both cans of beans, tomatoes, water, chili powder, cumin and pepper. Bring to a boil. Reduce heat; simmer, uncovered, for 10 minutes.
3. In prepared slow cooker, layer about a cup of bean mixture, one tortilla and ⅓ cup cheese. Repeat layers five times. Cover and cook on low for 4-5 hours or until heated through and cheese is melted.
4. Using foil strips as handles, remove the pie to a platter.

NOTE *Vegetarian meat crumbles are a nutritious protein source made from soy. Look for them in the natural foods freezer section.*
PER SERVING *1 piece equals 367 cal., 11 g fat (4 g sat. fat), 20 mg chol., 818 mg sodium, 41 g carb., 9 g fiber, 25 g pro.* **Diabetic Exchanges:** *3 starch, 2 lean meat, 1 fat.*

CORN BREAD-TOPPED FRIJOLES

My family often requests this savory entree. It's loaded with fresh Southwestern flavors.

—**SUZANNE CALDWELL** ARTESIA, NM

PREP: 20 MIN. • **COOK:** 3 HOURS
MAKES: 8 SERVINGS

- 1 **medium onion, chopped**
- 1 **medium green pepper, chopped**
- 1 **tablespoon canola oil**
- 2 **garlic cloves, minced**
- 1 **can (16 ounces) kidney beans, rinsed and drained**
- 1 **can (15 ounces) pinto beans, rinsed and drained**
- 1 **can (14½ ounces) diced tomatoes, undrained**
- 1 **can (8 ounces) tomato sauce**
- 1 **teaspoon chili powder**
- ½ **teaspoon pepper**
- ⅛ **teaspoon hot pepper sauce**

CORN BREAD TOPPING
- 1 **cup all-purpose flour**
- 1 **cup yellow cornmeal**
- 1 **tablespoon sugar**
- 1½ **teaspoons baking powder**
- ½ **teaspoon salt**
- 2 **large eggs, lightly beaten**
- 1¼ **cups fat-free milk**
- 1 **can (8¼ ounces) cream-style corn**
- 3 **tablespoons canola oil**

1. In a large skillet, saute onion and green pepper in oil until tender. Add garlic; cook 1 minute longer. Transfer to a greased 5-qt. slow cooker.
2. Stir in beans, tomatoes, tomato sauce, chili powder, pepper and pepper sauce. Cover and cook on high for 1 hour.
3. In a large bowl, combine flour, cornmeal, sugar, baking powder and salt. Combine the eggs, milk, corn and oil; add to the dry ingredients and mix well. Spoon evenly over bean mixture.
4. Cover and cook on high for 2 hours or until a toothpick inserted near the center of corn bread comes out clean.

PER SERVING *1 serving equals 367 cal., 9 g fat (1 g sat. fat), 54 mg chol., 708 mg sodium, 59 g carb., 9 g fiber, 14 g pro.*

CORN BREAD-TOPPED FRIJOLES

VEGETARIAN STUFFED PEPPERS

I slightly updated my mom's stuffed peppers, which were a favorite when I was growing up. Whenever I make them, I'm reminded of home.
—**MELISSA MCCABE** VICTOR, NY

PREP: 30 MIN. • **COOK:** 3½ HOURS
MAKES: 6 SERVINGS

- 2 **cups cooked brown rice**
- 3 **small tomatoes, chopped**
- 1 **cup frozen corn, thawed**
- 1 **small sweet onion, chopped**
- ¾ **cup cubed Monterey Jack cheese**
- ⅓ **cup chopped ripe olives**
- ⅓ **cup canned black beans, rinsed and drained**
- ⅓ **cup canned red beans, rinsed and drained**
- 4 **fresh basil leaves, thinly sliced**
- 3 **garlic cloves, minced**
- 1 **teaspoon salt**
- ½ **teaspoon pepper**
- 6 **large sweet peppers**
- ¾ **cup meatless spaghetti sauce**
- ½ **cup water**
- 4 **tablespoons grated Parmesan cheese, divided**

1. Place the first 12 ingredients in a large bowl; mix lightly to combine. Cut and discard tops from sweet peppers; remove seeds. Fill the peppers with rice mixture.

2. In a small bowl, mix spaghetti sauce and water; pour half of the mixture into an oval 5-qt. slow cooker. Add filled peppers. Top with remaining sauce. Sprinkle with 2 tablespoons cheese.

3. Cook, covered, on low for 3½-4 hours or until peppers are tender. Sprinkle with remaining Parmesan cheese.

PER SERVING *1 stuffed pepper equals 261 cal., 8 g fat (4 g sat. fat), 18 mg chol., 815 mg sodium, 39 g carb., 7 g fiber, 11 g pro.* **Diabetic Exchanges:** *2 starch, 1 lean meat, 1 vegetable, 1 fat.*

VEGETARIAN STUFFED PEPPERS

STRAWBERRY RHUBARB SAUCE,
PAGE 189

SNACKS & SWEETS

184

186

189

SWEET & SPICY PEANUTS

These crunchy peanuts have a caramel-like coating, and hot sauce gives them a touch of heat. They make a tasty snack any time of day.
—*TASTE OF HOME* TEST KITCHEN

PREP: 10 MIN.
COOK: 1½ HOURS + COOLING
MAKES: 4 CUPS

- 3 **cups salted peanuts**
- ½ **cup sugar**
- ⅓ **cup packed brown sugar**
- 2 **tablespoons hot water**
- 2 **tablespoons butter, melted**
- 1 **tablespoon Sriracha Asian hot chili sauce or hot pepper sauce**
- 1 **teaspoon chili powder**

1. Place the peanuts in a greased 1½-qt. slow cooker. In a small bowl, combine the sugars, water, butter, hot sauce and chili powder. Pour over peanuts. Cover and cook on high for 1½ hours, stirring once.
2. Spread on waxed paper to cool. Store in an airtight container.
PER SERVING *⅓ cup equals 284 cal., 20 g fat (4 g sat. fat), 5 mg chol., 214 mg sodium, 22 g carb., 3 g fiber, 10 g pro.*

SWEET & SPICY PEANUTS

SLOW-COOKED PEACH SALSA

Fresh peaches and tomatoes make my salsa a hands-down winner over store versions. As a treat, I give my co-workers several jars throughout the year.
—PEGGI STAHNKE CLEVELAND, OH

PREP: 20 MIN. • **COOK:** 3 HOURS
MAKES: 11 CUPS

- 4 **pounds tomatoes (about 12 medium), chopped**
- 1 **medium onion, chopped**
- 4 **jalapeno peppers, seeded and finely chopped**
- ½ **to ⅔ cup packed brown sugar**
- ¼ **cup minced fresh cilantro**
- 4 **garlic cloves, minced**
- 1 **teaspoon salt**
- 4 **cups chopped peeled fresh peaches (about 4 medium), divided**
- 1 **can (6 ounces) tomato paste**

1. In a 5-qt. slow cooker, combine the first seven ingredients; stir in 2 cups peaches. Cook, covered, on low 3-4 hours or until the onion is tender.
2. Stir tomato paste and remaining peaches into slow cooker. Transfer to covered containers. (If freezing, use freezer-safe containers and fill to within ½ in. of tops.) Refrigerate salsa up to 1 week or freeze up to 12 months. Thaw frozen salsa in refrigerator before serving.
NOTE *Wear disposable gloves when cutting hot peppers; the oils can burn skin. Avoid touching your face.*
PER SERVING *¼ cup equals 28 cal., trace fat (trace sat. fat), 0 chol., 59 mg sodium, 7 g carb., 1 g fiber, 1 g pro. Diabetic Exchange: ½ starch.*

**SLOW-COOKED
PEACH SALSA**

WARM SPICED CIDER PUNCH

sticks on a double thickness of cheesecloth; bring up corners of cloth and tie with string to form a bag. Place bag in slow cooker.

2. Cover and cook on low for 4-5 hours or until heated through. Remove and discard spice bag. Garnish with orange slices and additional cinnamon sticks if desired.

PER SERVING ¾ cup equals 108 cal., trace fat (trace sat. fat), 0 chol., 13 mg sodium, 26 g carb., trace fiber, 1 g pro.

⑤INGREDIENTS

SLOW-COOKED APPLESAUCE

My chunky applesauce works as either a light snack or alongside main dishes. Because it's prepared in the slow cooker, you can fix it and forget it so you and the family can head out for some fun.

—SUSANNE WASSON
MONTGOMERY, NY

PREP: 20 MIN. • **COOK:** 6 HOURS
MAKES: 12 CUPS

- **6   pounds apples (about 18 medium), peeled and sliced**
- **1   cup sugar**
- **1   cup water**
- **1   teaspoon salt**
- **1   teaspoon ground cinnamon**
- **¼   cup butter, cubed**
- **2   teaspoons vanilla extract**

1. In a 5-qt. slow cooker, combine the apples, sugar, water, salt and cinnamon. Cover and cook on low for 6-8 hours or until tender.

2. Turn off heat; stir in butter and vanilla. Mash if desired. Serve warm or cold.

PER SERVING ½ cup equals 105 cal., 2 g fat (1 g sat. fat), 5 mg chol., 112 mg sodium, 23 g carb., 2 g fiber, trace pro. **Diabetic Exchanges:** 1 fruit, ½ starch, ½ fat.

WARM SPICED CIDER PUNCH

Nothing warms you up on a chilly night the way hot apple cider does, so ladle up some love!

—SUSAN SMITH FOREST, VA

PREP: 5 MIN. • **COOK:** 4 HOURS
MAKES: 8 SERVINGS

- **4   cups apple cider or unsweetened apple juice**
- **2¼   cups water**
- **¾   cup orange juice concentrate**
- **¾   teaspoon ground nutmeg**
- **¾   teaspoon ground ginger**
- **3   whole cloves**
- **2   cinnamon sticks**
      Orange slices and additional cinnamon sticks, optional

1. In a 3-qt. slow cooker, combine the apple cider, water, orange juice concentrate, nutmeg and ginger. Place the cloves and cinnamon

CHERRY & SPICE RICE PUDDING

Cinnamon and cherries sweeten the deal in this dessert. If you've never tried rice pudding, here's an excellent place to start.

—DEB PERRY TRAVERSE CITY, MI

PREP: 10 MIN. • **COOK:** 2 HOURS
MAKES: 12 SERVINGS

- 4 **cups cooked long grain rice**
- 1 **can (12 ounces) evaporated milk**
- 1 **cup 2% milk**
- ⅓ **cup sugar**
- ¼ **cup water**
- ¾ **cup dried cherries**
- 3 **tablespoons butter, softened**
- 2 **teaspoons vanilla extract**
- ½ **teaspoon ground cinnamon**
- ¼ **teaspoon ground nutmeg**

1. In a large bowl, combine the rice, evaporated milk, milk, sugar and water. Stir in the remaining ingredients. Transfer to a 3-qt. slow cooker coated with cooking spray.
2. Cover and cook on low for 2-3 hours or until the mixture is thickened. Stir pudding lightly before serving. Serve warm or cold. Refrigerate leftovers.
PER SERVING *½ cup equals 193 cal., 5 g fat (4 g sat. fat), 19 mg chol., 61 mg sodium, 31 g carb., trace fiber, 4 g pro.* **Diabetic Exchanges:** *2 starch, 1 fat.*

TOP TIP

MILK SAVINGS

Using 2% milk instead of whole milk in the Cherry & Spice Rice Pudding recipe cuts back on calories, fat and saturated fat. That means you can feel great about enjoying it.

CHERRY & SPICE
RICE PUDDING

APPLE PIE OATMEAL DESSERT

APPLE PIE OATMEAL DESSERT

This warm and comforting dessert brings back memories of time spent with my family around the kitchen table. I usually serve the dish with sweetened whipped cream or vanilla ice cream as a topper.
—**CAROL GREER** EARLVILLE, IL

PREP: 15 MIN. • **COOK:** 4 HOURS
MAKES: 6 SERVINGS

- 1 cup quick-cooking oats
- ½ cup all-purpose flour
- ⅓ cup packed brown sugar
- 2 teaspoons baking powder
- 1½ teaspoons apple pie spice
- ¼ teaspoon salt
- 3 large eggs
- 1⅔ cups 2% milk, divided
- 1½ teaspoons vanilla extract
- 3 medium apples, peeled and finely chopped
  Vanilla ice cream, optional

1. In a large bowl, whisk the oats, flour, brown sugar, baking powder, pie spice and salt. In a small bowl, whisk eggs, 1 cup milk and vanilla until blended. Add to oat mixture, stirring just until moistened. Fold in apples.
2. Transfer to a greased 3-qt. slow cooker. Cook, covered, on low 4-5 hours or until apples are tender and top is set.
3. Stir in remaining milk. Serve warm or cold, with ice cream if desired.
PER SERVING *¾ cup (calculated without ice cream) equals 238 cal., 5 g fat (2 g sat. fat), 111 mg chol., 306 mg sodium, 41 g carb., 3 g fiber, 8 g pro.*

STRAWBERRY RHUBARB SAUCE

A neighbor shared with me the recipe for this wonderful fruit sauce. It's a great way to use up a bumper crop of rhubarb. We like it over ice cream, pancakes and even fresh, hot biscuits.
—**NANCY COWLISHAW** BOISE, ID

PREP: 15 MIN. • **COOK:** 4¼ HOURS
MAKES: 4½ CUPS

- 6 cups sliced fresh or frozen rhubarb, thawed
- 1 cup sugar
- ½ cup unsweetened apple juice
- 3 cinnamon sticks (3 inches)
- ½ teaspoon grated orange peel
- ¼ teaspoon ground ginger
- 1 pint fresh strawberries, halved
  Vanilla ice cream

1. Place the rhubarb, sugar, juice, cinnamon sticks, orange peel and ginger in a 3-qt. slow cooker. Cover and cook on low for 4-5 hours or until rhubarb is tender.
2. Stir in strawberries; cover and cook 15 minutes longer or until heated through. Discard cinnamon sticks. Serve with ice cream.
PER SERVING *¼ cup (calculated without ice cream) equals 60 cal., trace fat (trace sat. fat), 0 chol., 2 mg sodium, 15 g carb., 1 g fiber, trace pro.* **Diabetic Exchange:** *1 fruit.*

CHOCOLATE COVERED CHERRY PUDDING CAKE

Remembering how much my grandfather loved the chocolate-covered cherries we brought him for Christmas, I came up with this rich recipe in his honor. It's delicious, especially when served with whipped topping.

—MEREDITH COE CHARLOTTESVILLE, VA

PREP: 20 MIN.
COOK: 2 HOURS + STANDING
MAKES: 8 SERVINGS

- ½ cup reduced-fat sour cream
- 2 tablespoons canola oil
- 1 tablespoon butter, melted
- 2 teaspoons vanilla extract
- 1 cup all-purpose flour
- ¼ cup sugar
- ¼ cup packed brown sugar
- 3 tablespoons baking cocoa
- 2 teaspoons baking powder
- ½ teaspoon ground cinnamon
- ⅛ teaspoon salt
- 1 cup fresh or frozen pitted dark sweet cherries, thawed
- 1 cup fresh or frozen pitted tart cherries, thawed
- ⅓ cup 60% cacao bittersweet chocolate baking chips

PUDDING

- ½ cup packed brown sugar
- 2 tablespoons baking cocoa
- 1¼ cups hot water

1. In a large bowl, beat the sour cream, oil, butter and vanilla until blended. Combine the flour, sugars, cocoa, baking powder, cinnamon and salt. Add to sour cream mixture just until combined. Stir in cherries and chips. Pour into a 3-qt. slow cooker coated with cooking spray.
2. In a small bowl, combine the brown sugar and cocoa. Stir in the hot water until blended. Pour over the batter (do not stir). Cover and cook on high for 2 to 2½ hours or until set. Let stand for 15 minutes. Serve warm.

PER SERVING *1 serving equals 291 cal., 9 g fat (3 g sat. fat), 9 mg chol., 167 mg sodium, 51 g carb., 2 g fiber, 4 g pro.*

SPICED POMEGRANATE SIPPER

Your entire house will fill with the wonderful aroma of spices and simmering fruit juices when you make this.

—LISA RENSHAW KANSAS CITY, MO

PREP: 10 MIN. • **COOK:** 1 HOUR
MAKES: 16 SERVINGS (¾ CUP EACH)

- 1 bottle (64 ounces) cranberry-apple juice
- 2 cups unsweetened apple juice
- 1 cup pomegranate juice
- ⅔ cup honey
- ½ cup orange juice
- 10 whole cloves
- 3 cinnamon sticks (3 inches)
- 2 tablespoons grated orange peel

In a 5-qt. slow cooker, combine the first five ingredients. Place cloves, cinnamon sticks and orange peel on a double thickness of cheesecloth. Gather up corners of cloth to wrap seasonings; tie securely with string. Add to slow cooker. Cook, covered, on low 1-2 hours or until heated through. Discard spice bag.
PER SERVING ¾ *cup equals 131 cal., trace fat (trace sat. fat), 0 chol., 21 mg sodium, 33 g carb., trace fiber, trace pro.*

CREAMY ARTICHOKE DIP

Enjoy a lighter take on a treasured family favorite. It's just as ooey-gooey good as before!

—MARY SPENCER GREENDALE, WI

PREP: 20 MIN. • **COOK:** 1 HOUR
MAKES: 5 CUPS

- 2 cans (14 ounces each) water-packed artichoke hearts, rinsed, drained and coarsely chopped
- 1 package (8 ounces) reduced-fat cream cheese, cubed
- ¾ cup (6 ounces) plain yogurt
- 1 cup (4 ounces) shredded part-skim mozzarella cheese
- 1 cup reduced-fat ricotta cheese
- ¾ cup shredded Parmesan cheese, divided
- ½ cup shredded reduced-fat Swiss cheese
- ¼ cup reduced-fat mayonnaise
- 2 tablespoons lemon juice
- 1 tablespoon chopped seeded jalapeno pepper
- 1 teaspoon garlic powder
- 1 teaspoon seasoned salt
- Tortilla chips

1. In a 3-qt. slow cooker, combine artichokes, cream cheese, yogurt, mozzarella cheese, ricotta cheese, ½ cup Parmesan cheese, Swiss cheese, mayonnaise, lemon juice, jalapeno, garlic powder and seasoned salt. Cover and cook on low for 1 hour or until heated through.
2. Sprinkle with remaining cheese. Serve with tortilla chips.
NOTE *Wear disposable gloves when cutting hot peppers; the oils can burn skin. Avoid touching your face.*
PER SERVING ¼ *cup (calculated without tortilla chips) equals 104 cal., 6 g fat (3 g sat. fat), 20 mg chol., 348 mg sodium, 5 g carb., trace fiber, 7 g pro.*

CREAMY ARTICHOKE DIP

CHOCOLATE COVERED CHERRY PUDDING CAKE

SPICED POMEGRANATE SIPPER

HEIRLOOM TOMATO
& ZUCCHINI SALAD, PAGE 197

BONUS:
QUICK SIDES, SALADS & BREADS

198

209

209

BRUSSELS SPROUTS
WITH GARLIC

(5) INGREDIENTS

BRUSSELS SPROUTS WITH GARLIC

These Brussels sprouts are special enough for company, and so I like to serve them for Thanksgiving dinner. If you can't find fresh sprouts, try using frozen ones.

—MYRA INNES AUBURN, KS

START TO FINISH: 30 MIN.
MAKES: 6 SERVINGS

- 1½ **pounds fresh Brussels sprouts**
- 2 **teaspoons olive oil**
- 3 **teaspoons butter, divided**
- 4 **garlic cloves, chopped**
- ½ **cup reduced-sodium chicken broth**
- ¼ **teaspoon salt**
- ⅛ **teaspoon pepper**

1. Trim Brussels sprout stems. Using a paring knife, cut an "X" in the bottom of each.
2. In a large saucepan, heat oil and 1 teaspoon butter over medium heat. Add the garlic; cook and stir 1-2 minutes or until garlic begins to color. Immediately add Brussels sprouts, stirring to coat.
3. Stir in broth, salt and pepper; bring to a boil. Reduce the heat;

simmer, covered, 8-10 minutes or until Brussels sprouts are tender. Drain. Add the remaining butter; toss to coat.
PER SERVING ⅔ *cup equals 83 cal., 3 g fat (1 g sat. fat), 5 mg chol., 198 mg sodium, 11 g carb., 4 g fiber, 4 g pro.* **Diabetic Exchanges:** *2 vegetable, ½ fat.*

SPRINGTIME BARLEY

While working as a sorority house mother, I would occasionally cook for the girls. They loved this medley.

—SHARON HELMICK COLFAX, WA

START TO FINISH: 30 MIN.
MAKES: 4 SERVINGS

- 1 **small onion, chopped**
- 1 **medium carrot, chopped**
- 1 **tablespoon butter**
- 1 **cup quick-cooking barley**
- 2 **cups reduced-sodium chicken broth, divided**
- ½ **pound fresh asparagus, trimmed and cut into 1-inch pieces**
- ¼ **teaspoon dried marjoram**
- ⅛ **teaspoon pepper**
- 2 **tablespoons shredded Parmesan cheese**

1. In a large skillet, saute onion and carrot in butter until crisp-tender. Stir in the barley; cook and stir for 1 minute. Stir in 1 cup broth. Bring to a boil. Reduce heat; cook and stir until most of the liquid is absorbed.
2. Add the asparagus. Cook for 15-20 minutes or until the barley is tender and liquid is absorbed, stirring occasionally and adding more broth as needed. Stir in the marjoram and pepper; sprinkle with cheese.
PER SERVING ¾ *cup equals 226 cal., 5 g fat (2 g sat. fat), 9 mg chol., 396 mg sodium, 39 g carb., 9 g fiber, 9 g pro.* **Diabetic Exchanges:** *2 starch, 1 vegetable, ½ fat.*

(5) INGREDIENTS

MINTY WATERMELON-CUCUMBER SALAD

Capturing many of the fantastic flavors of summer, this refreshing, beautiful salad will be the talk of any picnic or potluck.

—ROBLYNN HUNNISETT GUELPH, ON

START TO FINISH: 20 MIN.
MAKES: 16 SERVINGS (¾ CUP EACH)

- 8 **cups cubed seedless watermelon**
- 2 **English cucumbers, halved lengthwise and sliced**
- 6 **green onions, chopped**
- ¼ **cup minced fresh mint**
- ¼ **cup balsamic vinegar**
- ¼ **cup olive oil**
- ½ **teaspoon salt**
- ½ **teaspoon pepper**

In a large bowl, combine the watermelon, cucumbers, green onions and mint. In a small bowl, whisk the remaining ingredients. Pour over salad and toss to coat. Serve immediately or refrigerate, covered, for up to 2 hours before serving the salad.
PER SERVING ¾ *cup equals 60 cal., 3 g fat (trace sat. fat), 0 chol., 78 mg sodium, 9 g carb., 1 g fiber, 1 g pro.* **Diabetic Exchanges:** *½ fruit, ½ fat.*

MINTY WATERMELON-
CUCUMBER SALAD

LEMON HERB QUINOA

⑤INGREDIENTS

LEMON HERB QUINOA

My family is turning to quinoa more and more these days. It's a super grain that's packed with nutrients. Plus, it can be paired with any kind of main course.

—**JENN TIDWELL** FAIR OAKS, CA

START TO FINISH: 25 MIN.
MAKES: 4 SERVINGS

- 2   cups water
- 1   cup quinoa, rinsed
- ½   teaspoon salt, divided
- 1   tablespoon minced fresh basil
- 1   tablespoon minced fresh cilantro
- 1½ teaspoons minced fresh mint
- 1   teaspoon grated lemon peel

1. In a small saucepan, bring the water to a boil. Add the quinoa and ¼ teaspoon salt. Reduce heat; cover and simmer for 12-15 minutes or until liquid is absorbed.

2. Remove from the heat. Add the basil, cilantro, mint, lemon peel and remaining salt; fluff with a fork.

NOTE *Look for quinoa in the cereal, rice or organic food aisle.*

PER SERVING ⅔ *cup equals 160 cal., 2 g fat (trace sat. fat), 0 chol., 304 mg sodium, 29 g carb., 3 g fiber, 6 g pro.* **Diabetic Exchange:** *2 starch.*

TOP TIP

WHY QUINOA?

Quinoa (really a seed) is often referred to as the "the perfect grain" because, unlike most grains, it offers complete proteins. So it's an excellent choice for vegetarian and vegan meals, which can be low in protein.

DILLED NEW POTATOES

(5)INGREDIENTS

DILLED NEW POTATOES

With six kids at home, I try to grow as much of our food as possible. Our big potato patch means easy and affordable meals for a good part of the year. And this side is a hit!

—JENNIFER FERRIS BRONSON, MI

START TO FINISH: 25 MIN.
MAKES: 8 SERVINGS

- 2 **pounds baby red potatoes (about 24)**
- ¼ **cup butter, melted**
- 2 **tablespoons snipped fresh dill**
- 1 **tablespoon lemon juice**
- 1 **teaspoon salt**
- ½ **teaspoon pepper**

1. Place potatoes in a Dutch oven; add water to cover. Bring to a boil. Reduce heat; cook, uncovered, 15-20 minutes or until tender.

2. Drain; return to the pan. Mix remaining ingredients; drizzle over potatoes and toss to coat.
PER SERVING *¾ cup equals 180 cal., 8 g fat (5 g sat. fat), 20 mg chol., 447 mg sodium, 27 g carb., 2 g fiber, 3 g pro. **Diabetic Exchanges:** 2 starch, 1½ fat.*

HEIRLOOM TOMATO & ZUCCHINI SALAD

Tomato wedges give this salad a juicy bite. It's a smart use of fresh herbs and veggies from your own garden or the farmers market.

—MATTHEW HASS FRANKLIN, WI

START TO FINISH: 25 MIN.
MAKES: 12 SERVINGS (¾ CUP EACH)

- 7 **large heirloom tomatoes (about 2½ pounds), cut into wedges**
- 3 **medium zucchini, halved lengthwise and thinly sliced**
- 2 **medium sweet yellow peppers, thinly sliced**
- ⅓ **cup cider vinegar**
- 3 **tablespoons olive oil**
- 1 **tablespoon sugar**
- 1½ **teaspoons salt**
- 1 **tablespoon each minced fresh basil, parsley and tarragon**

1. In a large bowl, combine the tomatoes, zucchini and peppers. In a small bowl, whisk vinegar, oil, sugar and salt until blended. Stir in herbs.
2. Just before serving, drizzle dressing over salad; toss gently to coat.
PER SERVING *1 cup equals 68 cal., 4 g fat (1 g sat. fat), 0 chol., 306 mg sodium, 8 g carb., 2 g fiber, 2 g pro. **Diabetic Exchanges:** 1 vegetable, ½ fat.*

⑤ INGREDIENTS

MUSHROOM & PEA RICE PILAF

Almost anything can be in a rice pilaf, so add peas and portobello mushrooms for a burst of color and a variety of textures.

—**STACY MULLENS** GRESHAM, OR

START TO FINISH: 25 MIN.
MAKES: 6 SERVINGS

- 1 package (6.6 ounces) rice pilaf mix with toasted almonds
- 1 tablespoon butter
- 1½ cups fresh or frozen peas
- 1 cup sliced baby portobello mushrooms

1. Prepare pilaf according to the package directions.
2. In a large skillet, heat butter over medium heat. Add the peas and mushrooms; cook and stir 6-8 minutes or until tender. Stir in the rice.
PER SERVING ⅔ cup equals 177 cal., 6 g fat (2 g sat. fat), 10 mg chol., 352 mg sodium, 28 g carb., 3 g fiber, 5 g pro. **Diabetic Exchanges:** 2 starch, ½ fat.

HONEY-THYME BUTTERNUT SQUASH

Instead of potatoes, try whipping up mashed butternut squash with honey, butter and thyme. More than a delightful Thanksgiving side, this 30-minute dish is a new fall favorite for weeknight meals, too.

—**BIANCA NOISEUX** BRISTOL, CT

START TO FINISH: 30 MIN.
MAKES: 10 SERVINGS

- 1 large butternut squash (about 5 pounds), peeled and cubed
- ¼ cup butter, cubed
- 3 tablespoons half-and-half cream
- 2 tablespoons honey
- 2 teaspoons dried parsley flakes
- ½ teaspoon salt

- ⅛ teaspoon dried thyme
- ⅛ teaspoon coarsely ground pepper

1. In a large saucepan, bring 1 in. of water to a boil. Add squash; cover and cook for 10-15 minutes or until tender.
2. Drain. Mash squash with the remaining ingredients.
PER SERVING ¾ cup equals 145 cal., 5 g fat (3 g sat. fat), 14 mg chol., 161 mg sodium, 26 g carb., 7 g fiber, 2 g pro. **Diabetic Exchanges:** 1½ starch, 1 fat.

EASY GARDEN TOMATOES

Simple as it is, this is one of my go-to dishes. I made three batches the first time, and a few stray olive slices were the only things left on the platter by the end of the meal.

—**HEATHER AHRENS** COLUMBUS, OH

START TO FINISH: 15 MIN.
MAKES: 6 SERVINGS

- 3 large tomatoes, thinly sliced
- 1 large red onion, thinly sliced
- ⅓ cup olive oil
- ¼ cup red wine vinegar
- 2 garlic cloves, minced
- 1 tablespoon minced fresh basil or 1 teaspoon dried basil
- 1½ teaspoons minced fresh oregano or ½ teaspoon dried oregano
- ¾ cup crumbled feta cheese
- 1 can (2¼ ounces) sliced ripe olives, drained

Arrange the tomatoes and onion on a serving platter. In a small bowl, whisk the oil, vinegar, garlic, basil and oregano; drizzle over the salad. Top salad with cheese and olives. Chill until serving.
PER SERVING 1 serving equals 184 cal., 16 g fat (3 g sat. fat), 8 mg chol., 234 mg sodium, 8 g carb., 2 g fiber, 4 g pro.

⑤ INGREDIENTS

FAVORITE MASHED SWEET POTATOES

My family begs me to make this recipe during the holidays. They like it because pumpkin pie spice really brings out the best in the sweet potatoes. And I love that I can make it the day before!

—**SENJA MERRILL** SANDY, UT

START TO FINISH: 25 MIN.
MAKES: 8 SERVINGS

- 3 pounds sweet potatoes (about 6 medium), peeled and cubed
- 3 tablespoons orange juice
- 2 tablespoons brown sugar
- 2 tablespoons maple syrup
- ¼ teaspoon pumpkin pie spice

Place the sweet potatoes in a 6-qt. stockpot; add water to cover. Bring to a boil. Reduce heat; cook, uncovered, 10-15 minutes or until tender. Drain; return to pan. Mash potatoes, gradually adding orange juice, brown sugar, syrup and pie spice to reach desired consistency.
PER SERVING ⅔ cup equals 117 cal., trace fat (trace sat. fat), 0 chol., 10 mg sodium, 28 g carb., 3 g fiber, 1 g pro. **Diabetic Exchange:** 2 starch.

TOP TIP

SWEET PERKS

In addition to tasting delicious, sweet potatoes contain a lot of good-for-you nutrients! They're an excellent source of vitamin A and a good source of vitamins C and B6, fiber and potassium. All the more reason to enjoy these taters!

MUSHROOM & PEA
RICE PILAF

FAVORITE MASHED
SWEET POTATOES

EASY GARDEN
TOMATOES

LEMON
PARMESAN ORZO

(5) INGREDIENTS
LEMON PARMESAN ORZO

Fresh lemon peel and minced parsley make this springtime orzo side. My family asks for it all the time. It's fantastic with chicken, pork and fish.

—LESLIE PALMER SWAMPSCOTT, MA

START TO FINISH: 20 MIN.
MAKES: 4 SERVINGS

- 1 **cup uncooked whole wheat orzo pasta**
- 1 **tablespoon olive oil**
- ¼ **cup grated Parmesan cheese**
- 2 **tablespoons minced fresh parsley**
- ½ **teaspoon grated lemon peel**
- ¼ **teaspoon salt**
- ¼ **teaspoon pepper**

Cook orzo according to package directions; drain. Transfer to a small bowl; drizzle with oil. Stir in the remaining ingredients.

PER SERVING *½ cup equals 191 cal., 6 g fat (1 g sat. fat), 4 mg chol., 225 mg sodium, 28 g carb., 7 g fiber, 7 g pro.* **Diabetic Exchanges:** *2 starch, ½ fat.*

(5) INGREDIENTS
ROASTED CARROT FRIES

Turn carrot sticks into crispy baked fries with a healthy twist. They are simply delicious with sweet and spicy ketchup.

—TASTE OF HOME TEST KITCHEN

START TO FINISH: 20 MIN.
MAKES: 5 SERVINGS

- 1 **pound fresh carrots, cut into ½-inch sticks**
- 2 **teaspoons olive oil**
- ½ **teaspoon salt**

Place the carrots in a greased 15x10x1-in. baking pan. Drizzle with oil and sprinkle with salt; toss to coat. Bake, uncovered, at 450° for 10-12 minutes or until crisp-tender.

HOLIDAY BRUSSELS SPROUTS

PER SERVING *½ cup equals 53 cal., 2 g fat (trace sat. fat), 0 chol., 299 mg sodium, 9 g carb., 3 g fiber, 1 g pro.* **Diabetic Exchange:** *2 vegetable.*

HOLIDAY BRUSSELS SPROUTS

Make Brussels sprouts extra special for the holidays with peas, celery and, of course, bacon. It's easy to double the recipe if needed.

—JODIE BECKMAN COUNCIL BLUFFS, IA

START TO FINISH: 25 MIN.
MAKES: 6 SERVINGS

- 1 **package (16 ounces) frozen Brussels sprouts**
- 1 **package (10 ounces) frozen peas**
- 2 **tablespoons butter**
- 2 **celery ribs, chopped**
- 2 **bacon strips, cooked and crumbled**
- 2 **tablespoons minced fresh chives**

1. Cook Brussels sprouts and peas according to the package directions; drain.
2. In a large skillet, heat the butter over medium-high heat. Add celery; cook and stir until crisp-tender. Add Brussels sprouts, peas, bacon and chives; toss to combine.

PER SERVING *⅔ cup equals 115 cal., 5 g fat (3 g sat. fat), 12 mg chol., 147 mg sodium, 13 g carb., 5 g fiber, 6 g pro.* **Diabetic Exchanges:** *2 vegetable, 1 fat.*

(5) INGREDIENTS

ROASTED ASPARAGUS WITH FETA

Pretty and easy to assemble, this simple side dish is delicious. With its festive appearance, it fits right in during the holidays.

—**PHYLLIS SCHMALZ** KANSAS CITY, KS

START TO FINISH: 25 MIN.
MAKES: 6 SERVINGS

- 2 **pounds fresh asparagus, trimmed**
- 1 **tablespoon olive oil**
  Kosher salt to taste
- 2 **medium tomatoes, seeded and chopped**
- ½ **cup crumbled feta cheese**

1. Arrange the asparagus in an ungreased 13x9-in. baking dish. Drizzle with the oil and sprinkle with salt.
2. Bake, uncovered, at 400° for 15-20 minutes or until tender. Transfer to a serving dish; sprinkle with tomatoes and feta cheese. Serve immediately.
PER SERVING *1 serving (calculated without salt) equals 72 cal., 4 g fat (1 g sat. fat), 5 mg chol., 103 mg sodium, 6 g carb., 2 g fiber, 4 g pro.* ***Diabetic Exchanges:*** *1 vegetable, 1 fat.*

(5) INGREDIENTS

SAUTEED SQUASH WITH TOMATOES & ONIONS

I love cooking food for family. My zucchini dish with tomatoes is like ratatouille without the eggplant.

—**ADAN FRANCO** MILWAUKEE, WI

START TO FINISH: 20 MIN.
MAKES: 8 SERVINGS

- 2 **tablespoons olive oil**
- 1 **medium onion, finely chopped**
- 4 **medium zucchini, chopped**
- 2 **large tomatoes, finely chopped**
- 1 **teaspoon salt**
- ¼ **teaspoon pepper**

1. In a large skillet, heat oil over medium-high heat. Add the onion; cook and stir 2-4 minutes or until tender. Add zucchini; cook and stir for 3 minutes.
2. Stir in tomatoes, salt and pepper; cook and stir 4-6 minutes longer or until squash is tender. Serve with a slotted spoon.
PER SERVING *¾ cup equals 60 cal., 4 g fat (1 g sat. fat), 0 chol., 306 mg sodium, 6 g carb., 2 g fiber, 2 g pro.* ***Diabetic Exchanges:*** *1 vegetable, ½ fat.*

TOP TIP

WHEN SHOULD YOU BUY ORGANIC?

Most of us have a budget to watch. So when should you buy organic fruit and veggies to avoid high levels of pesticide residue (ick!), and when can you buy conventional ones that don't have so much (yay!)?

- **Splurge on organic:** peppers, zucchini, celery, tomatoes, cucumbers, grapes, leafy greens, apples, nectarines, peaches, potatoes, snap peas and strawberries.
- **Save with conventional:** pineapple, avocados, cabbage, cantaloupe, eggplant, asparagus, cauliflower, kiwifruit, onions, sweet corn and mangoes.

SAUTEED SQUASH WITH TOMATOES & ONIONS

PESTO PASTA & POTATOES

PESTO PASTA & POTATOES

Although this healthy pasta dish is pretty easy to begin with, the cooking method makes it even easier. You can throw the green beans and pasta into one big pot.

—**LAURA FLOWERS** MOSCOW, ID

START TO FINISH: 30 MIN.
MAKES: 12 SERVINGS

- 1½ **pounds small red potatoes, halved**
- 12 **ounces uncooked whole grain spiral pasta**
- 3 **cups cut fresh or frozen green beans**
- 1 **jar (6½ ounces) prepared pesto**
- 1 **cup grated Parmigiano-Reggiano cheese**

1. Place the potatoes in a large saucepan; add water to cover. Bring to a boil. Reduce heat; cook, uncovered, 9-11 minutes or until tender. Drain water; transfer to a large bowl.

2. Meanwhile, cook the pasta according to package directions, adding green beans during the last 5 minutes of cooking; drain, reserving ¾ cup pasta water.

3. Add the pasta and green beans to potatoes. Stir in the pesto, cheese and enough reserved pasta water to coat.

PER SERVING *¾ cup equals 261 cal., 10 g fat (3 g sat. fat), 11 mg chol., 233 mg sodium, 34 g carb., 5 g fiber, 11 g pro.* **Diabetic Exchanges:** *2 starch, 2 fat.*

PROSCIUTTO BREADSTICKS

⑤ INGREDIENTS

PARTY TORTELLINI SALAD

Introduce this crowd-pleasing salad with a light vinaigrette dressing at your next gathering. It's an appealing addition to cookouts and picnics.
—**MARY WILT** IPSWICH, MA

START TO FINISH: 25 MIN.
MAKES: 10 SERVINGS

- 1 **package (19 ounces) frozen cheese tortellini**
- 2 **cups fresh broccoli florets**
- 1 **medium sweet red pepper, chopped**
- ½ **cup pimiento-stuffed olives, halved**
- ¾ **cup reduced-fat red wine vinaigrette**
- ½ **teaspoon salt**

1. Cook tortellini according to the package directions; drain and rinse in cold water.
2. In a large bowl, combine the tortellini, broccoli, red pepper and olives. Drizzle with dressing and sprinkle with salt; toss to coat. Cover and refrigerate until serving.
PER SERVING *¾ cup equals 156 cal., 7 g fat (2 g sat. fat), 8 mg chol., 596 mg sodium, 19 g carb., 1 g fiber, 6 g pro.* **Diabetic Exchanges:** *1 starch, 1 lean meat, ½ fat.*

THE SKINNY

VEGGIE-FULL SALAD

This pasta salad gets over a third of its volume from healthy veggies. Adding veggies is a great way to stretch fat- and calorie-loaded ingredients (meat, cheese and tortellini for example), so toss in even more if you'd like.

---

⑤ INGREDIENTS

PROSCIUTTO BREADSTICKS

Pair these breadsticks with your favorite pasta or egg dish. They're a tasty substitute for bacon and toast at brunch or any time.
—**MARIA REGAKIS** SAUGUS, MA

START TO FINISH: 30 MIN.
MAKES: 1 DOZEN

- 6 **thin slices prosciutto or deli ham**
- 1 **tube (11 ounces) refrigerated breadsticks**
- 1 **large egg, lightly beaten**
- ¼ **teaspoon fennel seed, crushed**
- ¼ **teaspoon pepper**

1. Preheat oven to 375°. Cut each slice of prosciutto into four thin strips. Unroll dough; separate into breadsticks. Top each with two strips prosciutto, pressing gently to adhere. Twist each breadstick; place on ungreased baking sheet, pressing the ends down firmly. Brush with beaten egg.
2. Combine fennel and pepper; sprinkle over breadsticks. Bake breadsticks for 10-13 minutes or until golden brown.
PER SERVING *1 breadstick equals 86 cal., 2 g fat (1 g sat. fat), 8 mg chol., 323 mg sodium, 13 g carb., trace fiber, 4 g pro.* **Diabetic Exchange:** *1 starch.*

PEAS A LA FRANCAISE

I love peas, especially in this recipe. With tiny pearl onions and accents of thyme and chervil, the dish is lovely to present.

—CHRISTINE FRAZIER
AUBURNDALE, FL

START TO FINISH: 30 MIN.
MAKES: 12 SERVINGS (½ CUP EACH)

- 1½ cups pearl onions, trimmed
- ¼ cup butter, cubed
- ¼ cup water
- 1 tablespoon sugar
- 1 teaspoon salt
- ¼ teaspoon dried thyme
- ¼ teaspoon dried chervil
- ¼ teaspoon pepper
- 2 packages (16 ounces each) frozen peas, thawed
- 2 cups shredded lettuce

1. In a Dutch oven, bring 6 cups water to a boil. Add pearl onions; boil for 3 minutes. Drain and rinse in cold water; peel and set aside.
2. In the same saucepan, melt butter over medium heat. Stir in the onions, water, sugar and seasonings. Add peas and lettuce; stir until blended. Cover and cook for 6-8 minutes or until vegetables are tender. Serve vegetables with a slotted spoon.
PER SERVING ½ cup equals 112 cal., 4 g fat (2 g sat. fat), 10 mg chol., 315 mg sodium, 15 g carb., 4 g fiber, 4 g pro. **Diabetic Exchanges:** 1 starch, 1 fat.

FREEZE IT
BLUEBERRY OATMEAL MUFFINS

Grab one of these tender muffins and go. Oats, blueberries and yogurt make them tasty and nutritious.

—DONNA BROCKETT KINGFISHER, OK

START TO FINISH: 30 MIN.
MAKES: 1 DOZEN

- 1¼ cups all-purpose flour
- 1 cup quick-cooking oats
- ½ cup packed brown sugar
- 2 teaspoons baking powder
- ½ teaspoon salt
- ½ teaspoon ground cinnamon
- ¼ teaspoon baking soda
- ¼ teaspoon ground nutmeg
- 1 large egg, lightly beaten
- 1 cup (8 ounces) plain yogurt
- ¼ cup butter, melted
- 1 cup fresh blueberries

1. In a large bowl, combine the first eight ingredients. Combine the egg, yogurt and butter; stir into the dry ingredients just until moistened. Fold in blueberries.
2. Coat the muffin cups with cooking spray or use paper liners; fill three-fourths full with batter. Bake at 400° for 18-22 minutes or until a toothpick inserted in the muffin comes out clean. Cool for 5 minutes before removing from pan to a wire rack. Serve warm.
FREEZE OPTION *Wrap muffins in foil; transfer to a resealable plastic freezer bag. May be frozen for up to 3 months. To use frozen muffins: Remove the foil. Thaw at room temperature. Serve warm.*
PER SERVING *1 muffin equals 167 cal., 6 g fat (3 g sat. fat), 31 mg chol., 249 mg sodium, 26 g carb., 1 g fiber, 4 g pro.* **Diabetic Exchanges:** *1½ starch, 1 fat.*

ARTICHOKE TOMATO SALAD

Dress up this salad by adding shredded rotisserie chicken or crumbling feta cheese on top.

—DEBORAH WILLIAMS PEORIA, AZ

START TO FINISH: 20 MIN.
MAKES: 8 SERVINGS

- 5 large tomatoes (about 2 pounds), cut into wedges
- ¼ teaspoon salt
- ¼ teaspoon pepper
- 1 jar (7½ ounces) marinated quartered artichoke hearts, drained
- 1 can (2¼ ounces) sliced ripe olives, drained
- 2 tablespoons minced fresh parsley
- 2 tablespoons white wine vinegar
- 2 garlic cloves, minced

Arrange the tomato wedges on a large platter; sprinkle with salt and pepper. In a small bowl, toss the remaining ingredients; spoon over tomatoes.
PER SERVING *¾ cup equals 74 cal., 5 g fat (1 g sat. fat), 0 chol., 241 mg sodium, 7 g carb., 2 g fiber, 1 g pro.* **Diabetic Exchanges:** *1 vegetable, 1 fat.*

HOW-TO
MINCE PARSLEY

1. Holding the handle of a chef's knife with one hand, rest fingers of your other hand on the top of the blade near tip.
2. Using the handle to guide and apply pressure, move knife in an arc across the parsley leaves, cutting with a rocking motion until the pieces are no larger than ⅛ in.

ARTICHOKE
TOMATO SALAD

THYME-ROASTED
CARROTS

(5) INGREDIENTS
THYME-ROASTED CARROTS

Cutting the carrots lengthwise makes this dish look extra pretty. For even more elegance, garnish with sprigs of either fresh thyme or parsley.

—DEIRDRE COX KANSAS CITY, MO

START TO FINISH: 30 MIN.
MAKES: ABOUT 12 SERVINGS
(2 CARROT HALVES EACH)

- 3 pounds medium carrots, halved lengthwise
- 2 tablespoons minced fresh thyme or 2 teaspoons dried thyme
- 2 tablespoons canola oil
- 1 tablespoon honey
- 1 teaspoon salt

Preheat the oven to 400°. Divide the carrots between two greased 15x10x1-in. baking pans. In a small bowl, mix the thyme, oil, honey and salt; brush over the carrots. Roast 20-25 minutes or until tender.
PER SERVING *2 carrot halves equals 73 cal., 3 g fat (trace sat. fat), 0 chol., 275 mg sodium, 12 g carb., 3 g fiber, 1 g pro.* **Diabetic Exchanges:** *1 vegetable, ½ starch, ½ fat.*

TENDER BISCUITS

These rolls are low in fat but not in flavor. They'll dress up a weeknight meal with ease.

—ANE BURKE BELLA VISTA, AR

START TO FINISH: 30 MIN.
MAKES: 2 BISCUITS

- ⅓ cup self-rising flour
- 1 tablespoon grated Parmesan cheese
- ⅛ teaspoon garlic salt
- 3 tablespoons reduced-fat cream cheese
- 3 tablespoons fat-free milk
- 1 tablespoon fat-free plain yogurt

1. In a small bowl, combine the flour, Parmesan cheese and garlic salt. Cut in cream cheese until mixture resembles coarse crumbs. Stir in milk and yogurt just until mixture is moistened.
2. Drop by scant ⅓ cupfuls 2 in. apart onto a baking sheet coated with cooking spray. Bake biscuits at 400° for 12-15 minutes or until golden brown. Serve warm.
PER SERVING *1 biscuit equals 142 cal., 5 g fat (4 g sat. fat), 18 mg chol., 497 mg sodium, 17 g carb., trace fiber, 6 g pro.* **Diabetic Exchanges:** *1 starch, 1 fat.*

TENDER BISCUITS

ORANGE POMEGRANATE
SALAD WITH HONEY

⑤ INGREDIENTS

ORANGE POMEGRANATE SALAD WITH HONEY

I discovered this special fruit salad in a cooking class. If you can, try to find orange flower water (also called orange blossom water)—it perks up the orange segments. But orange juice works well, too!

—CAROL RICHARDSON MARTY
LYNWOOD, WA

START TO FINISH: 15 MIN.
MAKES: 6 SERVINGS

- 5 medium oranges or 10 clementines
- ½ cup pomegranate seeds
- 2 tablespoons honey
- 1 to 2 teaspoons orange flower water or orange juice

1. Cut a thin slice from top and bottom of each orange; stand orange upright on a cutting board. With a knife, cut off peel and outer membrane from oranges. Cut crosswise into ½-in. slices.

2. Arrange the orange slices on a serving platter; sprinkle with pomegranate seeds. In a small bowl, mix the honey and orange flower water; drizzle over fruit.

PER SERVING ⅔ *cup equals 62 cal., trace fat (trace sat. fat), 0 chol., 2 mg sodium, 15 g carb., trace fiber, 1 g pro.* **Diabetic Exchange:** *1 fruit.*

TOP TIP

EDIBLE SEEDS

Yes, pomegranate seeds are edible! The seeds and surrounding juice sacs (arils) are the only parts of the pomegranate you can eat. One medium pomegranate (weighing about 8 ounces) yields roughly ¾ cup arils.

GRILLED SWEET POTATO WEDGES

I love it when an entire meal can be cooked outside on the grill and I don't have to fuss around in the kitchen. This recipe is easy and healthy at the same time. It's fun dipping the wedges in spicy sauce.
—NATALIE KNOWLTON KAMAS, UT

START TO FINISH: 30 MIN.
MAKES: 8 SERVINGS

- 4 **large sweet potatoes, cut into ½-inch wedges**
- ½ **teaspoon garlic salt**
- ¼ **teaspoon pepper**

DIPPING SAUCE

- ½ **cup reduced-fat mayonnaise**
- ½ **cup fat-free plain yogurt**
- 1 **teaspoon ground cumin**
- ½ **teaspoon seasoned salt**
- ½ **teaspoon paprika**
- ½ **teaspoon chili powder**

1. Place the potatoes in a large saucepan and cover with water. Bring to a boil. Reduce heat; cover and simmer 4-5 minutes or until crisp-tender. Drain; pat dry with paper towels. Sprinkle potatoes with garlic salt and pepper.

2. Grill, covered, over medium heat for 10-12 minutes or until tender, turning once. In a small bowl, combine the mayonnaise, yogurt and seasonings. Serve with sweet potato wedges.

PER SERVING ¾ *cup with 2 tablespoons sauce equals 166 cal., 5 g fat (1 g sat. fat), 6 mg chol., 349 mg sodium, 28 g carb., 3 g fiber, 3 g pro.* **Diabetic Exchanges:** *1½ starch, 1 fat.*

GRILLED SWEET POTATO WEDGES

CRUNCHY
BROCCOLI SALAD

CRUNCHY BROCCOLI SALAD

I never liked broccoli when I was younger, but now I'm hooked on this salad's light, sweet taste. It gives broccoli a whole new look and taste, in my opinion.
—**JESSICA CONREY** CEDAR RAPIDS, IA

START TO FINISH: 25 MIN.
MAKES: 10 SERVINGS

- 8 cups fresh broccoli florets (about 1 pound)
- 1 bunch green onions, thinly sliced
- ½ cup dried cranberries
- 3 tablespoons canola oil
- 3 tablespoons seasoned rice vinegar
- 2 tablespoons sugar
- ¼ cup sunflower kernels
- 3 bacon strips, cooked and crumbled

In a large bowl, combine broccoli, green onions and cranberries. In a small bowl, whisk oil, vinegar and sugar until blended; drizzle over broccoli mixture and toss to coat. Refrigerate until serving. Sprinkle with sunflower kernels and bacon before serving.

PER SERVING *¾ cup equals 121 cal., 7 g fat (1 g sat. fat), 2 mg chol., 233 mg sodium, 14 g carb., 3 g fiber, 3 g pro.* **Diabetic Exchanges:** *1 vegetable, 1 fat, ½ starch.*

⑤ INGREDIENTS
SWISS CHARD WITH ONIONS & GARLIC

I like to serve Swiss chard prepared this way with pasta, but it's also a tasty side dish on its own. My boys love it and ask for it often.
—**REBEKAH CHAPPEL** PORTALES, NM

START TO FINISH: 25 MIN.
MAKES: 6 SERVINGS

- 2 tablespoons olive oil
- 2 medium onions, chopped
- 6 garlic cloves, sliced
- ½ cup white balsamic vinegar
- 2 bunches Swiss chard, coarsely chopped (about 16 cups)
- ½ cup walnut halves, toasted
- ¼ teaspoon salt
- ¼ teaspoon pepper

1. In a 6-qt. stockpot, heat oil over medium-high heat. Add onions; cook and stir until tender. Add garlic; cook 1 minute longer.
2. Add vinegar, stirring to loosen any browned bits from pot. Add the remaining ingredients; cook for 4-6 minutes or until chard is tender, stirring occasionally.

NOTE *To toast the nuts, bake in a shallow pan in a 350° oven for 5-10 minutes or cook in a skillet over low heat until they are lightly browned, stirring occasionally.*

PER SERVING *⅔ cup equals 159 cal., 10 g fat (1 g sat. fat), 0 chol., 381 mg sodium, 16 g carb., 3 g fiber, 4 g pro.* **Diabetic Exchanges:** *2 fat, 1 starch.*

HOW-TO

TOAST NUTS IN MICROWAVE

Really in a pinch and need toasted nuts for a recipe? Place nuts in a microwave-safe dish. Microwave, uncovered, on high for 2-3 minutes or until lightly toasted, stirring twice. Watch carefully to avoid burning the nuts. You may need to adjust the time, depending on your microwave's power and the amount of nuts you are toasting.

EASY BAKED MUSHROOMS

Bet you've never had mushrooms quite like these! Skipping the deep fryer keeps them low in fat.

—**DENISE DIPACE** MEDFORD, NJ

START TO FINISH: 30 MIN.
MAKES: 4 SERVINGS

- 1 **pound medium fresh mushrooms, halved**
- 2 **tablespoons olive oil**
- ¼ **cup seasoned bread crumbs**
- ¼ **teaspoon garlic powder**
- ¼ **teaspoon pepper**
  Fresh parsley, optional

1. Place mushrooms on a baking sheet. Drizzle with oil; toss to coat. In a small bowl, combine the bread crumbs, garlic powder and pepper; sprinkle over mushrooms.
2. Bake, uncovered, at 425° for 18-20 minutes or until lightly browned. Garnish with parsley if desired.
PER SERVING *¾ cup equals 116 cal., 8 g fat (1 g sat. fat), 0 chol., 112 mg sodium, 10 g carb., 2 g fiber, 4 g pro.* **Diabetic Exchanges:** *1½ fat, ½ starch.*

LEMON-THYME ASPARAGUS

Out of thyme? No worries, the beauty of this dish is its versatility. Use another herb instead.

—**SARAH REID** OSHAWA, ON

START TO FINISH: 20 MIN.
MAKES: 4 SERVINGS

- 1 **pound fresh asparagus, trimmed and cut into 1-inch pieces**
- ½ **pound sliced fresh mushrooms**
- 1 **tablespoon butter**
- 1 **teaspoon olive oil**
- 1½ **teaspoons minced fresh thyme or ½ teaspoon dried thyme**
- 1 **teaspoon grated lemon peel**
- ½ **teaspoon salt**
- ½ **teaspoon lemon juice**
- ¼ **teaspoon pepper**

In a large skillet, saute asparagus and mushrooms in butter and oil until tender. Stir in the remaining ingredients.
PER SERVING *1 cup equals 64 cal., 4 g fat (2 g sat. fat), 8 mg chol., 324 mg sodium, 5 g carb., 2 g fiber, 3 g pro.* **Diabetic Exchanges:** *1 vegetable, 1 fat.*

CRUNCHY APPLE SALAD

A salad with fiber-rich fruit, creamy dressing and crunchy walnuts wins lots of fans. Add some low-fat granola for even more crunch.

—**KATHY ARMSTRONG** POST FALLS, ID

START TO FINISH: 15 MIN.
MAKES: 5 SERVINGS

- ⅓ **cup fat-free sugar-free vanilla yogurt**
- ⅓ **cup reduced-fat whipped topping**
- ¼ **teaspoon plus ⅛ teaspoon ground cinnamon, divided**
- ¼ **cup dried cranberries**
- 2 **medium red apples, chopped**
- 1 **large Granny Smith apple, chopped**
- 2 **tablespoons chopped walnuts**

In a large bowl, combine yogurt, whipped topping and ¼ teaspoon cinnamon. Add cranberries and apples; toss to coat. Refrigerate until serving. Sprinkle with the walnuts and remaining cinnamon before serving.
PER SERVING *¾ cup equals 109 cal., 3 g fat (1 g sat. fat), trace chol., 12 mg sodium, 22 g carb., 3 g fiber, 2 g pro.* **Diabetic Exchanges:** *1 fruit, ½ starch, ½ fat.*

HOW-TO

MAKE YOUR OWN SEASONED BREAD CRUMBS

Break slices of dried bread into pieces and process in a blender or food processor until you have fine crumbs, then season the crumbs as you like. A basic recipe might include dried basil and oregano, garlic and onion powder, grated Parmesan cheese, salt and paprika. Start with small amounts of the seasonings and add more as needed. One slice of dried bread will yield about ¼ cup of fine, dry bread crumbs.

EASY BAKED
MUSHROOMS

LEMON-THYME
ASPARAGUS

CRUNCHY
APPLE SALAD

SHREDDED GINGERED
BRUSSELS SPROUTS

(5) INGREDIENTS
SHREDDED GINGERED BRUSSELS SPROUTS

If you know folks who usually turn away from Brussels sprouts, have them try these. One bite just might make them converts.

—JAMES SCHEND
PLEASANT PRAIRIE, WI

START TO FINISH: 25 MIN.
MAKES: 6 SERVINGS

- 1 **pound fresh Brussels sprouts (about 5½ cups)**
- 1 **tablespoon olive oil**
- 1 **small onion, finely chopped**
- 1 **tablespoon minced fresh gingerroot**
- 1 **garlic clove, minced**
- ½ **teaspoon salt**
- 2 **tablespoons water**
- ¼ **teaspoon pepper**

1. Trim Brussels sprouts. Cut sprouts lengthwise in half; cut crosswise into thin slices.
2. Place a large skillet over medium-high heat. Add Brussels sprouts; cook and stir 2-3 minutes or until sprouts begin to brown lightly. Add oil and toss to coat. Stir in the onion, ginger, garlic and salt. Add water; reduce heat to medium and cook, covered, for 1-2 minutes or until vegetables are tender. Stir in the pepper.
PER SERVING *¾ cup equals 56 cal., 2 g fat (trace sat. fat), 0 chol., 214 mg sodium, 8 g carb., 3 g fiber, 2 g pro. **Diabetic Exchanges:** 1 vegetable, ½ fat.*

TENDER WHOLE WHEAT MUFFINS

Want oven-baked treats but need something to fit your diet? Simple whole wheat muffins are wonderful paired with soup or spread with a little jam for breakfast.

—KRISTINE CHAYES SMITHTOWN, NY

START TO FINISH: 30 MIN.
MAKES: 10 MUFFINS

- 1 **cup all-purpose flour**
- 1 **cup whole wheat flour**
- 2 **tablespoons sugar**
- 2½ **teaspoons baking powder**
- 1 **teaspoon salt**
- 1 **large egg**
- 1¼ **cups milk**
- 3 **tablespoons butter, melted**

1. Preheat oven to 400°. In a large bowl, whisk flours, sugar, baking powder and salt. In another bowl, whisk egg, milk and melted butter until blended. Add to flour mixture; stir just until moistened.
2. Fill greased muffin cups three-fourths full. Bake muffins 15-17 minutes or until a toothpick inserted in the center comes out clean. Cool for 5 minutes before removing from pan to a wire rack. Serve warm.
PER SERVING *1 muffin equals 152 cal., 5 g fat (3 g sat. fat), 35 mg chol., 393 mg sodium, 22 g carb., 2 g fiber, 5 g pro. **Diabetic Exchanges:** 1½ starch, 1 fat.*

TENDER WHOLE WHEAT MUFFINS

STRAWBERRY CREAM
CHEESE PIE, PAGE 239

BONUS:
LIGHT DESSERTS

243

229

220

CHOCOLATE ANGEL CUPCAKES WITH COCONUT CREAM FROSTING

Sweeten any meal with these fun, creamy frosted chocolate cupcakes that take just minutes to make. Their finger-licking flavor packs far fewer calories and less fat than you'll find in most traditional desserts!

—**MANDY RIVERS** LEXINGTON, SC

PREP: 15 MIN.
BAKE: 15 MIN. + COOLING
MAKES: 2 DOZEN

- 1 package (16 ounces) angel food cake mix
- ¾ cup baking cocoa
- 1 cup (8 ounces) reduced-fat sour cream
- 1 cup confectioners' sugar
- ⅛ teaspoon coconut extract
- 2½ cups reduced-fat whipped topping
- ¾ cup flaked coconut, toasted

1. Prepare cake mix according to package directions for cupcakes, adding cocoa when mixing.
2. Fill foil- or paper-lined muffin cups two-thirds full. Bake at 375° for 11-15 minutes or until the cake springs back when lightly touched and the cracks feel dry. Cool for 10 minutes before removing the cupcakes from pans to wire racks to cool completely.
3. For frosting, in a large bowl, combine sour cream, confectioners' sugar and extract until smooth. Fold in whipped topping. Frost cupcakes. Sprinkle with coconut. Refrigerate leftovers.
PER SERVING *1 cupcake equals 142 cal., 3 g fat (2 g sat. fat), 3 mg chol., 154 mg sodium, 27 g carb., 1 g fiber, 3 g pro.* **Diabetic Exchanges:** *1½ starch, ½ fat.*

 **INGREDIENTS**

LEMON-APRICOT FRUIT POPS

With just 31 calories, a kiss of sugar and lots of vitamin C, this is one lightly refreshing summer dessert everyone can find room for.

—**AYSHA SCHURMAN** AMMON, ID

PREP: 15 MIN. + FREEZING
MAKES: 6 SERVINGS

- ¼ cup orange juice
- 1 teaspoon grated lemon peel
- ¼ cup lemon juice
- 4 teaspoons sugar
- 1 cup sliced fresh apricots (4-5 medium)
- ½ cup ice cubes
- 1 teaspoon minced fresh mint, optional
- 6 freezer pop molds or 6 paper cups (3 ounces each) and wooden pop sticks

1. Place the first six ingredients in a blender; cover and process until blended. If desired, stir in mint.
2. Pour into molds or paper cups. Top molds with holders. If using cups, top with foil and insert sticks through foil. Freeze until firm.
PER SERVING *1 pop equals 31 cal., trace fat (trace sat. fat), 0 chol., trace sodium, 8 g carb., 1 g fiber, trace pro.* **Diabetic Exchange:** *½ fruit.*

THE SKINNY

NO-GUILT POPS

With only 11 little calories from added sugar in these pops, they're a fresh and tasty, low-cal way to beat the heat.

CHOCOLATE ANGEL CUPCAKES WITH COCONUT CREAM FROSTING

**LEMON-APRICOT
FRUIT POPS**

HOT FUDGE
CAKE

HOT FUDGE CAKE

What better way to top off a great meal than with a rich, chocolaty cake that makes its own sauce? Mom served it with a scoop of ice cream or a drizzle of cream, but why not try the lower fat versions?

—**VERA REID** LARAMIE, WY

PREP: 20 MIN. • **BAKE:** 35 MIN.
MAKES: 9 SERVINGS

- 1 **cup all-purpose flour**
- ¾ **cup sugar**
- 6 **tablespoons baking cocoa, divided**
- 2 **teaspoons baking powder**
- ¼ **teaspoon salt**
- ½ **cup 2% milk**
- 2 **tablespoons canola oil**
- 1 **teaspoon vanilla extract**
- 1 **cup packed brown sugar**
- 1¾ **cups hot water**
  Ice cream or whipped cream, optional

1. Preheat oven to 350°. In a bowl, whisk flour, sugar, 2 tablespoons cocoa, baking powder and salt. In another bowl, whisk milk, oil and vanilla until blended. Add to flour mixture; stir just until moistened.
2. Transfer to an ungreased 9-in. square baking pan. In a small bowl, mix brown sugar and remaining cocoa; sprinkle over batter. Pour hot water over all; do not stir.
3. Bake 35-40 minutes. Serve cake warm. If desired, top with ice cream or whipped cream.
PER SERVING *1 serving (calculated without whipped cream or ice cream) equals 253 cal., 4 g fat (1 g sat. fat), 2 mg chol., 171 mg sodium, 54 g carb., 1 g fiber, 3 g pro.*

BANANA PUDDING

My son enlisted in the Marines after high school and I didn't see him for more than two years. When he finally arrived back home, I grabbed hold of him at the airport and burst out crying. And when we got to our house, the first thing he ate was two bowls of my banana pudding.

—STEPHANIE HARRIS
MONTPELIER, VA

PREP: 35 MIN. + CHILLING
MAKES: 9 SERVINGS

- ¾ cup sugar
- ¼ cup all-purpose flour
- ¼ teaspoon salt
- 3 cups 2% milk
- 3 large eggs
- 1½ teaspoons vanilla extract
- 8 ounces vanilla wafers (about 60 cookies), divided
- 4 large ripe bananas, cut into ¼-inch slices

1. In a large saucepan, mix sugar, flour and salt. Whisk in milk. Cook and stir over medium heat until thickened and bubbly. Reduce heat to low; cook and stir for 2 minutes longer. Remove from heat.

2. In a small bowl, whisk the eggs. Whisk a small amount of the hot mixture into eggs; return all to pan, whisking constantly. Bring to a gentle boil; cook and stir 2 minutes. Remove from the heat. Stir in vanilla. Cool 15 minutes, stirring occasionally.

3. In an ungreased 8-in. square baking dish, layer 25 vanilla wafers, half of the banana slices and half of the pudding. Repeat layers.

4. Press plastic wrap onto surface of pudding. Refrigerate 4 hours or overnight. Just before serving the pudding, crush remaining wafers and sprinkle over top.

PER SERVING *1 serving equals 302 cal., 7 g fat (2 g sat. fat), 80 mg chol., 206 mg sodium, 55 g carb., 2 g fiber, 7 g pro.*

BANANA
PUDDING

ZUCCHINI CHOCOLATE
CAKE WITH ORANGE GLAZE

ZUCCHINI CHOCOLATE CAKE WITH ORANGE GLAZE

This lightened-up version of a family favorite has a lovely chocolate flavor with a hint of orange—and crunch from walnuts. Applesauce takes the place of some fat, cutting calories.
—**BARBARA WORREL** GRANBURY, TX

PREP: 20 MIN.
BAKE: 50 MIN. + COOLING
MAKES: 16 SERVINGS

- ½ **cup butter, softened**
- 1½ **cups sugar**
- 2 **large eggs**
- ¼ **cup unsweetened applesauce**
- 1 **teaspoon vanilla extract**
- 2½ **cups all-purpose flour**
- ½ **cup baking cocoa**
- 1¼ **teaspoons baking powder**
- 1 **teaspoon salt**
- 1 **teaspoon ground cinnamon**
- ½ **teaspoon baking soda**
- ½ **cup fat-free milk**
- 3 **cups shredded zucchini**
- ½ **cup chopped walnuts**
- 1 **tablespoon grated orange peel**

GLAZE
- 1¼ **cups confectioners' sugar**
- 2 **tablespoons orange juice**
- 1 **teaspoon vanilla extract**

1. Coat a 10-in. fluted tube pan with cooking spray and sprinkle with flour.
2. In a large bowl, cream the butter and sugar until light and fluffy. Add the eggs, one at a time, beating well after each addition. Beat in the applesauce and vanilla.
3. Combine flour, cocoa, baking powder, salt, cinnamon and baking soda; add to the creamed mixture alternately with milk, beating well after each addition. Fold in the zucchini, walnuts and orange peel.
4. Transfer to prepared pan. Bake at 350° for 50-60 minutes or until a toothpick inserted near the center comes out clean.
5. Cool for 10 minutes before removing from pan to a wire rack to cool completely. Combine glaze ingredients; drizzle over cake.
PER SERVING *1 slice equals 282 cal., 9 g fat (4 g sat. fat), 42 mg chol., 273 mg sodium, 47 g carb., 2 g fiber, 4 g pro.*

APPLE OATMEAL COOKIES

When I took these yummy cookies to work, they were gone in seconds. They're a wonderfully welcome snack that's low in calories!
—**NICKI WOODS** SPRINGFIELD, MO

PREP: 10 MIN. • **BAKE:** 15 MIN./BATCH
MAKES: ABOUT 5 DOZEN

- 1 **package yellow cake mix (regular size)**
- 1½ **cups quick-cooking oats**
- ½ **cup packed brown sugar**
- 2 **teaspoons ground cinnamon**
- 1 **large egg**
- ¾ **cup unsweetened applesauce**
- 1 **cup finely chopped peeled apple**
- ½ **cup raisins**

1. In a large bowl, combine the cake mix, oats, brown sugar and cinnamon. In a small bowl, combine the egg, applesauce, apple and raisins. Stir into oat mixture and mix well.
2. Drop by heaping teaspoonfuls 2 in. apart onto baking sheets coated with cooking spray. Bake at 350° for 12-14 minutes or until cookies are golden brown. Let stand 2 minutes before removing to wire racks to cool.
PER SERVING *1 cookie equals 57 cal., 1 g fat (trace sat. fat), 0 chol., 55 mg sodium, 12 g carb., 1 g fiber, 1 g pro.* **Diabetic Exchange:** *1 starch.*

LEMON MERINGUE CUPCAKES

Classic lemon meringue pie was the inspiration for these gorgeous little cupcakes. The tangy treats hide an indulging lemon pie filling beneath the fluffy toasted meringue. Make them for your next gathering—they'll be a big hit.

—**ANDREA QUIROZ** CHICAGO, IL

PREP: 30 MIN.
BAKE: 25 MIN. + COOLING
MAKES: 2 DOZEN

- 1 package lemon cake mix (regular size)
- 1⅓ cups water
- ⅓ cup canola oil
- 3 large eggs
- 1 tablespoon grated lemon peel
- 1 cup lemon creme pie filling

MERINGUE
- 3 large egg whites
- ½ teaspoon cream of tartar
- ½ cup sugar

1. In a large bowl, combine cake mix, water, oil, eggs and lemon peel; beat on low speed for 30 seconds. Beat on medium for 2 minutes.
2. Fill paper-lined muffin cups two-thirds full. Bake at 350° for 18-22 minutes or until a toothpick inserted near the center comes out clean.
3. Cut a small hole in corner of a pastry or plastic bag; insert a very small tip. Fill with pie filling. Push tip into top of each cupcake to fill.
4. In a large bowl, beat the egg whites and cream of tartar on medium speed until soft peaks form. Gradually beat in the sugar, 1 tablespoon at a time, on high until stiff glossy peaks form and the sugar is dissolved. Pipe meringue over tops of cupcakes.
5. Bake at 400° for 5-8 minutes or until the meringue is golden brown. Cool the cupcakes for 10 minutes before removing from pans to wire racks to cool completely. Store in an airtight container in refrigerator.

PER SERVING *1 cupcake equals 153 cal., 5 g fat (1 g sat. fat), 28 mg chol., 176 mg sodium, 25 g carb., trace fiber, 2 g pro.* **Diabetic Exchanges:** 1½ starch, 1½ fat.

UPSIDE-DOWN BERRY CAKE

Here's a summery cake that's delicious warm or cold. It soaks up loads of flavor from the berries.

—**CANDICE SCHOLL**
WEST SUNBURY, PA

PREP: 20 MIN.
BAKE: 30 MIN. + COOLING
MAKES: 15 SERVINGS

- ½ cup chopped walnuts
- 1 cup fresh or frozen blueberries
- 1 cup fresh or frozen raspberries, halved
- 1 cup sliced fresh strawberries
- ¼ cup sugar
- 1 package (3 ounces) raspberry gelatin
- 1 package yellow cake mix (regular size)
- 2 large eggs
- 1¼ cups water
- 2 tablespoons canola oil
- 1½ cups miniature marshmallows

1. In a well-greased 13x9-in. baking pan, layer the walnuts and berries; sprinkle with sugar and gelatin. In a large bowl, combine the cake mix, eggs, water and oil; beat on low speed for 30 seconds. Beat on medium 2 minutes. Fold in marshmallows. Pour over top.
2. Bake at 350° for 35-40 minutes or until a toothpick inserted near the center comes out clean. Cool for 5 minutes before inverting onto a serving platter. Refrigerate any leftovers.

PER SERVING *1 piece equals 276 cal., 7 g fat (2 g sat. fat), 28 mg chol., 249 mg sodium, 51 g carb., 1 g fiber, 3 g pro.*

WARM CHOCOLATE MELTING CUPS

These creamy, chocolaty desserts are surprisingly decadent and oh so smooth. Even more surprising, each one has fewer than 200 calories and only 6 grams of fat.

—**KISSA VAUGHN** TROY, TX

PREP: 20 MIN. • **BAKE:** 20 MIN.
MAKES: 10 SERVINGS

- 1¼ cups sugar, divided
- ½ cup baking cocoa
- 2 tablespoons all-purpose flour
- ⅛ teaspoon salt
- ¾ cup water
- ¾ cup plus 1 tablespoon semisweet chocolate chips
- 1 tablespoon brewed coffee
- 1 teaspoon vanilla extract
- 2 large eggs
- 1 large egg white
- 10 fresh strawberry halves, optional

1. In a small saucepan, combine ¾ cup sugar, cocoa, flour and salt. Gradually stir in water. Bring to a boil; cook and stir for 2 minutes or until thickened. Remove from the heat; stir in the chocolate chips, coffee and vanilla until smooth. Transfer to a large bowl.
2. In another bowl, beat eggs and egg white until slightly thickened. Gradually add the remaining sugar, beating until thick and lemon-colored. Fold the egg mixture into the chocolate mixture.
3. Transfer to ten 4-oz. ramekins coated with cooking spray. Place the ramekins in a baking pan; add 1 in. of boiling water to pan. Bake, uncovered, at 350° for 20-25 minutes or just until centers are set. Garnish with strawberry halves if desired. Serve immediately.

PER SERVING *1 dessert equals 197 cal., 6 g fat (3 g sat. fat), 42 mg chol., 51 mg sodium, 37 g carb., 2 g fiber, 3 g pro.*

LEMON MERINGUE
CUPCAKES

WARM CHOCOLATE
MELTING CUPS

UPSIDE-DOWN
BERRY CAKE

CHOCOLATY
S'MORES BARS

(5) INGREDIENTS
CHOCOLATY S'MORES BARS

One night, my husband had some friends over to play poker, and he asked for these bars. When they polished off the pan, I shared the recipe so his friends could make them at home, too.

—REBECCA SHIPP BEEBE, AR

PREP: 15 MIN. + COOLING
MAKES: 1½ DOZEN

- ¼ **cup butter, cubed**
- 1 **package (10 ounces) large marshmallows**
- 1 **package (12 ounces) Golden Grahams**
- ⅓ **cup milk chocolate chips, melted**

1. In a large saucepan, melt the butter over low heat. Add the marshmallows; cook and stir until blended. Remove from heat. Stir in cereal until coated.

2. Using a buttered spatula, press evenly into a greased 13x9-in. pan. Drizzle with the melted chocolate chips. Cool completely. Cut into bars. Store in an airtight container.

PER SERVING *1 bar equals 159 cal., 4 g fat (2 g sat. fat), 7 mg chol., 197 mg sodium, 30 g carb., 1 g fiber, 1 g pro.*

HOW-TO

MELT CHOCOLATE

Place chocolate in a microwave-safe bowl. Microwave for 1 minute; stir. Then microwave for additional 10- to 20-second intervals; stir until smooth. Do not overheat.

ROOT BEER FLOAT PIE

(5) INGREDIENTS
ROOT BEER FLOAT PIE

Your kids will always remember this pie. And you can stay cool in the kitchen making it—no need to turn on the oven or stand over a stove!

—CINDY REAMS PHILIPSBURG, PA

PREP: 15 MIN. + CHILLING
MAKES: 8 SERVINGS

- 1 **carton (8 ounces) frozen reduced-fat whipped topping, thawed, divided**
- ¾ **cup cold diet root beer**
- ½ **cup fat-free milk**
- 1 **package (1 ounce) sugar-free instant vanilla pudding mix**
- 1 **graham cracker crust (9 inches)**
  Maraschino cherries, optional

1. Set aside and refrigerate ½ cup whipped topping for garnish. In a large bowl, whisk the root beer, milk and pudding mix for 2 minutes. Fold in half of remaining whipped topping. Spread into the graham cracker crust.

2. Spread the remaining whipped topping over pie. Refrigerate for at least 8 hours or overnight.

3. Dollop the reserved whipped topping over each serving; top with a maraschino cherry if desired.

PER SERVING *1 piece equals 185 cal., 8 g fat (4 g sat. fat), trace chol., 275 mg sodium, 27 g carb., trace fiber, 1 g pro.* **Diabetic Exchanges:** *2 starch, 1 fat.*

RHUBARB-PINEAPPLE CRISP

We grow our own rhubarb, so I enjoy finding new ways to use it. I first tried this combination with tropical fruit years ago, becoming an instant fan.

—**JUDY SCHUT** GRAND RAPIDS, MI

PREP: 15 MIN. • **BAKE:** 30 MIN.
MAKES: 6 SERVINGS

- **2 cups sliced fresh or frozen rhubarb, thawed and drained**
- **1 can (20 ounces) unsweetened pineapple tidbits, drained**
- **½ cup sugar, divided**
- **2 tablespoons plus ⅓ cup all-purpose flour, divided**
- **⅓ cup quick-cooking oats**
- **¾ teaspoon ground cinnamon**
- **⅛ teaspoon salt**
- **¼ cup cold butter**
  Whipped cream, optional

1. In a large bowl, combine the rhubarb, pineapple, ¼ cup sugar and 2 tablespoons flour. Transfer to a 9-in. deep-dish pie plate coated with cooking spray.

2. In a small bowl, combine the oats, cinnamon, salt and remaining sugar and flour. Cut in the butter until crumbly. Sprinkle over the fruit. Bake, uncovered, at 350° for 30-35 minutes or until the filling is bubbly and the topping is golden brown. Cool for 5 minutes; serve with whipped cream if desired.

NOTE *If using frozen rhubarb, measure rhubarb while still frozen, then thaw completely. Drain in a colander, but do not press liquid out.*

PER SERVING *1 serving (calculated without whipped cream) equals 232 cal., 8 g fat (5 g sat. fat), 20 mg chol., 106 mg sodium, 39 g carb., 2 g fiber, 2 g pro.*

RHUBARB-PINEAPPLE CRISP

---

(5) INGREDIENTS

OLD-FASHIONED RICE PUDDING

As a child, I always waited eagerly for the first heavenly bite of this rice pudding. Talk about a dish with the taste of homemade love!

—**SANDRA MELNYCHENKO** GRANDVIEW, MB

PREP: 10 MIN. • **BAKE:** 1 HOUR
MAKES: 6 SERVINGS

- **3½ cups 2% milk**
- **½ cup uncooked long-grain rice**
- **⅓ cup sugar**
- **½ teaspoon salt**
- **½ cup raisins**
- **1 teaspoon vanilla extract**
  Ground cinnamon, optional

1. In a large saucepan, combine milk, rice, sugar and salt. Bring to a boil over medium heat, stirring constantly. Pour into a greased 1½-qt. baking dish.

2. Cover and bake at 325° for 45 minutes, stirring the pudding every 15 minutes. Add the raisins and vanilla; cover and bake for 15 minutes longer or until rice is tender. Sprinkle with cinnamon if desired. Serve warm or chilled. Store in the refrigerator.

PER SERVING *¾ cup equals 208 cal., 3 g fat (2 g sat. fat), 11 mg chol., 270 mg sodium, 40 g carb., 1 g fiber, 6 g pro.*

OLD-FASHIONED
RICE PUDDING

VANILLA MERINGUE COOKIES

VANILLA MERINGUE COOKIES

These sweet little swirls are light as can be. They're all you need after a big, special dinner.

—**JENNI SHARP** MILWAUKEE, WI

PREP: 20 MIN.
BAKE: 40 MIN. + STANDING
MAKES: ABOUT 5 DOZEN

- 3 **large egg whites**
- 1½ **teaspoons clear or regular vanilla extract**
- ¼ **teaspoon cream of tartar**
  Dash salt
- ⅔ **cup sugar**

1. Place the egg whites in a small bowl; let stand at room temperature 30 minutes.

2. Preheat the oven to 250°. Add vanilla, cream of tartar and salt to egg whites; beat on medium speed until foamy. Gradually add sugar, 1 tablespoon at a time, beating on high after each addition until sugar is dissolved. Continue beating until stiff glossy peaks form, about 7 minutes.

3. Cut a small hole in the tip of a pastry bag or in a corner of a food-safe plastic bag; insert a #32 star tip. Transfer meringue to bag. Pipe 1¼-in.-diameter cookies 2 in. apart onto parchment paper-lined baking sheets.

4. Bake 40-45 minutes or until firm to the touch. Turn off oven (do not open oven door); leave meringues in oven 1 hour. Remove from oven; cool completely on baking sheets. Remove meringues from paper; store in an airtight container at room temperature.

PER SERVING *1 cookie equals 10 cal., trace fat (0 sat. fat), 0 chol., 5 mg sodium, 2 g carb., 0 fiber, trace pro.* **Diabetic Exchange:** *Free food.*

LEMON-BERRY SHORTCAKE

Bake a simple cake using fresh strawberries, and enjoy this summertime classic with whipped topping and more berries.

—MERYL HERR GRAND RAPIDS, MI

PREP: 30 MIN.
BAKE: 20 MIN. + COOLING
MAKES: 8 SERVINGS

- 1⅓ **cups all-purpose flour**
- ½ **cup sugar**
- 2 **teaspoons baking powder**
- ¼ **teaspoon salt**
- 1 **large egg**
- ⅔ **cup buttermilk**
- ¼ **cup butter, melted**
- 1 **teaspoon grated lemon peel**
- 1 **tablespoon lemon juice**
- 1 **teaspoon vanilla extract**
- 1 **cup sliced fresh strawberries**

TOPPING

- 1 **cup fresh blackberries**
- 1 **cup sliced fresh strawberries**
- 1 **tablespoon lemon juice**
- 1 **teaspoon sugar**
- 2 **cups reduced-fat whipped topping**

1. Preheat oven to 350°. Grease and flour a 9-in. round baking pan.
2. In a large bowl, whisk the flour, sugar, baking powder and salt. In another bowl, whisk the egg, buttermilk, melted butter, lemon peel, lemon juice and vanilla. Add to the dry ingredients; stir just until moistened. Fold in 1 cup of strawberries. Transfer to the prepared pan.
3. Bake 20-25 minutes or until a toothpick inserted in center comes out clean. Cool 10 minutes before removing from pan to a wire rack to cool completely.
4. For topping, toss berries with lemon juice and sugar. To serve, spread whipped topping over cake. Top with berries.

PER SERVING *1 slice equals 252 cal., 9 g fat (6 g sat. fat), 42 mg chol., 245 mg sodium, 40 g carb., 2 g fiber, 4 g pro.*

LEMON-BERRY SHORTCAKE

**STRAWBERRY
SORBET SENSATION**

(5) INGREDIENTS
STRAWBERRY SORBET SENSATION

On hot days in Colorado, we chill out with slices of this berries-and-cream dessert. The layered effect is so much fun. Use any flavor of sorbet you like.
—**KENDRA DOSS** COLORADO SPRINGS, CO

PREP: 20 MIN. + FREEZING
MAKES: 8 SERVINGS

- 2 **cups strawberry sorbet, softened if necessary**
- 1 **cup cold fat-free milk**
- 1 **package (1 ounce) sugar-free instant vanilla pudding mix**
- 1 **carton (8 ounces) frozen reduced-fat whipped topping, thawed**
  Sliced fresh strawberries

1. Line an 8x4-in. loaf pan with foil. Spread sorbet onto bottom of pan; place in freezer 15 minutes.
2. In a small bowl, whisk milk and pudding mix 2 minutes. Let stand 2 minutes or until soft-set. Fold the whipped topping into the pudding; spread over sorbet. Freeze, covered, 4 hours or overnight.
3. Remove dessert from freezer 10-15 minutes before serving. Unmold dessert onto a serving plate; remove foil. Cut into slices. Serve with strawberries.
PER SERVING *1 slice equals 153 cal., 3 g fat (3 g sat. fat), 1 mg chol., 163 mg sodium, 27 g carb., 2 g fiber, 1 g pro.* **Diabetic Exchanges:** *2 starch, ½ fat.*

RHUBARB OAT BARS

These soft rhubarb bars provide just the right balance of tartness and sweetness. They're hard to beat when you're craving a sweet treat.
—**RENETTE CRESSEY** FORT MILL, SC

PREP: 20 MIN.
BAKE: 25 MIN. + COOLING
MAKES: 16 BARS

- 1½ **cups chopped fresh or frozen rhubarb**
- 1 **cup packed brown sugar, divided**
- 4 **tablespoons water, divided**
- 1 **teaspoon lemon juice**
- 4 **teaspoons cornstarch**
- 1 **cup old-fashioned oats**
- ¾ **cup all-purpose flour**
- ½ **cup flaked coconut**
- ½ **teaspoon salt**
- ⅓ **cup butter, melted**

1. In a large saucepan, combine rhubarb, ½ cup brown sugar, 3 tablespoons water and lemon juice. Bring to a boil. Reduce the heat to medium; cook and stir for 4-5 minutes or until the rhubarb is tender.
2. Combine the cornstarch and remaining water until smooth; gradually stir into rhubarb mixture. Bring to a boil; cook and stir for 2 minutes or until thickened. Remove from the heat; set aside.
3. In a large bowl, combine oats, flour, coconut, salt and remaining brown sugar. Stir in butter until mixture is crumbly.
4. Press half of the oats mixture into a greased 8-in. square baking dish. Spread with rhubarb mixture. Sprinkle with the remaining oat mixture and press down lightly.
5. Bake at 350° for 25-30 minutes or until golden brown. Cool on a wire rack. Cut into squares.
NOTE *If using frozen rhubarb, measure rhubarb while still frozen, then thaw completely. Drain in a colander, but do not press liquid out.*

PER SERVING *1 bar equals 145 cal., 5 g fat (3 g sat. fat), 10 mg chol., 126 mg sodium, 24 g carb., 1 g fiber, 2 g pro.* **Diabetic Exchanges:** *1½ starch, 1 fat.*

TROPICAL CRISP

One bite of this juicy, crunchy fruit crisp and you just might hear the crash of ocean waves!
—*TASTE OF HOME TEST KITCHEN*

PREP: 20 MIN. • **BAKE:** 30 MIN.
MAKES: 9 SERVINGS

- 1 **fresh pineapple, peeled and cubed**
- 4 **medium bananas, sliced**
- ¼ **cup packed brown sugar**
- 2 **tablespoons all-purpose flour**

TOPPING
- ⅓ **cup old-fashioned oats**
- ¼ **cup all-purpose flour**
- 2 **tablespoons flaked coconut, toasted**
- 2 **tablespoons brown sugar**
- ¼ **teaspoon ground nutmeg**
- ¼ **cup cold butter, cubed**

1. Preheat oven to 350°. In a large bowl, combine the pineapple and bananas. Sprinkle with brown sugar and flour; toss to coat. Transfer to an 11x7-in. baking dish coated with cooking spray.
2. In a small bowl, mix the first five topping ingredients; cut in the butter until crumbly. Sprinkle over the pineapple mixture.
3. Bake 30-35 minutes or until filling is bubbly and topping is golden brown. Serve warm or at room temperature.
NOTE *To toast coconut, bake in a shallow pan in a 350° oven for 5-10 minutes or cook in a skillet over low heat until golden brown, stirring occasionally.*
PER SERVING *1 serving equals 188 cal., 6 g fat (4 g sat. fat), 13 mg chol., 44 mg sodium, 34 g carb., 3 g fiber, 2 g pro.* **Diabetic Exchanges:** *1 starch, 1 fruit, 1 fat.*

GRAN'S APPLE CAKE

My grandmother would occasionally bring over this wonderful cake while it was still warm from the oven. The spicy apple flavor, plus the sweet cream cheese frosting, made the dessert a standout. I've lightened up the recipe, but we love this family favorite just as much as ever.

—**LAURIS CONRAD** TURLOCK, CA

PREP: 20 MIN.
BAKE: 35 MIN. + COOLING
MAKES: 18 SERVINGS

- 1⅔ cups sugar
- 2 large eggs
- ½ cup unsweetened applesauce
- 2 tablespoons canola oil
- 2 teaspoons vanilla extract
- 2 cups all-purpose flour
- 2 teaspoons baking soda
- 2 teaspoons ground cinnamon
- ¾ teaspoon salt
- 6 cups chopped peeled tart apples
- ½ cup chopped pecans

FROSTING

- 4 ounces reduced-fat cream cheese
- 2 tablespoons butter, softened
- 1 teaspoon vanilla extract
- 1 cup confectioners' sugar

1. Preheat the oven to 350°. Coat a 13x9-in. baking pan well with cooking spray.
2. In a large bowl, beat sugar, eggs, applesauce, oil and vanilla until well blended. In another bowl, whisk flour, baking soda, cinnamon and salt; gradually beat into the sugar mixture. Fold in apples and pecans.
3. Transfer to prepared pan. Bake 35-40 minutes or until top is golden brown and a toothpick inserted in the center comes out clean. Cool completely in pan on a wire rack.
4. In a small bowl, beat cream cheese, butter and vanilla until smooth. Gradually beat in the confectioners' sugar (the mixture will be soft). Spread over the cake. Refrigerate leftovers.

PER SERVING *1 piece equals 241 cal., 7g fat (2g sat. fat), 29mg chol., 284mg sodium, 42g carb., 1g fiber, 3g pro.*

⑤INGREDIENTS
BANANA BOATS

This recipe, a long-ago gift from a good friend, is quick, fun to make and scrumptious. My family always requests it when we go camping.

—**BRENDA LOVELESS** GARLAND, TX

START TO FINISH: 20 MIN.
MAKES: 4 SERVINGS

- 4 medium unpeeled ripe bananas
- 4 teaspoons miniature chocolate chips
- 4 tablespoons miniature marshmallows

1. Cut the banana peel lengthwise about ½ in. deep, leaving ½ in. at both ends. Open peel wider to form a pocket. Fill each with 1 teaspoon chocolate chips and 1 tablespoon marshmallows. Crimp and shape four pieces of heavy-duty foil (about 12 in. square) around the bananas, forming boats.
2. Grill bananas, covered, over medium heat for 5-10 minutes or until the marshmallows melt and are golden brown.

PER SERVING *1 banana boat equals 136 cal., 2 g fat (1 g sat. fat), 0 chol., 3 mg sodium, 32 g carb., 3 g fiber, 1 g pro.*

MAKEOVER DIRT DESSERT

Break out the spoons and make sure you get a bite before everyone else when you take this lightened-up treat to your next potluck, because it won't be around very long.

—**KRISTI LINTON** BAY CITY, MI

PREP: 30 MIN. + CHILLING
MAKES: 20 SERVINGS

- 1 package (8 ounces) fat-free cream cheese
- 3 ounces cream cheese, softened
- ¾ cup confectioners' sugar
- 3½ cups cold fat-free milk
- 2 packages (1 ounce each) sugar-free instant vanilla pudding mix
- 1 carton (12 ounces) frozen reduced-fat whipped topping, thawed
- 1 package (15½ ounces) reduced-fat Oreo cookies, crushed

1. In a large bowl, beat cream cheeses and confectioners' sugar until smooth. In a large bowl, whisk the milk and pudding mixes for 2 minutes; let stand for 2 minutes or until soft-set. Gradually stir into cream cheese mixture. Fold in the whipped topping.
2. Spread 1⅓ cups of the crushed Oreo cookies into an ungreased 13x9-in. dish. Layer with half the pudding mixture and half of the remaining cookies. Repeat layers. Refrigerate the dessert for at least 1 hour before serving.

PER SERVING *½ cup equals 208 cal., 6 g fat (4 g sat. fat), 6 mg chol., 364 mg sodium, 33 g carb., 1 g fiber, 5 g pro.* **Diabetic Exchanges: 2 starch, 1 fat.**

THE SKINNY

LIGHTER DESSERT

By finding a low-fat or no-fat equivalent for almost every ingredient in the original Dirt Dessert, we trimmed more than 100 calories and 10g of fat from every serving!

GRAN'S APPLE CAKE

BANANA BOATS

MAKEOVER DIRT DESSERT

ARCTIC
ORANGE PIE

(5) INGREDIENTS
ARCTIC ORANGE PIE

This frosty pie is so easy to make—and versatile. Instead of orange, I have tried lemonade, mango and pineapple juice concentrates, and my family loves each version.
—**MARIE PRZEPIERSKI** ERIE, PA

PREP: 20 MIN. + FREEZING
MAKES: 8 SERVINGS

- 1 package (8 ounces) fat-free cream cheese
- 1 can (6 ounces) frozen orange juice concentrate, thawed
- 1 carton (8 ounces) frozen reduced-fat whipped topping, thawed
- 1 reduced-fat graham cracker crust (8 inches)
- 1 can (11 ounces) mandarin oranges, drained

In a large bowl, beat cream cheese and orange juice concentrate until smooth. Fold in whipped topping; pour into crust. Cover and freeze for 4 hours or until firm. Remove from the freezer about 10 minutes before cutting. Garnish with oranges.
PER SERVING 1 piece equals 241 cal., 7 g fat (4 g sat. fat), 2 mg chol., 251 mg sodium, 36 g carb., 1 g fiber, 6 g pro. **Diabetic Exchanges:** 1½ fat, 1 starch, 1 fruit.

DATE OAT BARS

My mother found this recipe many years ago. I love the surprise citrus zip just as much now as I did then.
—**JOYCE EASTMAN**
GARDEN GROVE, CA

PREP: 30 MIN.
BAKE: 30 MIN. + COOLING
MAKES: 3 DOZEN

- 1¾ cups chopped dates
- ½ cup water
- 2 tablespoons brown sugar
- 1 teaspoon grated orange peel
- 2 tablespoons orange juice
- 1 teaspoon lemon juice

CRUST
- 1½ cups all-purpose flour
- 1 teaspoon baking powder
- ½ teaspoon baking soda
- ¼ teaspoon salt
- 1 cup cold butter
- 1½ cups old-fashioned oats
- 1 cup packed brown sugar

1. In a small saucepan, combine the dates, water, brown sugar and orange peel. Cook and stir over medium heat until mixture comes to a boil, about 4 minutes. Cook and stir 3 minutes longer or until liquid is absorbed. Remove from the heat. Stir in the orange and lemon juices. Cool to room temperature.
2. In a large bowl, combine flour, baking powder, baking soda and salt. Cut in butter until crumbly. Add oats and brown sugar; mix well. Set aside half for the topping. Press remaining crumb mixture into a greased 13x9-in. baking pan.
3. Drop the date mixture by small spoonfuls onto crust. Sprinkle with the reserved crumb mixture; press down gently. Bake at 325° for 30-35 minutes or until golden brown. Cool on a wire rack. Cut into bars.
PER SERVING 1 bar equals 126 cal., 5 g fat (3 g sat. fat), 14 mg chol., 100 mg sodium, 19 g carb., 1 g fiber, 1 g pro. **Diabetic Exchanges:** 1 starch, 1 fat.

STRAWBERRY CREAM CHEESE PIE

Cheesecake lovers will savor every bite of this creamy strawberry pie. Everyone in my family is a fan.
—**KIM VAN RHEENEN** MENDOTA, IL

PREP: 20 MIN. + CHILLING
BAKE: 30 MIN. + COOLING
MAKES: 8 SERVINGS

- Pastry for a single-crust pie (9 inches)
- 1 package (8 ounces) reduced-fat cream cheese

- ½ cup egg substitute
- 3 tablespoons honey
- 1 teaspoon vanilla extract
- 3½ cups sliced fresh strawberries
- 1 tablespoon cornstarch
- ½ cup cold water
- ½ cup reduced-sugar strawberry preserves
- Fat-free whipped topping, optional

1. Roll out pastry to fit a 9-in. pie plate; transfer pastry to plate. Trim pastry to ½ in. beyond edge of plate; flute edges. Bake at 350° for 13-15 minutes or until the crust is lightly browned.
2. Meanwhile, in a large bowl, beat the cream cheese, egg substitute, honey and vanilla until smooth. Pour into crust. Bake 15-18 minutes longer or until center is almost set. Cool completely on a wire rack.
3. Arrange strawberries over the filling. In a saucepan, combine cornstarch and water until smooth. Stir in preserves. Bring to a boil; cook and stir for 2 minutes or until thickened. Spoon or brush over the strawberries. Refrigerate pie for 2 hours before cutting. Garnish with whipped topping if desired.
PER SERVING 1 piece (calculated without whipped topping) equals 268 cal., 12 g fat (6 g sat. fat), 21 mg chol., 119 mg sodium, 34 g carb., 2 g fiber, 5 g pro.

THE SKINNY

EGG SUB

By using egg substitute instead of whole eggs in this pie, you save about 10 calories per slice. In addition, egg substitute cuts back on cholesterol while keeping the protein.

PUMPKIN
OATMEAL BARS

APPLE-SPICE ANGEL FOOD CAKE

Angel food cake mix is lower in fat and calories than regular cake mix. Apple pie spice and toasted nuts add a festive fall flavor, but you'll want to make this year-round!

—JOAN BUEHNERKEMPER
TEUTOPOLIS, IL

PREP: 10 MIN.
BAKE: 35 MIN. + COOLING
MAKES: 16 SERVINGS

- 1 **package (16 ounces) angel food cake mix**
- 1 **cup water**
- ⅔ **cup unsweetened applesauce**
- ½ **cup finely chopped pecans, toasted**
- 1 **teaspoon apple pie spice**
  Reduced-fat whipped topping and/or apple slices, optional

1. In a large bowl, combine cake mix and water. Beat on low speed for 30 seconds. Beat on medium speed for 1 minute. Fold in the applesauce, pecans and pie spice.
2. Gently spoon into an ungreased 10-in. tube pan. Cut through batter with a knife to remove air pockets. Bake on the lowest oven rack at 350° for 35-45 minutes or until lightly browned and entire top appears dry. Immediately invert pan; cool completely, about 1 hour.
3. Run a knife around side and center tube of pan. Remove cake to a serving plate. Garnish with whipped topping and/or apple slices if desired.

PER SERVING *1 slice (calculated without optional ingredients) equals 136 cal., 3 g fat (trace sat. fat), 0 chol., 209 mg sodium, 26 g carb., 1 g fiber, 3 g pro.* **Diabetic Exchanges:** *1½ starch, ½ fat.*

PUMPKIN OATMEAL BARS

It took me a long time to perfect these bars, but I'm so happy with how they turned out in the end. They have it all: sugar and spice and a light, creamy pumpkin layer that's especially nice!

—ERIN ANDREWS EDGEWATER, FL

PREP: 30 MIN.
BAKE: 30 MIN. + COOLING
MAKES: 2 DOZEN

- 1 **package yellow cake mix (regular size)**
- 2½ **cups quick-cooking oats**
- 5 **tablespoons butter, melted**
- 3 **tablespoons honey**
- 1 **tablespoon water**

FILLING

- 1 **can (15 ounces) solid-pack pumpkin**
- ¼ **cup reduced-fat cream cheese**
- ¼ **cup fat-free milk**
- 3 **tablespoons brown sugar**
- 2 **tablespoons maple syrup**
- 1 **teaspoon ground cinnamon**
- 1 **teaspoon vanilla extract**
- ¼ **teaspoon ground allspice**
- ¼ **teaspoon ground cloves**
- 1 **large egg**
- 1 **large egg white**
- ¼ **cup chopped walnuts**
- 1 **tablespoon butter, melted**

1. In a large bowl, combine the cake mix and oats; set aside ½ cup for topping. Add the butter, honey and water to the remaining cake mixture. Press onto the bottom of a 13x9-in. baking pan coated with cooking spray.
2. For the filling, in a large bowl, beat the pumpkin, cream cheese, milk, brown sugar, maple syrup, cinnamon, vanilla, allspice and cloves until blended. Add egg and egg white; beat on low speed just until combined. Pour over crust. In a small bowl, combine the walnuts, butter and reserved cake mixture; sprinkle over filling.
3. Bake at 350° for 30-35 minutes or until set and edges are lightly browned. Cool on a wire rack. Cut into bars.

PER SERVING *1 bar equals 186 cal., 7 g fat (3 g sat. fat), 18 mg chol., 180 mg sodium, 30 g carb., 2 g fiber, 3 g pro.* **Diabetic Exchanges:** *2 starch, 1 fat.*

**APPLE-SPICE
ANGEL FOOD CAKE**

**RASPBERRY
SORBET**

⑤INGREDIENTS

RASPBERRY SORBET

With an abundant crop of fresh raspberries from the backyard, I rely on this recipe for a tasty frozen dessert that's pure simplicity.

—**KAREN BAILEY** GOLDEN, CO

PREP: 5 MIN. + FREEZING
MAKES: 6 SERVINGS

¼ cup plus 1½ teaspoons fresh lemon juice
3¾ cups fresh or frozen unsweetened raspberries
2¼ cups confectioners' sugar

Place all ingredients in a blender or food processor; cover and process until smooth. Transfer to a freezer container; freeze until firm.

PER SERVING *1 serving equals 216 cal., trace fat (trace sat. fat), 0 chol., 1 mg sodium, 55 g carb., 5 g fiber, 1 g pro.*

TOP TIP

KEEP THE SUGAR

When making sorbet, don't skimp on the amount of sugar in the recipe. The high sugar content keeps it from freezing into a block of ice. Sugar also helps give sorbet its smooth texture, so keep things sweet.

LOW-FAT PEANUT BUTTER COOKIES

When you bite into one of these yummy cookies, you'll never guess it's low in fat. It's our little secret.

—MARIA REGAKIS SAUGUS, MA

PREP: 15 MIN. + FREEZING
BAKE: 10 MIN. + COOLING
MAKES: ABOUT 2 DOZEN

- 3 **tablespoons butter**
- 2 **tablespoons reduced-fat peanut butter**
- ½ **cup packed brown sugar**
- ¼ **cup sugar**
- 1 **large egg white**
- 1 **teaspoon vanilla extract**
- 1 **cup all-purpose flour**
- ¼ **teaspoon baking soda**
- ⅛ **teaspoon salt**

1. In a large bowl, cream butter, peanut butter and sugars until light and fluffy. Add egg white; beat until blended. Beat in vanilla. Combine the flour, baking soda and salt; gradually add to the creamed mixture and mix well. Shape into an 8-in. roll; wrap in plastic wrap. Freeze for 2 hours or until firm.

2. Unwrap and cut into slices, just over ¼-in. thick. Place 2 in. apart on baking sheets coated with cooking spray. Press with a fork to make crisscross pattern. Bake at 350° for 6-8 minutes for chewy cookies or 8-10 minutes for crisp cookies. Cool for 1-2 minutes before removing cookies to wire racks; cool completely.

PER SERVING *1 cookie equals 62 cal., 2 g fat (1 g sat. fat), 4 mg chol., 64 mg sodium, 11 g carb., trace fiber, 1 g pro.* **Diabetic Exchanges:** *½ starch, ½ fat.*

LOW-FAT PEANUT BUTTER COOKIES

PICNIC BERRY
SHORTCAKES

PICNIC BERRY SHORTCAKES

You can make the berry sauce ahead of time and chill. Then assemble the entire dessert a couple of hours before serving.
—*TASTE OF HOME* TEST KITCHEN

PREP: 20 MIN. + CHILLING
MAKES: 4 SERVINGS

- 2 **tablespoons sugar**
- ½ **teaspoon cornstarch**
- 2 **tablespoons water**
- 2 **cups sliced fresh strawberries, divided**
- ½ **teaspoon grated lime peel**
- 2 **individual round sponge cakes**
- 2 **cups fresh blueberries**
  Whipped topping, optional

1. In a small saucepan, mix sugar and cornstarch. Stir in water. Add 1 cup strawberries; mash mixture. Bring to a boil; cook and stir for 1-2 minutes or until thickened. Remove from heat; stir in the lime peel. Transfer to a small bowl; refrigerate, covered, until chilled.
2. Cut sponge cakes crosswise in half; trim each to fit in the bottoms of four wide-mouth half-pint canning jars. In a small bowl, mix the blueberries and remaining strawberries; spoon over cakes. Top with sauce. If desired, serve with whipped topping.
PER SERVING *1 dessert (calculated without whipped topping) equals 124 cal., 1 g fat (trace sat. fat), 10 mg chol., 67 mg sodium, 29 g carb., 3 g fiber, 2 g pro.* **Diabetic Exchanges:** *1 starch, 1 fruit.*

IRISH CREAM CUPCAKES

IRISH CREAM CUPCAKES

If you're looking for big, grown-up taste in a lightened-up little package, give these cute cupcake treats a try. No need to wait for St. Patrick's Day.
—**JENNY LEIGHTY** WEST SALEM, OH

PREP: 25 MIN.
BAKE: 20 MIN. + COOLING
MAKES: 2 DOZEN

- ½ **cup butter, softened**
- 1½ **cups sugar**
- 2 **large eggs**
- ¾ **cup unsweetened applesauce**
- 2 **teaspoons vanilla extract**
- 2½ **cups all-purpose flour**
- 3 **teaspoons baking powder**
- ½ **teaspoon salt**
- ½ **cup Irish cream liqueur**

FROSTING

- ⅓ **cup butter, softened**
- 4 **ounces reduced-fat cream cheese**
- 6 **tablespoons Irish cream liqueur**
- 4 **cups confectioners' sugar**

1. In a large bowl, beat the butter and sugar until crumbly, about 2 minutes. Add eggs, one at a time, beating well after each addition. Beat in the applesauce and vanilla (the mixture may appear curdled). Combine flour, baking powder and salt; add to the creamed mixture alternately with liqueur, beating well after each addition.
2. Fill paper-lined muffin cups two-thirds full. Bake at 350° for 18-22 minutes or until a toothpick inserted near the center comes out clean. Cool for 10 minutes before removing from pans to wire racks to cool completely.
3. For frosting, in a large bowl, beat butter and cream cheese until fluffy. Beat in liqueur. Add confectioners' sugar; beat until smooth. Pipe over tops of the cupcakes. Refrigerate the leftovers.
PER SERVING *1 cupcake equals 273 cal., 9 g fat (5 g sat. fat), 38 mg chol., 170 mg sodium, 45 g carb., trace fiber, 2 g pro.*

GENERAL RECIPE INDEX
Find every recipe by food category and major ingredient.

ALPHABETICAL RECIPE INDEX

Find every recipe by title.